Best Cover Letters For $100,000+ Jobs

Wendy S. Enelow, CPRW, JCTC, CCM

IMPACT PUBLICATIONS
Manassas Park, VA

Library of Congress Cataloging-in-Publication Data

Enelow, Wendy S.
    Best cover letters for $100,000+ jobs / Wendy S. Enelow.
      p. cm.
    Rev. ed. of: 201 winning cover letters for $100,000+ jobs: cover letters that can change your life! / Wendy S. Enelow. c1998
    ISBN 1-57023-169-9 (alk. paper)
    1. Cover letters. 2. Resumes (Employment) I. Title: Best resumes for one hundred thousand dollar plus jobs. II. Enelow, Wendy S. 201 winning cover letters for $100,000+ jobs. III. Title.

HF5383.E477 2001
808'.06665 – dc21   2001024153

Publisher: For information, including current and forthcoming publications, authors, press kits, and submission guidelines, visit Impact's website: *www.impactpublications. com*

Publicity/Rights: For information on publicity, author interviews, and subsidiary rights, contact Media Relations: Tel. 703-361-7300 or Fax 703-335-9486.

Sales/Distribution: For information on distribution or quantity discount rates, call (703-361-7300), fax (703-335-9486), email (*info@impactpublications.com*) or write: Sales Department, Impact Publications, 9104 Manassas Drive, Suite N, Manassas Park, VA 20111. Bookstore orders should be directed to our trade distributor: National Book Network, 15200 NBN Way, Blue Ridge Summit, PA 17214, Tel. 1-800-462-6420.

Contents

Job Search, Career Management, Coaching, Counseling,
Cover Letter Writing and Other Career Resources

Preface

LET'S GET THINGS STRAIGHT FROM THE BEGINNING. WHEN I wrote this book, I wrote it for individuals, like yourself, who *are the best* or aspire *to be the best* – in their professions, their careers, and their lives. This book was *not* written for the faint of heart nor faint of career. It was written for those who strive to move forward and upward in their careers, who push themselves to reach new heights, and who are energized, not intimidated, by challenge.

This book was written for Chairmen, Presidents, Chief Executive Officers (CEOs), Chief Operating Officers (COOs), Chief Financial Officers (CFOs), Chief Information Officers (CIOs), and Chief Knowledge Officers (CKOs). It was written for General Managers, Directors, Executive Vice Presidents, and Vice Presidents who are already earning $100,000 a year or more.

This book was also written for mid-level professionals and managers aspiring to reach new heights, assume greater professional responsibilities, and pursue new career opportunities. It was written for the Sales Representative making $65,000 a year and working toward that $100,000+ salary. It was written for the Purchasing Supervisor making $75,000 a year and applying for a position with a starting salary of $100,000. It was written for the MBA graduate who is just launching his career and knows that, in years to come, he will be making $100,000 a year or more.

In summary, this book was written for *you* – the leaders and aspiring leaders of the business world.

Best Cover Letters For $100,000+ Jobs

Books by Wendy S. Enelow

1500+ Keywords for $100,000+ Jobs
Best Cover Letters for $100,000+ Jobs
Best Resumes for $100,000+ Jobs
Resume Winners From the Pros
Winning Interviews for $100,000+ Jobs

1

Writing Your Best Cover Letter

OVER THE PAST DECADE, AS THE U.S. ECONOMY HAS UNDER-gone dramatic and long-lasting changes, the business world has globalized and the employment market become more competitive, the job search process has evolved into a much more complex and more sophisticated process. Remember the days when you could type a brief resume of your work history and educational background, submit a few copies to friends, and in response to advertisements, go on a few interviews and accept a new offer, all within a few weeks? Well, forget those days, for they are long since gone! The times have changed, the employment market has changed and the competition for top-flight opportunities has increased at an unprecedented rate.

Showcase Your Talents and Strengths

Step one, and perhaps the most critical step in planning, preparing, and launching a successful job search for a $100,000+ position, involves the writing and design of your portfolio of job search marketing communications. These documents should be written to showcase your talents and strengths, highlight your achievements, and excite prospective employers to extend you the opportunity for an interview.

Without these tools, you can go nowhere in your job search. They are the foundation for everything else that follows – responses to job postings, email campaigns to recruiters, direct mail to companies, Internet postings, networking, and other activities you'll engage in to market yourself into your next position. They are what get you in the door for interviews; they are what you leave behind after the interview as a reminder of who you are and the value you bring to an organization; they are your calling card. These documents are crucial in building your visibility throughout the job search market and ultimately facilitating your success.

To succeed in your job search, there are several different documents that you must include in your portfolio of marketing communications:

- Your Resume (multiple versions if necessary)

- Your Cover Letter (multiple versions if necessary)

- Your Interview Follow-Up Letters (personalized to each company and position)

- Your Networking Letters (customized to each of your colleagues)

This book is devoted to the latter three items – cover letters, interview follow-up letters and networking letters – along with other special types of letters you may have the opportunity to use in your job search. For detailed information on writing and designing resumes for $100,000+ management and executive opportunities, you can refer to the companion book in this series, *Best Resumes For $100,000+ Jobs* (Impact Publications, 2001).

Critical Cover Letter Concepts

Over the past decade, the cover letter has undergone a massive transformation. In years past, a cover letter was really just a transmittal letter, a short note indicating that you were "transmitting" your resume for review. Today's cover letters are true marketing communications, focusing on your achievements, experience, and credentials as they directly relate to a particular company's or recruiter's needs. They are proactive, designed to market and to sell, not just passively communicate "Here's my resume."

To understand the value of your cover letter to your job search process, it is best to start with a clear definition of what a cover letter is. It is defined as:

- A marketing document that is a "teaser," designed to entice someone to read your resume and extend you the opportunity for a personal interview.

- A tool designed to sell the high points of your career – your successes, achievements, and most notable and relevant qualifications.

- A document that demonstrates the value you bring to a prospective employer.

- A document that is fairly quick to read and easy to peruse.

- A visual presentation that communicates an executive image.

A cover letter is not:

- A transmittal letter that simply states "Enclosed is my resume … may we meet for an interview?"

- A document containing lengthy text and long paragraphs that is slow to read.

- A passive, low-energy, and narrative summary of your work history.

Writing cover letters, just like writing resumes, is a creative process where your challenge is to highlight the "greatest" things about yourself and your career in the least amount of space possible while relating those "great" things to the company's specific needs. No problem! We'll explore this concept in much greater detail in the next chapter. However, to get you started, pay close attention to the following.

Five Critical Cover Letter Rules

Effective cover letters are ones that conform to these five critical rules for writing cover letters:

1. **Complement and don't repeat**. Cover letters should complement your resume, not repeat it. Do not take text, word for word, from your resume and simply drop it into your cover letter. Find different ways to communicate the same messages, achievements, and qualifications. For example, if you highlighted specific revenue achievements in your resume, consider highlighting cumulative revenue achievements over the past 5-10 years in your cover letter. You'll still be communicating a message of success without being repetitive.

2. **Ask for the interview!** The whole purpose of writing a cover letter and sending it with a resume is to get an interview. Don't be shy – do ask for the interview! Consider ending your letter with something like this: "I look forward to meeting with you to pursue the Director of Manufacturing position and will follow up next week to schedule an interview."

3. **Create a theme**. Cover letters must clearly communicate who you are (e.g., purchasing director, sales manager, VP of Information Technology, CEO), the value you bring to an organization, and your track record of success. Paint a clear picture of who you are; no one will take the time to figure it out if you don't spell it out.

4. **Write to sell**. Stay away from the old-school transmittal letters that say, "Here's my resume … give me a job." Be sure that your cover letters communicate *"Why"* someone should give you a job, or at least an interview. The best strategy is, "Here's my resume … this is *why* I'm such a great candidate … now, give me the job." (Preferably, your own wording should be a bit more suave!)

5. **Presentation is critical**. Cover letters for $100,000+ positions must be perfect! They must be 100% error-free, visually pleasing and dynamic.

Today's Competitive $100,000+ Cover Letter

Above is a precise outline of what a cover letter is and is not. Common sense would have it that if you followed that outline, you'd know precisely what to do. However, as an executive job seeker, you face unique challenges in developing, writing, and designing a cover letter that will position you for a $100,000+ position.

What is it that makes your cover letter so very different from others? What must you do to competitively position your cover letter and get noticed in the crowd of other qualified candidates? What makes your cover letter so special and so unique? The answers are straightforward:

- **$100,000+ cover letters** are marketing tools, written to "sell" a job seeker into his or her next position.

- **$100,000+ cover letters** are dynamic, distinctive, and hard-hitting.

- **$100,000+ cover letters** present a clear and concise picture of "who" the job search candidate is.

- **$100,000+ cover letters** are sharp and upscale in their visual presentation.

- **$100,000+ cover letters** focus on success and achievement.

- **$100,000+ cover letters** clearly communicate the value of a job seeker.

- **$100,000+ cover letters** highlight the experiences, qualifications, and knowledge that make each candidate unique.

Most significantly, the writing, tone, style, and presentation of a $100,000+ cover letter must be superb. The wording must be aggressive and the presentation top-of-the-line. The impression it leaves the reader with must be that of an accomplished and successful executive who has delivered strong results and demonstrated outstanding leadership skills. The cover letter must communicate "I bring value to you and to your organization." If you are ever going to "toot your own horn," *this is the time to do it!*

Translating Your Qualifications Into Hard-Hitting Cover Letter Content

Etch these words into your head, your heart, and your soul ... ***Cover Letter Writing Is Sales !!!*** Say that phrase over and over until it becomes a part of you, for it is this mindset that will propel you to write a top-notch cover letter.

Your cover letter is a document that should be written specifically to market and merchandise *your* talents. Critical to that concept is the "*sell it to me, don't tell it to me*" strategy. Think about that. You do not want to tell someone what you have done. Rather, you want to *sell* what you have accomplished. How do you do that? You do that by writing powerful sentences, highlighting your achievements and qualifications, using action verbs, and creating a cover letter that communicates success.

To better understand the concept of selling your qualifications, here are a few examples:

Poor Example:

- Managed budgeting for 15 operating locations in the Dow Chemical Corporation.

Good Example:

- Closed 1999 at 20% under projected costs while directing all budgeting functions for 15 of Dow Chemical's operating locations.

Poor Example:

- Directed sales and business development in the Eastern U.S.

Good Example:

- Increased sales revenues 22% and market share 24% while leading all corporate sales and business development programs in the Eastern U.S.

Poor Example:
- Hired to reorganize the entire IT organization.

Good Example:

- Transitioned Monarch's data center into a state-of-the-art information technology and support organization with advanced networking, database, and e-commerce applications.

"*Sell it to me, don't tell it to me*" ... see what a difference it makes in the words, the tone, the style, and the impact? Always remember that you are selling whenever you are writing any job search materials

Use the Language of Key Words

The words that you select create the tone and energy of your cover letter. If you use words such as "responsible for" and "duties included," your cover letter becomes passive, boring, and repetitive. But when you use words such as ... directed, designed, created, achieved, delivered, increased, improved, launched, revitalized ... your resume comes to life and communicates energy, drive, and achievement.

There are four strategies to follow that will help you determine your word choice. All except #3 are critical to every cover letter you will write. Strategy #3 is important only if your job search is focused on a particular industry or related group of industries.

✓ *Strategy #1:* Write in the active first-person (dropping the "I's"); never the third-person. What does this mean? Here's an example:

Active First-Person: Improved bottom-line profits by 18%.

Third-Person: Mr. Smith improved bottom-line profits by 18%.

Can you see the difference? The first example communicates "I did this." The second example communicates "Mr. Smith, the other guy, did that" and it moves ownership away from you. Your cover letter must be a part of who you are and not a distant third-party voice.

✓ *Strategy #2:* Use key words specific to your current professional goals. If you're looking for a job in sales, use sales, marketing, and customer service words. If you're looking for a position in manufacturing, use words related to production, product management, inventory, and workforce management. These key words are essential if you want to communicate you have the "right" set of skills and experience for the type of position you are seeking. What's more, key words are an essential component in the resume and cover letter scanning process (when companies and recruiters use scanners to determine if you have the appropriate skills and qualifications for a particular opportunity). The computer, not a person, "reads" your letter. Therefore, word choice is critical.

✓ *Strategy #3:* Use key words specific to your current preferences for type of industry. Strategy #3 is applicable only if your job search is industry-specific. If you are looking for a position in a technology industry, use the appropriate technology acronyms. If you're looking for a position in the retail industry, talk about buying, merchandising, and loss prevention. If the insurance industry is your objective, use words such as indemnity, E&O, and risk assessment. These key words are essential if you want to communicate you have the "right" set of skills and experience for the industry. What's more, just as with "professional" key words, "industry" key words have become an essential component in the resume and cover letter scanning process.

Here are a few sample key words for 28 different professions and industries. Use this list to get you thinking about the key words that are specific to your profession (Strategy #2) and your industry (Strategy #3).

➤ **Accounting:** Payables, Receivables, General Ledger, Financial Analysis, Reporting, Audit, Budgeting, Month-End Closings

➤ **Administration:** Executive Liaison Affairs, Board of Directors, Minutes, Recordkeeping, Scheduling, Project Administration

➤ **Association Management:** Fundraising, Corporate Sponsorships, Member Services, Outreach, Advocacy, Regulatory & Legal Affairs

➤ **Banking:** De Novo Banking, Commercial, Retail, Back Office, Lending, Cross-Border Transactions, Regulatory Compliance

➤ **Construction:** Commercial, Industrial & Residential, Project Planning, Scheduling, Contracts, Environmental Assessment

➤ **Corporate Finance:** Tax, Treasury, Mergers, Acquisitions, Budgeting, Cost Avoidance, Investment Management, Forecasting, Analysis

➤ **Education:** Curriculum Development, Instructional Systems Design, Program Administration, Testing & Placement, Training

➤ **Engineering:** Prototype Development, Project Management, Failure Analysis, Reliability, Experimental Design, Product Functionality

➤ **Government:** Regulatory Compliance & Reporting, Public/Private Sector, Competitive Bidding, Fixed Price Contracts, VIP Relations

➤ **Health Care:** Patient Management, Treatment Planning, Emergency Intervention, Invasive Therapies, Utilization Review

➤ **Hospitality:** Food & Beverage, Guest Relations, Facilities Management, Meetings & Events, Amenities, Labor & Food Cost Controls

➤ **Human Resources:** Staffing, Training & Development, Compensation, Benefits Administration, Employee Assistance, HRIS Technology

- **Human Services:** Diagnostic Assessment, Case Management, Inter-Agency Relations, Crisis Intervention, Treatment Planning

- **Information Technology:** Client/Server, Web-Enabling, Internet/Intranet, Integration, Migration, Configuration, Platform, Hardware, Software

- **Insurance:** Claims Administration, Risk Management, Liability, P&C, E&O, LLC, Portfolio Management, Client Development

- **Investment Finance:** Mergers, Acquisitions, Joint Ventures, Venture Funding, ROI, ROA, ROE, Portfolio Management, NASD, Cross-Border

- **Law/Legal:** Legal Research & Writing, Case Management, Judicial Proceedings, Investigations, Client Representation

- **Logistics:** Purchasing, Supply Chain, Inventory Planning, Warehousing, Distribution, Transportation, Resource & Asset Management

- **Manufacturing:** Productivity & Yield Improvement, Cost Reduction, MRP, JIT, Manufacturing Cell, Quality, Materials, Scheduling, Control

- **Marketing:** Multimedia Communications & Presentations, New Market Development, Product Launch, Advertising, Branding

- **Media:** New Media, Production, Direction, Broadcasting, On-Air Talent, Studio Engineering, E-Commerce, Press Relations

- **Purchasing:** Supply Chain Management, Vendor Sourcing, Contract Negotiations, Fixed Price, Inventory Planning,

- **Quality:** Engineering, Reliability, ISO, TQM, Quality Assurance, Failure Analysis & Reporting, Product Performance, Quality Audits

- **Real Estate:** Residential, Commercial & Industrial Properties, Buy/Sell Negotiations, Contracts, Regulatory Compliance, Marketing

> **Retail:** Multi-Site Operations, Merchandising, Loss Prevention, Sales, Customer Service, Training, Facilities, Buying, In-Store Events

> **Sales:** Customer Presentations, Negotiations, Sales Closings, New Product Launch, Contracts, Competitive Positioning

> **Security:** Corporate Security, VIP Protection, Risk Assessment, Perimeter & Facilities Control, Emergency Preparedness

> **Telecommunications:** Infrastructure, Technology, Networking, Internet/Intranet, Cellular, Base Station, Voice & Data, Secure Transmissions

✓ *Strategy #4:* Write for the level of position you are pursuing – professional, managerial and executive. Use hard-hitting words and phrases that communicate the level of expertise that you bring to an organization. Do not write about "controlling revenues"; write about "P&L management." Do not write about "supervising staff"; write about "building and leading a 20-person management team." Use words and phrases such as:

- Accelerating Revenue Growth

- Aggressive Turnaround Leadership

- Best-in-Class Operations

- Capturing Cost Reductions

- Competitively Positioning Products, Services & Technologies

- Continuous Improvement

- Cross-Cultural Communications

- Cross-Culturally Sensitive

- Cross-Functional Team Leadership

- Distinguished Performance

- Driving Product Development & Innovation

- E-Commerce & E-Business

- Emerging Ventures

- Entrepreneurial Drive & Vision

- Executive Presentations & Negotiations

- Fast-Track Promotion

- Global Business Development

- High-Performance

- International Business Expansion

- Matrix Management

- Mergers & Acquisitions

- Multinational Organizations

- Negotiating Strategic Alliances

- New Media

- Organization(al) Leadership

- Outperforming Global Competition

- Outsourcing Operations

- Partnerships & Joint Ventures

- Performance Revitalization

- Pioneering Technologies

- Proactive Change Agent

- Process Redesign & Optimization

- Start-Up, Turnaround & High-Growth Organizations

- Strong & Sustainable Revenue Gains

- Technologically Sophisticated Organizations

- Visionary Leadership

2

Writing a Powerful Cover Letter

Making the Best Choices

Before you ever begin to write your cover letter, you need to make six critical decisions that will impact the type of letter you develop:

1. **Use** – Is this a letter that you are going to use over and over again, or are you writing a specific letter to a specific individual for a specific opportunity?

2. **Recipient** – Whom are you writing to (recruiter, company, network contact, venture capital firm, etc.)?

3. **Message** – What is the overall message you want to communicate and the image you want to project?

4. **Presentation Style** – What style of letter do you want to write?

5. **Length** – Will your letter be 1 page or 2 pages?

6. **Distribution Strategy** – How are you going to distribute your letter (mail, fax, email, website)?

We will explore each of these six concepts in detail. Once you understand them, it should only take you a few quick minutes to make these decisions each time you are ready to write a letter.

Use

The very first question to ask yourself is "How am I going to use this letter?" Generally, you will have one of two answers. Either you are writing a letter (template letter) that you want to be able to use over and over and over in your job search, or you are writing a specific letter to a specific company, recruiter, or venture capital firm for a specific opportunity (or type of opportunity if you are not aware of a particular position).

Chances are much more likely that you will have more versions of your cover letter than your resume. Your resume is a marketing document that highlights your entire career. Your cover letter, on the other hand, is a marketing document that highlights just a few specifics of your career most related to a particular company or opportunity. Let's consider each of these two letters in more detail.

Template Cover Letters

If you're in a situation where you can write just one cover letter and then use it again and again, with just a few minor changes here and there, great! It will certainly make your cover letter writing process easier and faster. This will be most appropriate for you if your job search objectives are (1) narrow in focus and (2) closely related to your past career history.

Here's a good example: Your entire background has been in the sale of consumer electronics to retailers and mass merchandisers nationwide. You've set your sights on a higher-level management position within the same industry and *only* that industry. As such, most positions you apply for will call for the same type of qualifications in a candidate; namely, individuals with strong sales experience, a track record of revenue and profit growth, contacts with major customers, experience in building new markets, success in launching new products, and more. Therefore, it stands to reason, that you can write one cover letter and only have to modify it a bit here and there to meet the specifications for each position.

As you can see, a template letter can be a real time-saver and allow you to quickly and easily get resumes out into the market. However, its use is somewhat limited in scope to positions that are all closely related to one another.

Individual Cover Letters

The more diversified your career and the more diversified the types of positions for which you will be applying, the greater the need for individualized cover letters. These letters provide you with a vehicle to highlight specific qualifications, achievements, experiences, credentials, and more as they directly relate to the needs of a particular company.

Consider this example. You're a Vice President of Engineering with 10 years experience in the petrochemical industry. At this point in your career, you're interested in remaining in the engineering field and will be pursuing opportunities in both the petrochemical industry as well as other non-related industries. When you write your petrochemical letter, you are not only focusing on your engineering expertise, but also your industry and product knowledge. On the other hand, when you're writing to companies outside of your industry, chances are you won't even mention the word petrochemical. Instead, your focus is on engineering projects, products and technologies, while downplaying your particular industry experience. It is essential that you "paint the picture" you want someone to see by highlighting those experiences, and only those experiences, related to a particular company's needs.

Obviously, writing individual cover letters requires a great deal more effort on your part and will slow your job search process down a bit. However, if you are interested enough to contact a company, recruiter, or venture capital firm, then be willing to devote the time necessary to develop a cover letter that will spark their interest in you. It's well worth it in the long run.

Recipient

A key consideration when writing a cover letter is who the recipient will be. Are you writing to an HR manager, a company executive, a search firm, a venture capital firm or a network contact? Who you are writing to will dictate what you write and how you present it. Think about it as you read through the following section.

Letters to HR Managers

When you're writing to an HR manager in response to an advertisement in the *Wall Street Journal*, you're going to focus on responding to the specific qualifications as stated in the advertisement. You'll summarize the relevant highlights and achievements of your career as they relate to that specific position. You want to quickly and accurately demonstrate that you have exactly the experience and credentials they are seeking in a qualified candidate.

Be sure to respond to any particular requests that have been presented in an advertisement. This may include salary history, salary requirements, geographic preferences, technology skills, citizenship, foreign language skills, and more. I maintain a hard-and-fast rule that if the information has been requested, I am obligated to supply it or, at a minimum, refer to it in the letter with the comment that it can be discussed at the time of a personal interview.

Letters to Company Executives

When you're writing to a company executive, you're going to speak the language of the company and the industry. If you're writing to the CEO of a plastics manufacturing company, you'll highlight your industry-related experience and knowledge about products, technologies, industry trends, and the like. If you're writing to the VP of Marketing of an early-stage Internet company, your focus will be on your success in building market presence, launching new technologies, and generating revenues. Demonstrate that you understand the industry, the company, and their needs. What's more, let them know that you're the solution.

When writing to an executive, be sure to use "executive-level" language. Your cover letter should have an executive tone and style, and communicate energy, enthusiasm, dedication and success. Most important, it should leave the reader with a clear representation of the value you bring to the organization and to him/her.

Letters to Recruiters

When you're writing to a recruiter at a national search firm, you'll focus your letter on precisely the professions and industries in which the recruiter specializes. If the recruiter places executive management candidates in the insurance industry, you'll accentuate your executive leadership experience and your knowledge of the insurance industry. If the recruiter specializes in the placement of sales candidates in the technology and telecommunications industries, you'll focus on your sales achievements within those industries. Make these letters both industry-specific and job-specific.

When you're writing to recruiters, you want to be upfront about who you are and what you want. This may entail including information that you would generally not include in letters to companies, venture capital firms, or your personal network of contacts. Such information might include your specific salary requirements (see the upcoming section on *Salary History and Salary Requirements*), relocation preferences, citizenship or residency status, any physical limitations, and any special health care or educational requirements for special needs children.

You and the recruiter will be working together to find a good match and the above issues may directly impact that. For example, if you're not a U.S. citizen, you won't be eligible for a position that requires a high-level security clearance. Or, if you have a special needs child, chances are you won't be able to relocate to a remote area of Montana with no high-tech health care facilities. Sharing this type of information makes sure that neither you nor the recruiter are wasting your time.

Letters to Venture Capital Firms

When you're writing to a venture capital firm, you'll highlight your success in key areas of most interest, concern, and value to the venture capital and investment communities. If this is an audience you're interested in, be sure to highlight your involvement in launching profitable new ventures, raising private equity and/or institutional capital, increasing bottom-line profits, leading road shows, and participating in mergers, acquisitions, divestitures, IPOs, and other corporate transactions. These are just some of the hot buttons for the VC community.

Remember, however, that VC firms also need strong general management, financial management, sales management, and other senior-level leadership. Be sure to not only highlight the major "projects" of your career, but place equal emphasis on the overall management, strategic planning, and leadership value to you would bring to the firm.

Letters to Your Personal Network of Contacts

When you're writing to your network of contacts, your letters will be quite different than any of the above. Most often, they will be more casual in tone and may reference some personal issues such as family, kids, recreational activities and the like that are common denominators between you, the job seeker, and your contact. Of course, you'll also include relevant career information and perhaps even an achievement or two. Most important, however, you're writing to ask these individuals for their *help – not* for a job! (If they have an appropriate position, or know of one, chances are likely that they will mention it to you.)

How personal these letters are will depend on how well you know each contact. I often recommend you create a tiered system of networking, with Tier 1 being your closest colleagues, Tier 2 a step further away, and Tier 3 comprised of individuals whom you've had some contact with but don't really know well. Refer to the last section in this book for samples of the various styles of networking letters.

Message

Who are you? Are you a finance guy, a general management guy or an international business development gal? Do you build revenues, cut costs, launch new ventures, or optimize productivity? Is your expertise in new product development, customer relationship management, or government affairs? Who are you and how do you want to be perceived?

These are critical questions you must ask yourself before you write a single word of your letter. If you're not clear as to "who you are," then no one else will be. Fortunately, this is most likely a process that you completed while you were preparing your resume, so when you get to your cover letters, you already know the answer. Be advised, however, that the "who you are" can change a bit with each cover letter, based on the specific hiring requirements of each position and each company.

Just as critical, not only do you have to determine "who you are," you must communicate that information at the very start of your cover letter. Tell the reader right at the beginning that you're a senior-level IT executive, an insurance industry sales professional, or a member of a 3-person executive management team of a leading-edge E-commerce company. Don't make the recipient struggle through your letter trying to figure out who you are. Prospective employers generally won't take the time!

Presentation Style

There are three basic cover letter presentation styles. Which of these styles you use for any particular letter will depend on the specific information you want to communicate and to whom.

Paragraph-Style Letters

The paragraph-style is best used when you are "telling a story" about yourself, your career and your achievements. It provides a strong overview of your experience and qualifications, and highlights significant achievements within the body of the letter. Paragraph-style letters use narrative text and look much like the following:

```
Dear Ms. Alexander:

    When I reflect back on my career at J&J, it's hard to believe
that I left more than eight years ago. Seems like only yesterday!
Despite all the transition, what a great company it was and what a
tremendous learning ground for so many of us.

    As you're aware, I resigned my position with J&J to assume a VP
of Finance position with a high-growth communications company. Our
growth was phenomenal, building Thompson from $18 million in annual
revenues to more than $120 million with 28 distinct operating
companies/divisions. In fact, after just five years, I was promoted
to the #1 finance position in the company's largest and most profit-
able operating division.

    Then, in 1998, I was enticed to join an early-stage merchant
banking group in need of strong financial and operating leadership.
I thought this would be a tremendous opportunity and, in many ways,
it has been. Over the past two years, I orchestrated a major acqui-
sition and its complete reorganization and have recently launched
the start-up of a new high-tech venture. Our long-term goal is an
IPO; however, there have been so many changes within the investor
group that I have begun to question their long-term commitment.

    As such, I'm contacting a select group of my colleagues to
inquire if you are aware of any executive opportunities for a
candidate with my qualifications. I'm interested in a position that
will combine my financial and operating expertise, and would con-
sider a start-up venture, a rapid turnaround situation or a high-
growth company. I need a new challenge!
```

Bullet-Style Letters

The bullet-style is best used when you want to highlight specific achievements and qualifications in a letter format that is quick and easy to review. The text is often short phrases and sentences, each communicating one specific qualification or achievement. It looks much like the following:

```
Dear Mr. Greene:

I am forwarding my resume in response to your advertisement for a PR
Professional. Highlights of my professional career include:

    • More than 10 years' experience in both Broadcast and Print
      Journalism.

    • Strong background in marketing, public relations, customer
      relations, and copyrighting/editing.

    • Extensive network of contacts throughout the New York metro
      medical community developed through in-depth reporting and
      feature stories on the healthcare industry.

    • Excellent research, data collection, data synthesis and
      documentation skills.

    • Ability to independently plan, prioritize and manage special
      projects.

    • Outstanding skills and competencies in editorial content
      development.
```

Combination-Style Letters

My favorite, as you'll be able to tell from all of the samples in this book, is the combination-style letter. It is best used when you want to give a bit of your career story, share some of your personality, and highlight a few of your most notable accomplishments. The body of a combination-style letter looks much like the following:

Dear Ms. Hamilton:

I am a 12-year employee of Kesson Oil with a career in Sales & Marketing. Although secure in my current position, I am confidentially exploring new professional opportunities in the oil and gas industry, and have enclosed my resume for your review. Highlights of my professional career that may be of particular interest to you include:

- Current leadership of sales, marketing and business development programs for the South Florida market ($52 million in annual sales from 175 franchise locations). Closed 1999 at $6.5 million OVER profit plan.

- Selection for Kesson's Global Leadership Council, an honor bestowed on the top 1% of employees worldwide. Graduated #1 from Kesson's 5-month Technical Sales & Marketing Training Program.

- Delivered a 25% reduction in field/customer support costs while Acting Manager of Business Performance (involving best-in-class practices, benchmarking, consolidation and business unit revitalization).

- Outstanding communication, presentation, negotiation and customer relationship management skills. Accomplished sales trainer and team leader with an entrepreneurial spirit and solid decision-making and problem-solving skills. Thinks and performs independently.

Length

It is generally accepted that cover letters should be one page long. Remember, cover letters are designed to "tease" a prospective employer by highlighting your most notable qualifications and achievements as they relate to a particular company or professional opportunity. As we've learned earlier, they are NOT designed to encapsulate your entire career. Your only objective is to sell your career highlights and achievements as they are relevant to a particular situation.

However, there may be occasions when a second page is appropriate and necessary to communicate your message. Only you can be make this determination based on why you're writing a specific letter and to whom. Circumstances when you may want to consider a second page include:

- You are writing a broadcast letter and not a traditional cover letter. When you send a broadcast letter, you send it alone, without a resume. Therefore, it is often the case that you need to include a bit more information than you normally would in a letter – information about your specific employment experience and educational credentials.

- You have critical information to include and it simply will not fit onto one page. Just be sure that the information is indeed critical and valuable in generating interest in you and your qualifications.

- You are interested in an opportunity that does not quite fit your background and the information you have highlighted on your resume. However, you do have the experience. It simply has not been the focal point of your career. In this situation, you want to bring these skills, qualifications and achievements to the forefront in your cover letter and, as such, it may take an additional page.

- An advertisement has asked you to supply specific information in your cover letter, more information than will fit on one page.

- Your letter is long and dense, and there is little white space on the page. Well all know that readability is everything. If you cannot fit it comfortably onto one page, increase the type size, add in white space, push it onto two pages, and allow your letter to breathe.

It is never recommended that a cover letter be longer than two pages. If you find that your letter goes onto a third page, edit it and cut it. Your only objective with your cover letter (and resume) is to get in the door for an interview. If it's too long, people will be inclined to toss it into the "I'm going to look at this later" pile. If that happens, chances are you've lost the opportunity.

Distribution Strategy

The method in which a specific letter will be distributed will dictate several key points about its presentation. Is your letter going to be distributed via mail, fax, and/or email? Or, are you going to post your cover letter on your own website for review by prospective employers and recruiters? In today's electronic age, chances are you will be sending just as many resumes electronically as you will on paper. As such, it is critical to understand the similarities and the differences in visual presentation.

If you are going to be printing and mailing copies, you'll want to use a Printed Cover Letter. If you plan to send your letters via email, an Electronic Cover Letter will be right for you. And, if you want to combine the aesthetic qualities of the Printed Letter with the ease in transmission of the Electronic Letter, you may consider a Web Cover Letter.

Printed Cover Letters

The single most important thing to remember when you are preparing a printed cover letter is that you are writing a sales document. You have a product to sell – yourself – and it must be attractively packaged and presented. To compete against hundreds, if not thousands, of other qualified candidates, your letters must be sharp, distinct, and dynamic.

Use an up-to-date typestyle that is bold and attracts attention. This doesn't mean using an italic typeface, cute logos, or an outrageous paper color. Instead, be *conservatively distinctive*. Choose a sharp-looking typeface such as Bookman, Soutane, Krone, Garamond, or Fritz, or if your font selection is limited, the more common Times Roman, CG Omega, or Arial typefaces. The samples in this book will further demonstrate how to create documents that are sharp and upscale while still remaining conservative and "to the point."

Paper color should be clean and conservative, preferably white, ivory or light gray. You can even consider a bordered paper (e.g., light gray paper with small white border around the perimeter). It is only for "creative" positions (e.g., graphic arts, theater, media) where colored papers can be appropriate and are an important part of the packaging. In these situations, your challenge is to visually demonstrate your creative talents.

If possible, adhere to these formatting guidelines when preparing your printed cover letter:

- Do not expect readers to struggle through 10-15 line paragraphs. Substitute 2-3 shorter paragraphs or use bullets to offset new sentences and sections.

- Do not overdo **bold** and *italics* type. Excessive use of either defeats the purpose of these enhancements. If half of the type on the page is bold, nothing will stand out.

- Use nothing smaller than 10-point type. If you want employers to read your letter, make sure they don't need a magnifying glass!

- Don't clutter your letter. Everything you have heard about "white space" is true. Let your document "breathe" so readers do not have to struggle through it.

- Use an excellent printer. Smudged, faint, heavy or otherwise poor quality print will discourage red-eyed readers.

Electronic Cover Letters

Electronic cover letters are "plain Jane" letters stripped to the bone to allow for ease in file transfer, email, and other technical applications. Professional resume writers, who work so hard to make each resume and cover letter look good, "freak out," while engineers love how neat and clean these letters are!

If possible, adhere to these formatting guidelines when preparing your electronic cover letter:

- Avoid **bold** print, <u>underlining</u>, *italics*, and other type enhancements. If you want to draw attention to a specific word, heading, or title, use CAPITALIZATION to make it stand out.

- Type all information starting on the left hand side of the page. Do not center or justify any of the text, or use columns, for they generally do not translate well electronically.
- Leave white space just as you would with a printed cover letter. Ease in readability is a key factor in any type of communication.

- It is important to keep these letters shorter than print letters. Email is a tool for quick and efficient communication. Be sure that your letter is quick and easy to read. Make your letter a quick read.

NOTE: *Your electronic cover letter will automatically be presented in* `Courier` *typestyle. You have no control over this, as it is the automatic default.*

Web Cover Letters

As one would expect, a new phenomenon is emerging that allows you to merge the visual distinction of a printed resume and cover letter with the ease of electronic access. The new web resume and cover letter are hosted on your own website where you can refer recruiters, colleagues, potential employers, and others. Rather than pasting your plain-looking documents into an email message, include a link to your URL. With just one click, your printed resume and letter instantly appear. It is easy and efficient while still maintaining the integrity of the aesthetic quality of your job search communications.

For those in technology industries, you can go one step further and create a multimedia presentation. Never before have you been able to create a resume and cover letter that actually demonstrate your technical expertise. Just think of the competitive advantage web-based career documents can give your job search.

Cover Letter Etiquette

Should a cover letter be on the same paper as the accompanying resume?

Generally, yes. When both documents are presented on the same paper, the presentation is sharp and professional. However, if you'd like your presentation to be a bit different, try using complementary papers. For example, type your resume on a light gray paper with white border and your cover letters on matching white paper for an upscale and distinctive presentation.

How should you address a cover letter if you do not have a contact name?

"Dear Sir/Madam" is the most acceptable salutation if you do not have a contact name at a particular company or search firm. However, whenever possible, make a telephone call and get a contact name. It is certainly much better to write to someone specifically rather than to anyone. Further, you then have a contact name for future follow up.

Should you mail your resumes and cover letters in large envelopes (9"x12") or regular #10 envelopes?

I have listened to 45-minute discussions about envelope size! Have you ever made a hiring decision based on size of envelope? Probably not. Therefore, it honestly does not matter. However, I recommend that you use #10 envelopes for most of your mailings. Use the larger 9x12 envelopes for high-level network contacts, direct mail to senior executives, and advertisements for senior management opportunities. It makes sense. If you are mailing your resume and cover letter to Bill Gates, don't fold them into a little envelope. However, if mailing to 500 recruiters, the small envelopes are fine and less expensive. Use your judgment and follow your instincts.

Should you use monarch size paper for your cover letters?

Monarch paper (7¼ x 10½) does stand out from the more traditional letter size paper (8½ x 11) and appears more personal. However, I have never found that size of paper made any difference in determining whether or not an individual was offered the opportunity for an interview. I leave monarch size paper to your discretion.

If writing "cold" to a company (not in response to a specific advertisement), should you send your resume and cover letter to the Human Resources Department?

No! HR departments process, review and evaluate resumes. They generally do not make hiring decisions, unless it is for a position in the HR Department. Instead, forward your resume and cover letter to the President, CEO, COO, Vice President of Sales & Marketing, or another senior executive with the authority to schedule an interview and make a hiring decision. It is much more efficient to work "down from the top" than to start with the HR Department and try to climb out.

Should you always follow up with a phone call after you've sent a letter and resume?

Telephone follow-up can be quite costly. Furthermore, it is often difficult to get the person you wish to speak to on the phone. Try calling during off-hours and be persistent but not annoying. Also, be sure to position yourself well with the secretary or assistant of the individual you are attempting to contact. They can be your single most valuable asset in opening the door and getting in.

I do not recommend telephone follow-up after each and every letter and resume you forward unless you have a contact at the company, consider yourself an ideal candidate, or are particularly interested in that company or position. Your time is better spent getting more resumes and cover letters out than leaving phone messages that may never be returned.

Salary History & Salary Requirements

If you've ever read any books on resume writing, you've heard it repeated time and time again that you should never include salary on your resume. The correct tool for communicating that information is your cover letter, where you can briefly respond to a request for compensation information.

To best begin our discussion, let's start with a clear definition of the differences between salary history and salary requirements. A **salary history** is a listing of your past positions with beginning and ending salaries. The salary history, if truly comprehensive, will include not only your salary, but your bonuses, incentives, and other compensation.

Salary requirements refers to your current salary objectives. This information can be presented as (1) a *specific number* ("My salary requirement is $100,000 annually plus complete benefits package"), or as (2) a *range* ("My salary requirements are $100,000 to $135,000 annually").

There are only two situations when it is appropriate to provide salary information:

- **Ad Responses**. When you are responding to a specific advertisement that has asked each candidate to supply salary history and/or salary requirements.

- **Recruiters**. Every time you write to a recruiter. You don't want to waste the recruiter's time or yours, so be sure to provide basic information about your current salary requirements. The recruiter doesn't want to call you for a job that pays $400,000 if you're only making $100,000 now. Conversely, you don't want to get a call for a job that pays $55,000 when your interests are in a $200,000+ position.

Other than the two situations above, salary is *not* a topic to be discussed in a cover letter. It is a much better strategy to discuss salary history and requirements in a person-to-person interview where you can ask questions (e.g., salary ranges of company executives, compensation paid to previous individuals in the position, bonus and incentive plans, stock options) and explore competitive market/industry data.

My recommendation when supplying salary information at such an early stage in the hiring process (when you are initially submitting your resume for consideration), is to "define the ballpark." Simply put, this means giving a broad-brushed overview that allows the reader to quickly ascertain "where you fit in." Salary is often a very difficult topic to discuss in a cover letter – particularly if you know little about a specific position or a specific company. You don't want to state a figure that is too high and will put you "out of the running." However, you don't want to "low ball" your worth either.

Consider the following examples:

- **When asked for a salary history**, it is not necessary to include a detailed salary review of your entire career. Rather, you might write, "As requested, my recent salary has averaged $95,000 to $135,000 over the past 5 years."

- **When asked for salary requirements**, you do not have to include a specific dollar value. Rather, you might write, "My salary requirements are $150,000+, but flexible based upon the requirements and demands of the position."

If an advertisement, a recruiter, or a specific company asks for a comprehensive salary history it is recommended that you prepare an additional page that lists the compensation history of your entire career, starting with the most recent position and working your way backwards in time. Consider one of the two following formats:

Position Title	Company	Dates	Starting Salary	Ending Salary
President	TDS Tech, Inc.	1999-Present	$150,000+	$250,000+

Position	Company	Dates	Starting Compensation	Ending Compensation
President	TDS Tech, Inc.	1999-Present	$150,000 base salary Stock options 10% year-end bonus Generous benefits	$250,000 base salary Stock options 10% year-end bonus Generous benefits

Expert Resources

In order to give yourself the competitive job search advantage, it is often wise to consult a resume, career, or job search expert. These individuals can provide you with insights and expert guidance as you plan and manage your search campaign. You have your choice of working with a professional resume and cover letter writer, executive career coach, career counselor, outplacement consultant, recruiter, and others who deliver job search services and support to candidates like yourself.

What's more, there are companies that will post your resume online, other companies that post position announcements on the Web, and others that produce targeted email and print campaigns to prospective employers that you select. There are reference-checking companies, coaches who specialize in interview training, and publications galore on executive job search and career marketing.

The list of potential resources is virtually endless, from the resume writer down the street to the global outplacement consulting firm with offices on 6 out of 7 continents. The emergence of all these firms has created a wealth of resources for job seekers, but also made the process much more difficult with so many choices. How do you determine exactly what help you need and from whom? Then, how do you find the right person?

Refer to Appendix A for a list of the professional members of the Career Masters Institute, a prestigious professional association whose members work with job seekers worldwide to help them plan and manage successful search campaigns. They are resume writers, career coaches, counselors, career development specialists, recruiters, outplacement consultants, and others, ready, willing and able to provide you with expert job search and career planning assistance.

3

Best Cover Letter Samples

The 200+ cover letters that follow are "real-life" letters written for "real-life" job seekers, all of whom either make $100,000+ a year or are close to that mark. Each was written with a specific objective in mind; each was written to showcase the talents, achievements, and career successes of each job seeker as they related to a specific opportunity or a specific career path. Most important, each has opened doors, generated interviews, and helped close top-level opportunities. Use the sample words, formats, styles, strategies, and concepts as the foundation for writing your own powerful executive cover letter.

Accounting & Audit

KeyWords, Action Verbs & High-Impact Phrases to "Nail" Your Cover Letter:

- General Accounting & Cost Accounting

- Accounting Information Systems Technology

- Cost Reductions & Avoidance

- Financial Planning, Analysis & Reporting

- Internal & External Audit Management

- Budgeting, Forecasting & Projections

- Process Design & Efficiency Improvement

- Integrated Accounting Systems & Consolidation

- Banking & Cash Flow Management

- Credit & Collections Management

STUART GRANT, CPA, CMA
stugrantcpa@cpa.com
21547 South Washington Avenue
Morristown, New Jersey 08654

Home (908) 491-5471

Office (201) 655-5410

March 12, 2001

Ronald Keeler
President
Pacific Manufacturing, Inc.
1234 Grant Highway, Suite 5472
Los Angeles, CA 90054

Dear Mr. Keeler:

Recruited to LLC Industries in 1984, I spearheaded the development and management of all corporate accounting operations for over 12 years as the company grew, expanded, acquired, merged and reconfigured itself several times. The challenges were enormous and the opportunity tremendous.

My role with the corporation expanded beyond corporate accounting to include active participation with the executive and operating management teams in strategic planning and corporate development. Involved in numerous mergers, acquisitions and divestitures, I not only provided the "numbers" but also the rationale, strategy and action plans to achieve our results.

As you review my resume, you will note that I have extensive qualifications in all corporate accounting and financial reporting functions in combination with extensive skills in debt management/restructuring, cash management and related corporate treasury functions. I am a decisive business manager with excellent planning and problem solving skills, eager to take on new challenges and deliver results.

Currently, I am exploring new professional opportunities and would welcome a personal interview for the position of Corporate Accounting Director as advertised in the Search Bulletin. I appreciate your time and consideration, and look forward to meeting with you.

Sincerely,

Stuart Grant, CPA, CMA

Enclosure

DOLORES M. LOREAN
9845 Beverley Glen Street #102
Los Angeles, California 90087
(310) 977-6544

August 12, 2000

Barbara Van Sprecken, HR Director
American Greeting Cards
9348 North Pacific Avenue
Los Angeles, CA 97764

Dear Ms. Van Sprecken:

I am a well-qualified Accounting Professional/Accounting Supervisor writing in response to your advertisement for a Manager of Accounting. Highlights of my professional career include:

* Thirteen years' experience in Accounts Receivable, Billing, Credit/Collection, Accounts Payable and Accounting/Financial Reporting.
* Introduction of leading edge MIS and PC applications to automate manual accounting functions, increase data accuracy and reduce monthly closing cycles.
* Training and development of accounting professionals and support staff.
* Extensive qualifications in customer relationship management and communications.
* Excellent analytical, decision making and problem-solving skills.

Recruited to Investment News in 1990, I was the driving force behind the development of a sophisticated accounts receivable system. During my five-year tenure, as the company sales increased 75%, I was able to build the systems, policies, procedures and standards to manage growth with no additional staff. Our results were significant and measurable.

Investment News has recently brought in a new management team and realigned the workforce. Thus my interest in your search and request for a personal interview. Thank you.

Sincerely,

Dolores M. Lorean

Enclosure

JENNIFER A. MARIETTA
5274 Roundabout Drive
Athens, Georgia 33858
Home (770) 414-6470
Office (770) 515-6547

February 27, 2001

W.R. Grace & Company
c/o Dept. TF
1 Town Center Road
Boca Raton, FL 33486-1010

Dear Sir/Madam:

In need of a **Director of Internal Audit**? Let me tell you why I'm the perfect candidate:

- Eight years of progressively responsible experience in the design, development and leadership of large-scale internal audit organizations (financial, IS and operational).

- Success in transitioning audit from an internal "regulatory" function into a cooperative business partner to all operating units, responsive to their constantly changing operating, market and financial demands.

- Extensive IS experience throughout my career with recent leadership responsibility (in cooperation with other management executives) for a multi-million dollar SAP implementation.

- Record of fast-track career promotion, based on combined strength of management, leadership, analytical, technology and project management skills. Current responsibility for financial affairs of 50 business units nationwide.

- Consistent and verifiable contributions to improved revenues and profits through process redesign, internal controls, cost reduction and performance improvement initiatives.

Although secure in my current position, I am confidentially exploring new professional challenges and opportunities. Thus my interest in interviewing for the position of Director of Internal Audit where I guarantee to provide strong, decisive and results-driven leadership.

I appreciate your time in reviewing my qualifications and look forward to speaking with you.

Sincerely,

Jennifer A. Marietta

Enclosure

Advertising & Public Relations

KeyWords, Action Verbs & High-Impact Phrases to "Nail" Your Cover Letter:

- Advertising Agency Relations
- Major Campaigns & Client Projects
- Internet & New Media Campaigns
- VIP Relations
- Press Relations & Coverage
- Corporate Communications
- Revenue & Profit Increases
- Special Events Management
- Crisis Communications
- Employee Communications

RACHEL S. THOMPSON

565 Lakeside Drive   (811) 234-0090
Spring, MT 65471

November 4, 2000

Matthew Atkinson
Dunn Corporation
525 University Avenue, Suite 1500
Menlo Park, CA 94025

Dear Mr. Atkinson:

Consider this. In 1996, millions of PR dollars were invested in the promotion of both emerging and well-established information, telecommunications, Internet and multimedia technology companies. Projections for 1997 and 1998 are even stronger, yet the number of PR firms offering such services is still quite limited. In fact, many of the technology companies that are headquartered in the Washington metro area are going to Philadelphia, New York and other major cities for high-quality, high-caliber PR representation.

This is where I can be of value to Dunn Corporation. With 16 years of top-flight PR and account management experience, I have provided both the strategy and the tactical implementation plans to leaders in the technology industry — Apple Computers, Novell, Cericor Technologies, Hewlett Packard, MCI and Landmark Systems Corporation. The scope of my responsibility has ranged from the conceptual design and implementation of PR campaigns for worldwide product launch to issues arising from complex and rapidly-changing regulatory requirements. Further, my success has included both the development of new client relationships as well as the growth, expansion and retention of existing accounts.

Working either as the Principal of my own PR agency or as the full-time Director of PR, I have been the driving force behind numerous successful PR, advertising and marketing initiatives for these organizations. In an agency setting, I have combined creative talents with more structured general business skills to deliver campaigns that are cost-effective, market-appropriate and profitable. In turn, I have created the market and established the image that has driven millions and millions of dollars in new revenues. Equally solid is my performance in strategic planning, P&L management, team building/leadership, organization development, project planning/management and general administrative affairs.

Now my goal is to launch a start-up PR function targeted exclusively to the technology industry, and I am contacting you to explore your potential interest in this and related market opportunities. I would welcome the chance to speak with you to evaluate your interest, share my ideas and determine the potential viability of such an endeavor. I'll follow up next week to discuss your interest and how we proceed from this point forward.

Sincerely,

Rachel S. Thompson

Enclosure

MARY R. GLEN
1511 McLean Avenue
Charleston, West Virginia 55413
(304) 917-0045

June 26, 2000

M. Marriot
Coplthorne & Bellows
1021 Crown Point Parkway #340
Atlanta, GA 30338

Dear M. Marriot:

The world of public relations has changed! No longer is PR a "behind the scenes" function churning out press releases. Today, PR is one of the most critical and most visible functions within an successful corporation. A qualified candidate must be strategist, writer, public speaker and more.

This is the expertise I bring to Coplthorne & Bellows. With 16 years professional experience with both PR agencies and directly with companies in the high-tech industry, I have demonstrated my ability to build market recognition, increase customer awareness, and provide the foundation for strong and sustainable revenue growth.

The breadth of my experience spans markets worldwide and includes the complete portfolio of PR functions (e.g., publicity, PR, print and broadcast communications, multimedia advertising, strategy, special events). I am successful in combining creative talents with more structured general business skills to deliver campaigns that are cost-effective, market-appropriate and profitable. Equally solid is my performance in strategic planning, team building/leadership, organization development, project management and general administrative affairs.

I would welcome the opportunity to interview for your Public Relations Search and can guarantee that the strength of my qualifications will add measurable value to both your operations and your clients. Thank you. I look forward to speaking with you.

Sincerely,

Mary R. Glen

Enclosure

NANCY FRIEDMAN

1511 Park Avenue, #409
New York, New York 10010
(212) 917-0045
nancy.friedman.22@mantech.com

March 31, 2001

Diane M. Woodson
Public Relations Inc.
9834 Commercial Drive, Suite 398
McLean, VA 20354

Dear Ms. Woodson:

Gaining positive public relations and publicity is an art that requires the ability to merge strategy with concept and action. It demands an individual who not only understands the product and the market, but knows the "PR game" and its significant players.

This is the expertise I bring to your organization. With 16 years of top-level public relations, publicity, advertising, marketing and special events experience, I have created winning campaigns that have received positive press coverage and facilitated strong market gains. Most notably, I have demonstrated my flexibility in transitioning PR programs from one industry to another, capitalizing upon the core competencies of each campaign while reinventing tactics to meet specific market demands.

I have often found myself challenged, working in a boardroom of "old line" companies unaware of the tremendous demands and influence of public relations. Being able to communicate the value of PR to these individuals has not only required strong and decisive presentation skills, but the ability to educate regarding the value of sophisticated creativity.

My career has spanned the entire spectrum of the PR market — from Wall Street investors to individual consumers — from leading broadcast media to large employee groups — from individual corporate sponsors to worldwide advertising agencies. To each, I have provided the strategic, tactical and operating leadership critical to communicating our messages and accelerating our growth.

At this juncture in my career, I am seeking a position that will allow me to continue spearheading successful, visible and results-driven publicity and PR campaigns. Thus my interest in your search for a Public Relations Director and request for a personal interview. Thank you.

Sincerely,

Nancy Friedman

Enclosure

BRYAN ALEXANDER
9834 South Atlantic Avenue - Garden City, NY 11550 - (516) 538-5261

November 13, 2000

Metropolitan Public Relations
Attn: Angela
934 Avenue of the Americas, 23rd Floor
New York, NY 10110

FAX (212) 138-6541

Dear Angela:

I am forwarding my resume in response to your advertisement for a Public Relations Professional. Highlights of my professional career that may be of particular interest to you include the following:

- More than 10 years' experience in both Broadcast and Print Journalism.

- Strong background in marketing, public relations, customer relations and copyrighting/editing.

- Extensive network of contacts throughout the New York metro medical community developed through in-depth reporting and feature stories on the healthcare industry.

- Excellent research, data collection, data synthesis and documentation skills.

- Ability to independently plan, prioritize and manage special projects.

- Outstanding skills and competencies in editorial content development.

My goal is to transition my experience into a high-profile marketing/public relations position where I can continue to drive forward growth and corporate recognition. You will find that the combination of my research, writing and reporting qualifications will make a positive and long-lasting impact upon the success of Metropolitan.

I appreciate your time and consideration, and look forward to meeting with you. Thank you.

Sincerely,

Bryan Alexander

Enclosure

Association & Not-For-Profit Management

KeyWords, Action Verbs & High-Impact Phrases to "Nail" Your Cover Letter:

- Board & Foundations Relations

- Staff Training & Leadership

- Operating Cost Reductions

- Member Services Development & Delivery

- Revenue Success

- Legislative & Regulatory Affairs

- Public & Private Partnerships

- Capital Giving & Fundraising

- Member Communications

- Press Affairs, Public Affairs & Public Relations

JACK ARTHUR
10415 Republican Lane
Topeka, Kansas 66673

Phone: (601) 469-5753   Fax: (601) 469-3826   Email: jarthur2393@aol.com

March 24, 2000

John D. Valenti
Chairman of the Board
International Association of Painters
2938 Main Street
Reading, MA 02837

Dear Mr. Valenti :

As one of the top three executives in a national nonprofit organization, I am recognized for my expertise in building strong, efficient, cost-effective and productive operations responsive to our members' needs. My efforts, and those of the two other members of the executive management team, were the foundation for the tremendous financial and operational success of NARP.

When we started years ago, the organization was an unknown entity. Through our efforts in building a strong business culture, developing sound financial policies, introducing advanced technology, and driving member development, we now boast of a national reputation and strong bottom-line. My contributions to that organization and the value I bring to IAP are best summarized as follows:

Financial Leadership

I built NARP's entire financial, accounting, internal auditing and budgeting infrastructure from the ground floor. This included developing a progressive cash management program, managing payroll and related tax affairs, negotiating lines of credit and managing investments valued in excess of $3 million. Further, I launched a series of aggressive cost reduction initiatives that reduced overhead costs within specific categories by as much as 40%. Through my efforts, NARP ended 1998 with a projected investment reserve of one year's operating expense.

Organizational & Administrative Leadership

My contributions to the Board of Directors, Executive Committee and Finance Committee were strong and active. Perhaps most notable were my efforts in relationship development – with legal counsel, bankers, investors, insurance managers, government officials and others – all critical to the long-term development and viability of the association. I am a strong communicator with keen negotiation and interpersonal relationship management skills.

43

Human Resources Leadership

When I joined NARP there was no HR function. Under my leadership, we developed a complete HR function, recruitment and benefit programs, retirement plans, training programs, job descriptions, employee manuals and more. Today, NARP has a fully-integrated HR organization able to support the association as it continues to grow, expand and strengthen its operations.

Office Technology

In an attempt to keep pace with the rapid emergence of new technologies, I spearheaded the acquisition and implementation of a host of computer systems designed specifically for association management. Further, I led the acquisition of several generations of telephone/ telecommunication systems. As such, I bring to IAP a good working knowledge of the technology and telecommunication tools available to meet industry needs and enhance productivity.

Program & Convention Management

My contributions to programming, conventions and meetings has focused on the planning and logistical "side of the house." Over the years, I coordinated efforts for up to 10 events per year which hosted up to 20,000 total participants. In addition, I have been active in providing content development concepts to better service our national membership.

As you can see, the strength of my experience in Association Management is broad and has always been devoted to forward action to achieve member support and strong financial performance. Please also note that I have an MBA in Finance and a BS in Business, both from Long Island University.

My goal is to continue within Association Management; however, my direction has changed. Throughout my entire career, I have been quite interested in the Building, Construction & Housing industry and, in fact, worked for a $200 million REIT early in my career. Through this experience, I developed a strong foundation and understanding of the industry, its partners, its financial demands and its operating requirements. Years later, I earned my real estate license, just to keep my "fingers in the pot." Now, I am ready to make a full transition to an association whose mission is to service that industry. I'm sure you will agree that my experience places me in a well qualified position for such an opportunity.

I would welcome a personal interview to discuss your current executive staffing requirements and would be pleased to provide any additional information you require. Thank you.

Sincerely,

Jack Arthur

Enclosure

DAVID R. MYERS, CAE, CIC
123 Lewiston Road
Reston, Virginia 22493

Home: 703-866-0836   Office: 703-888-3300

June 1, 2000

Elwood R. Filbert, III
Managing Partner
Association Recruitment Specialists
One Majors Lane, S.W.
Washington, DC 20009

Dear Mr. Filbert:

When I joined ARA in 1989, the Association was fraught with organizational challenges and issues. Today, our organization is strong, our cash flow is positive, our member retention is outstanding and we are technologically on the "cutting edge."

Previously, during my 5-year tenure with AMMA, I built a "best-in-class" business organization to support the Association through dramatic change, reorganization and relocation. In fact, my leadership was critical in transitioning from a negative cash flow to $6+ million positive.

These two examples clearly demonstrate the value I bring to one of your client organizations. I began my career in Association Management with a concentration in Finance, Administration and Information Technology, advancing rapidly through a series of increasingly responsible positions. In 1987, a unique opportunity presented itself and I successfully transitioned into general management. Today, as the CEO and EVP of a nationwide association, I have built an organization that is well-respected, innovative and financially solid.

Characterized by others as a strong business leader, I have been recognized for my success in partnership development, member services, regulatory affairs, marketing/product development and regulatory/government affairs. Perhaps most significant are my leadership capabilities and my success in building high-performance business teams to support association goals, objectives and member needs.

At this point in my career, I am confidentially exploring new professional challenges and opportunities, and would welcome the chance to discuss any specific search assignments that are appropriate for an executive with my background. Be advised that I am open to relocation and that my salary requirements are $125,000+. Thank you.

Sincerely,

David R. Myers, CAE, CIC

Enclosure

LESTER W. WATSON
9834 Chicago Avenue
Highland Park, Illinois 60547
Phone: (847) 547-6471
Email: leswatson@association.net

July 20, 2000

James P. Carter, Chairman
International Peanut Council
9485 Peanut Lane
Atlanta, Georgia 64721

Dear Mr. Carter:

With 20 years' experience in Association Management, I bring to the International Peanut Council strong management experience and a record of significant financial results. Directing associations with both corporate and individual members, I have consistently delivered strong performance in:

- Revenue & Profit Improvement
- New Member Development & Member Retention
- New Product & New Service Development
- Budgeting, Fundraising & Corporate Giving
- Administrative Management & Organizational Change/Reengineering

As President & CEO, the scope of my responsibility has spanned all association operations — from strategic planning, Board affairs and budgeting/financial management to member services, public relations and corporate liaison affairs. I combine strong leadership and communications skills with the ability to energize teams and initiate action. In turn, financial, service and operating results have improved year after year.

My goal is to secure a new executive position with an association in need of strong and decisive leadership. I guarantee to increase your membership, expand your services and improve your financial results. I appreciate your time and look forward to speaking with you.

Sincerely,

Lester W. Watson

Enclosure

MARTIN A. JURY
88 San Laguna Beach Trail
Santa Monica, CA 99983
903.737.8865
mjury@association.net

March 21, 2000

National Action Council for Minorities in Engineering
President & Chief Executive Officer Search
c/o Ayers and Associates, Inc.
1745 Jefferson Davis Highway, Suite 404
Arlington, VA 22202

Dear Sir/Madam:

I am currently employed as the Director of Education for one of the world's largest technology companies. In this position for the past five years, I have orchestrated a number of programs nationwide to facilitate minority access to educational, training and career opportunities in engineering, science and technology. The scope of my experience is directly in line with the search requirements for the President/CEO of NACME, and I have enclosed my resume, executive profile and references for your review. However, there are several key initiatives that I would like to bring to your attention:

- Forged industry-leading partnerships with major educational institutions nationwide to provide technological expertise in advancing their technology infrastructures and student educational opportunities. Currently, I am working on programs with the University of Miami, University of Georgia, University of Northern Arkansas, the State Departments of Education in Mississippi and Delaware, and several other institutions.

- Negotiated public/private partnerships to fund and develop emerging technologies (e.g., data mining, virtual learning, global learning, computer modeling/simulation, speech recognition, web-based ventures).

- Led development and funding for the corporation's Ph.D. Fellowship in Science, Engineering and Mathematics for Underrepresented Minorities and Women.

- Developed and funded several educational grant programs targeted exclusively to African-American, Latino and other minority groups.

- Pioneered innovative technology-based educational opportunities for university and school administrators, educators and students.

- Researched and prepared benchmark analysis of our company's performance in minority recruitment as compared to other major industry players.

National Action Council for Minorities in Engineering
March 21, 2000
Page Two

In each and every project we undertake, we are committed to not only increasing educational opportunities, but promoting increased student retention rates, improved academic performance, cultural diversity in the workplace and lifelong career decision-making. And, we have succeeded. To date, these initiatives have provided new and enriched educational opportunities for more than 10,000 students across the country.

Just as critical, my team and I have positioned our organization as a sought-after resource and the preferred method of action throughout the organization and with our customers to recruit and develop a diverse workforce with a special focus on underrepresented minorities. Collateral responsibilities have included:

- Steering Committee Team Leader – People of Color and Disabilities in Technology.

- Peer Reviewer – National Science Foundation's Centers for Research Excellence in Science and Technology (CREST).

- Guest Speaker – The Association of Departments of Computer & Information Science & Engineering at Harvard University Foundation's annual meeting. Presented to 200 minority students interested in science, engineering and mathematics from universities nationwide.

- Senior Advisor – Model Academic Institutions. Industry partner to six minority-serving institutions to increase the pipeline of well-trained minorities pursuing careers in mathematics, science and engineering.

Complementing all of this experience are my strengths in strategic planning, organizational leadership, team building, project management, finance and law. Further, I have extensive experience managing relationships with Board of Directors and other top-level executives. I am an independent thinker and decision-maker, creative in my program and project management efforts, and successful in building solid business systems and infrastructures. What's more, I thoroughly enjoy working with the academic community and know what it takes to win their support and cooperation.

Be advised that my job search is confidential. I am not actively in the market, but am intrigued by the opportunity with NACME and look forward to interviewing with you. Please let me know if you would like any additional information. Thank you.

Sincerely,

Martin A. Jury

Enclosure

Banking

KeyWords, Action Verbs & High-Impact Phrases to "Nail" Your Cover Letter:

- Revenue & Profit Increases

- Operating Cost Reductions

- New Services & New Products

- Technology Installations

- New Sources of Fee Income

- Asset & Portfolio Development & Management

- Bad Debt Recovery & Workout

- Large/High-Profile Financial Transactions

- Reorganization & Consolidation

- Regulatory Performance

WALTER H. CHRISTOPHSON
125 Pembroke Drive
Richmond, Virginia 25841

Home: (804) 253-2467   Office: (804) 727-0707

October 31, 2000

Jason Adler
Chairman
Fidelity Savings Bank
3942 Northeast 34th Street
Richmond, VA 25465

Dear Mr. Adler:

The dynamics of banking have changed so dramatically throughout my 20-year career that I often wonder if I really do work in the same industry!

With the tremendous regulatory changes, transition from "old-line" banking to customer service-driven organizations, and the unprecedented number of mergers and acquisitions, the challenges have been demanding. The latter has been most relevant to my career, having not only "survived" three major acquisitions, but playing a vital role in the integration of diverse operations, services, products and personnel.

Further, my achievements have included several successful business and product line start-ups, a number of aggressive reengineering and process redesign initiatives, and a constant focus on productivity, quality and financial gains. I am a strong operations manager, able to direct large staffs at multiple locations in the design and delivery of complete banking services to both corporate and consumer markets.

My financial results speak for themselves with recent achievements including:

* $7 million increase in new business volume through expanded marketing and direct sales initiatives.
*   30% gain in profit and revenue results despite near 50% workforce downsizing.
*   Ranking in Gallup's Top 3% on customer service benchmarks.

After a successful effort in private consulting, I am anxious to return to the banking industry and look forward to speaking with you to explore management opportunities with Central Fidelity Bank. Thank you.

Sincerely,

Walter H. Christophson

Enclosure

NEAL DOUGLAS
13458 S.W. 62nd Street
Portland, Oregon 96542
(801) 386-7991
douglasneal@aol.com

January 18, 2001

Allison Hentges
Director of Human Resources
National Bank of America, Inc.
9349 Fifth Avenue, 34th Floor
New York, NY 10031

Dear Ms. Hentges:

I am a well-qualified Banking Professional recognized for my expertise in solving operating problems, improving customer relations, accelerating fee income and asset growth, and strengthening personnel performance. Despite the competitive challenges, I have consistently delivered results.

- **If your goal is to increase lending volume**, I originated over $1 million in mortgages within less than two years.

- **If your goal is to increase deposit growth**, I captured $8.8 million in net deposits in 1995.

- **If your goal is to strengthen your market position and customer image**, I led a number of marketing, business development and outreach programs which dominated local markets and outperformed our competition.

- **If your goal is to enhance customer service**, I spearheaded a number of successful programs that not only increased customer satisfaction, but improved staff's focus on service, retention and performance.

My goal is to secure a management position with a leading financial institution seeking qualified, career-oriented professionals looking for long-term opportunities for employment and promotion. I appreciate your consideration and look forward to what I anticipate will be the first of many positive communications. Thank you.

Sincerely,

Neal Douglas

Enclosure

HENRICO L. SOLOMON
346 West 45rd Street * New York, NY 10185 * H (212) 763-2836 * hsolomon@aol.com

February 1, 2001

Jonathan Smith
President & CEO
Charter Banking Corporation
189 Elmwood Boulevard
Iowa City, IA 64638

Dear Mr. Smith:

I have but one professional goal – to continue to build high-growth private banking programs targeted specifically to high net worth Italian investors. It's where my career has focused for the past 10 years and where I have delivered outstanding performance results:

- Currently with Excelsior Bank's International Division, I created an entirely new market segment of Italian investors that currently have more than $450 million in invested and deposited assets with CitiGroup.

- During my tenure with one of Italy's largest and most diversified financial institutions, I personally brought more than $50 million in assets to the bank over four years.

- While working with Robey and Company, I was one of only three finance professionals responsible for establishing the company's initial market presence throughout Italy. First year results exceeded expectations by better than 200%.

I bring to your organization a strong blend of business development, marketing, sales and customer management expertise. Combine that with my solid financial, investment, portfolio management, asset management and analytical skills, and I guarantee my ability to produce. My only interest in leaving Exelsior (it's been a great experience for five years!) is my intrigue with Charter and your premier market position.

If you are interested in a candidate with my qualifications and objectives, I would welcome a personal interview at your earliest convenience. Be advised that I am open to relocation and extensive travel as may be required. Thank you.

Sincerely,

Henrico Solomon

Enclosure

FELICIA C. URENDA
6547 Collins Avenue
Coral Gables, Florida 31183
(954) 386-7991

January 2, 2001

John Rockwell
Florida National Bank
9485 Sunshine Corporate Center, Suite 3934
Miami, Florida 32654

Dear Mr. Rockwell:

I am looking for a great opportunity. With 12 years of increasingly responsible experience in retail and commercial banking operations, I bring to your organization excellent qualifications in:

- Introducing customer service driven initiatives to enhance customer retention, improve customer loyalty and promote new business development.

- Developing and implementing improved business processes to streamline operations,   reduce overhead costs and improve overall performance.

- Launching sales and marketing initiatives that have won dominant positioning despite extensive market competition.

Promoted rapidly throughout my career, I advanced to Branch Vice President with the Bank of Miami. My challenge was to enhance the performance of both domestic and international banking operations. Results were impressive and included the negotiation/closure of numerous commercial banking agreements and recognition as a top revenue producer for two consecutive years. Please also note that I have strong qualifications in consumer lending, and am currently managing a high-profile loan marketing and lending operation for Savings of America.

My goal is to join a leading banking institution offering opportunities in the Miami area for long-term employment and career advancement. In turn, I guarantee strong performance, consistently superior results and a real commitment to your organization.

Sincerely,

Felicia C. Urenda

Enclosure

Construction

KeyWords, Action Verbs & High-Impact Phrases to "Nail" Your Cover Letter:

- Project Planning, Administration & Management

- Large Dollar & Major Projects

- Regulatory Compliance & Reporting

- Environmental Issues & Hazardous Site Remediation

- Contract & Partner Negotiations

- Union & Trade Relations

- Investor Negotiations & Reporting

- Project Scheduling & Crewing

- Resource & Equipment Management

- Project Lifecycle Management

CHARLES G. PALMER
188 Grossman Drive
Ellington, Illinois 67654
(613) 832-0936

December 4, 2000

Dan Owens
President
Tiburon Construction & Development
1 Lakeside Drive
Tiburon, CA 99382

Dear Mr. Owens:

After a long and successful career as the Vice President of Engineering and Construction for EnvironCare, I have decided to resign my position and seek opportunities elsewhere. With the company for more than 10 years, I have "survived" countless mergers, reorganizations, spin-offs and other corporate initiatives. Throughout all the transition, I have continued to effectively, efficiently and profitably direct engineering and construction.

My goal is a position on your senior executive team where I can utilize the strength of my experience in both construction management as well as general management. Briefly summarized, my qualifications include:

- More than 20 years' experience in construction project management, from initial proposal and client presentation stages through complete design, engineering and construction to start-up staffing and operations. My specific areas of functional expertise are outlined on the enclosed resume.

- Equally solid performance as a general manager, including full P&L for departmental operations and projects worldwide. In addition, I have directed the entire purchasing function, corporate facilities design and management, a complex contracting and subcontracting function, human resources, M&A integration and a host of other senior-level operating responsibilities.

I would welcome the opportunity to meet with you, and can guarantee that the strength of my experience, strong reputation and ability to deliver results will add measurable value to your organization. Thank you.

Sincerely,

Charles G. Palmer

Enclosure

EDWARD BRENTWOOD
5647 Chapel Drive
New Orleans, Louisiana 43241
(971) 984-3413

March 16, 2001

Bradley Majors
United Development Corp
11540 Santa Monica Boulevard, Suite 643
Los Angeles, CA 90021

Dear Mr. Majors:

Throughout my real estate development and construction management career, I have planned, designed, built and marketed more than 50 residential, commercial, health care, technology and light industrial properties worldwide. Total project values within the past 10 years have exceeded $450 million and served as the catalyst for large-scale inner city redevelopment as well as new community development projects.

Critical to my success is my ability to build cooperation among diverse public and private interests groups to fund and support project development. This has often required sensitive negotiations and communications, allowing me to rally support and drive forward projects with significant community and commercial impact.

Equally significant is my expertise in facilities management, maintenance and renovation. With responsibility for up to 35 properties, staffs of more than 200 and annual operating budgets of $15+ million, I have delivered strong performance results, reduced annual facilities costs and improved functional capabilities.

Currently, I am exploring new professional challenges and opportunities and will call to schedule an interview. Thank you.

Sincerely,

Edward Brentwood

Enclosure

ERIC DOUGLAS

11249 Taylor Drive
Los Altos, CA 94021

Home (415) 531-9492
Email – ericdoug@aol.com

November 15, 2000

Michael Perry
Partner
Bastion Capital Corporation
972 Vallejo Street
Newport Beach, CA 92660

Dear Mr. Perry:

I am a well-qualified Construction Manager with extensive experience in the planning, staffing, budgeting and on-site field supervision of both new construction and renovation projects. With a total of 17 years' experience in construction and corporate facilities management, I bring to Bastion excellent skills in:

* All major construction trades including HVAC, electrical, roofing, framing, concrete forming and finishing, carpentry, ceramic tile and painting.

* Evaluating project costs and developing accurate project budgets.

* Selecting, negotiating contracts with and managing project subcontractors.

* Managing projects as per state and local building codes and regulations.

Most significant is my success in delivering projects on time and within budget, despite the many challenges often encountered in the field. I have accomplished this through my ability to effectively plan, schedule and prioritize.

Currently working as a General Contractor, I have completed more than 15 projects in the past two years. Now, however, I am seeking to transition my experience back into a corporate environment and would welcome the opportunity for a personal interview to explore your need for talented, decisive and strong field leadership.

I appreciate your consideration and look forward to speaking with you. Thank you.

Sincerely,

Eric Douglas

Enclosure

Consulting

**KeyWords, Action Verbs & High-Impact Phrases
to "Nail" Your Cover Letter:**

- Project Planning & Execution

- Major Projects & Quantifiable Results

- Major Clients (*if not confidential*)

- Operations Turnaround

- Quality, Efficiency & Productivity Improvements

- Interim Executive Positions

- Client Presentations & Contract Negotiations

- Marketing & New Business Development

- Matrix Management & Team Leadership

- Performance Reengineering & Change Management

DYNAMIC CONSULTING RESOURCES
Management, Operating & Marketing Solutions
230195 Pine Street Marketplace
Seattle, Washington 90641
Phone: (206) 496-0809
Email: dominion@msn.com

March 12, 2001

George Bergman
President
Impact Technology Manufacturing, Inc.
9394 Industrial Zone
Kent, WA 98321

Dear Mr. Bergman:

Are you struggling with core issues impacting the operation, revenues and profitability of your organization?

Are you in the midst of a start-up or emerging growth situation?

Are you spearheading an organization-wide reengineering and revitalization program?

Are you constantly evaluating all of your options to determine the most appropriate course of action?

Are you ready to make the next move?

Let Dynamic Consulting help. With more than 20 years of top-flight executive management experience with Microsoft, Fujitsu, Xerox, Control Data and several emerging technology ventures, I have delivered consistently strong performance results. At each organization, my contributions positively impacted operations and financial performance.

My expertise spans virtually all core management functions with particular emphasis in worldwide sales and marketing, product management, multichannel distribution, manufacturing/operations, and organizational change/performance improvement.

Today, I am the principal of Dynamic Consulting, a unique, performance-driven consulting practice working exclusively with firms in the information technology and telecommunications industries to solve problems, meet challenges and improve financial results.

Let's take a few minutes to explore the challenges you are facing and your need for strong, decisive and immediate project leadership. I am available at your request for a free consultation.

Sincerely,

Timothy Lee, President

Enclosure

RICHARD O'CONNOR
934 South Pearson Lane
Carmel, Indiana 45655
(404) 303-4398

January 17, 2001

Clifford Davis
Davis Consulting
1029 Brookline Drive
Indianapolis, IN 46731

Dear Mr. Davis:

Sometimes a fresh perspective, new strategies or an objective viewpoint are what's needed. When you're in the thick of the decision-making process, it is often difficult to "pull back" and identify what the best tactics are and how to accelerate your earnings.

This is the expertise I bring to an organization — my ability to quickly assess, evaluate, plan and initiate action. Whether challenged to launch a new technology venture, orchestrate the turnaround of an international business unit, or accelerate growth for an established technology leader, I have delivered strong financial results:

* 50%+ increase in ROI for ABC Technology Corporation.
* 35% increase in pre-tax profits for Australian Operations.
* 500% revenue growth for start-up turnkey systems supplier.
* $10 million revenue gain for one of IBM's largest reseller organizations.

Now, after a successful "corporate" career, I am interested in transitioning into the consulting arena where I can provide strong and decisive operating, marketing and/or development expertise. As such, my interest in your practice and request for a personal interview.

I will phone next week to follow up and look forward to meeting with you.

Sincerely,

Richard O'Connor

Enclosure

BRADLEY G. FOSTER
2013 Poplar Forest Drive
Lexington, Virginia 22071
(540) 986-7167

February 4, 2001

J. Herrmann
Herrmann Executive Consultants
1007 Broad Street
Philadelphia, PA 11663

Dear Mr. Herrmann:

After a successful career as President and CEO of diverse manufacturing organizations, I am transitioning my experience into the consulting arena. My goal is to affiliate with a well-established practice, recognized for their expertise and results.

Just as with consulting, my career has been "project-driven." In addition to general management and P&L operating unit management responsibilities, I have worked closely with affiliated business units and subsidiaries to provide expertise on a broad range of operating, financial, marketing, technology and product issues. I have been the crisis manager, troubleshooter and problem solver. For example:

- Assessed status of Rymer's $15 million Canadian Division, identified bottlenecks, redesigned business processes, and realigned staff and management teams.
  RESULT: Transition from $1.3 million loss to $850,000 profit.

- Evaluated efficiency and consolidated nine sites into six product-driven organizations.
  RESULT: $2.5 million cost reduction.

- Led corporate relocation to control escalating operating and labor costs.
  RESULT: $2.3 million reduction in labor, overhead and transportation expenses.

- Introduced leading edge technologies, processes and quality standards (including ISO 9000) to accelerate productivity within labor-intensive operations.
  RESULT: Annual efficiency gains of more than 22%.

- Identified and captured new market opportunities to exploit the core competencies of new business group formed following large corporate merger.
  RESULT: Revenue growth from $59 million to $80 million.

I am anxious to speak with you and appreciate your quick response. Please note that I am currently employed and would appreciate your confidentiality in this matter. Thank you.

Sincerely,

Bradley G. Foster

Enclosure

LEWIS GRANTFORD
Email: lgrant@myworld.com
1201 Univac Drive
Murray, Ohio 44874
440-689-1783
Lgrant@murray.net

August 24, 2000

Jeremy Greene
Managing Partner
GLASSER CONSULTANTS
787 Second Avenue
Lewiston, ME 09863

Dear Mr. Greene:

For the past 15+ years, I have worked as both a Consultant and Corporate Executive specializing in the strategic, financial and operational leadership of corporate development projects. Specifically, I have led and/or co-managed more than 10 mergers, acquisitions, joint ventures, strategic alliances and partnership programs throughout both the US and foreign markets.

The greatest value I bring to your clients is my ability to build relationships between top executives, often with vastly differing objectives and organizational requirements. I am a mediator, successful in facilitating positive results, bringing to fruition deals and opportunities never before attempted.

Further, I offer outstanding financial skills (MBA and CPA), and have led and/or participated in structuring and negotiating transactions valued from less than $1 million to more than $200 million.

Currently, I am operating a private consulting practice exclusively in corporate development and have managed several unique US/foreign partner projects. Now, I am interested in consulting opportunities where I can team with other professionals to identify, develop and execute new acquisitions, strategic projects, new ventures and other corporate deals.

As such, I would welcome a personal interview and can, of course, be available at your convenience. Thank you.

Sincerely,

Lewis Grantford

Enclosure

PATRICK M. DOUGHERTY
2492 Mission Road
Raleigh, North Carolina 24579
Phone (919) 282-6863   Fax (919) 286-0941

March 2, 2001

Thomas Wilder
Turnaround Consultants International
9845 Research Triangle
Raleigh, NC 27653

Dear Mr. Wilder:

As Acting CEO of a complex turnaround venture in the multimedia and broadcast industries, I am currently leading an aggressive reorganization, capital financing and market repositioning. My goal is to return the company to profitability within the first 12 months and position for long-term growth and diversification.

Previously, during my affiliation with Apple, Greene & West Co. (a well-respected turnaround management consulting group), I participated in several successful turnaround projects. My contributions were varied but focused on evaluating the feasibility of continued operations and how to redesign each organization for financial and operational revitalization.

Equally significant were my contributions to the successful turnaround of CCS Manufacturing. The company was faced with tremendous operating and financial challenges. Through the efforts of myself, the other executives and the entire workforce, we were able to reverse previous losses, lower corporate debt and enhance internal operating competencies.

My goal is to affiliate with a consulting and/or turnaround management organization seeking senior-level financial and operating leadership. I enjoy the challenges of turnaround situations and the opportunity to make immediate and substantive improvements.

I would, of course, be interested in pursuing any other opportunities you feel appropriate to my experience in not only turnaround management, but also start-up, emerging growth and high-growth ventures. Thank you.

Sincerely,

Patrick M. Dougherty

Enclosure

LAWRENCE NOLAN
3224 Malvern Drive
Pittsburgh, Pennsylvania 16532
(412) 396-2487
LNOLAN@bigdog.net

April 10, 2001

Mr. Steven Chappel
Global Technology Partners
349 Market Street
Philadelphia, PA 19601

Dear Mr. Chappel:

Although "technically" an employee, I have functioned as a consultant throughout the Westinghouse organization for more than 15 years. Working in a number of the company's operating divisions, my roles have ranged dramatically, from direct P&L responsibility for multi-site manufacturing operations to leadership of large-scale quality and business performance improvement initiatives. To each, I have contributed to measurable gains in revenues, profits and ROI.

My expertise lies in my ability to quickly and accurately assess a situation. What does each organization need in order to produce more, save money, increase earnings and strengthen its competitive position? These are been the challenges I faced and the results I delivered.

Currently, I am exploring the possibility for transitioning into a full-time consulting position specializing in quality, performance reengineering and/or operations. I believe the value of my experience — across broad industries, markets and functional disciplines — allows me to bring a unique perspective to your clients. More importantly, I will deliver results.

Please note that my strengths also include strategic planning, financial and operations analysis, team building and leadership, change management, process redesign, and executive presentations. I am direct and decisive in my leadership style, yet flexible in responding to constantly changing organizational, financial, operating and market demands.

I would welcome a personal interview to explore senior consulting opportunities and thank you for your time.

Sincerely,

Lawrence Nolan

Enclosure

JAMES H. MARTIN
4595 Birch Street
Knoxville, Tennessee 54453
(935) 647-3214

November 15, 2000

Michael P. Charles
Charles Interim Executives
7953 Ivanhoe Avenue
Colorado Springs, CO 80632

Dear Mr. Charles:

Delivering value to client organizations has been the focus of my career for the past 12 years. With more than 100 completed engagements, I have consistently provided my clients with strategies, action plans and leadership critical to performance improvement, revenue and profit growth, cost reduction and technology gain. Most notably, I:

- Guided Capital Enterprises in the development of their marketing and business plans, and led a successful effort to raise $5 million in start-up funding.

- Delivered a $1+ million operating cost savings to James Berglund & Sons through consolidation of multiple plant facilities into one centralized operation.

- Negotiated joint venture, built to $4+ million in revenues and sold for 100% ROI.

- Spearheaded product development, manufacturing process reengineering and operations planning efforts (emphasis in technological, pharmaceutical and medical device industries).

- Pioneered innovative global sales, marketing and business development initiatives for key corporate clients.

I enjoy the "project challenge" and the dynamics of diverse corporate cultures. I excel in building new client relationships and managing cross-functional project teams. My leadership style is direct and decisive, yet I am able to maintain the flexibility critical to successful consulting and long-term client retention.

I would welcome the opportunity to pursue senior-level consulting opportunities and appreciate your consideration. I'll phone next week to schedule an interview. Thank you.

Sincerely,

James H. Martin

Enclosure

BARRY YOUNG
5421 Duplin Drive, Greensboro, North Carolina 27242
Home (910) 927-4510 / Voice Mail (910) 342-9907

May 26, 2001

William C. Jones
International Consultants, Inc.
3145 Seaview Avenue
Myrtle Beach, SC 28742

Dear Mr. Jones:

I am forwarding my resume in anticipation that you may be interested in a well-qualified Senior Finance Executive to join your consulting team. My goal is to transition from the private sector into a high-profile consulting position where I can continue to provide strategic, transactions and financial management expertise.

Although I have worked within a large corporation, my career path has been unique, often as an internal consultant, advisor and special projects manager for several of the organization's largest subsidiaries. Highlights include:

* **Capital Financing**. Active participation in the 1994 $1 billion IPO of Malvern, Ltd.

* **Turnaround Management**. Leadership of cross-functional team that saved the IT Group $13 million in annual costs while capturing $650 million in new business.

* **Technology Advancement**. Introduction of leading edge PC technologies to automate core business functions for Electronic Naval Systems Group.

* **Financial Analysis**. Design of strategic and tactical financial modeling and budgeting methodologies for the $1 billion Astronautics Group.

Most notable has been my success in building partnerships with senior management executives, operating personnel, outside advisors and consultants. Further, I have demonstrated my flexibility, moving from one business group to another, quickly evaluating their specific requirements, and initiating the appropriate course of action.

I bring to International strong problem solving, negotiation and project management skills, each of which I believe critical to a successful consulting career. Thank you.

Sincerely,

Barry Young

Enclosure

Corporate Development

KeyWords, Action Verbs & High-Impact Phrases to "Nail" Your Cover Letter:

- Strategic Planning & Development

- Mergers & Acquisitions

- High-Profile Dealmaking & Transactions

- Joint Ventures & Strategic Alliances

- IPOs & Secondary Offerings

- Marketing & New Business Development

- Investor, Bank & Venture Capital "Road Shows"

- Financial Analysis & Projections

- Technology/Product Transfers & Licensing

- Revenue & Profit Growth

RONALD E. RILEY
PO Box 12
Lexington, Virginia 22873

Home (540) 898-3726   Fax (540) 898-3722

October 12, 2000

George Smithton
Chief Operating Officer
LBO Partners, LLC
One Greengate Lane
Minneapolis, MN 66537

Dear Mr. Smithton:

There is nothing that I have found throughout my career that offers more challenge or more satisfaction than transacting the "deal." The strategy, the partners and the money involved can be daunting and complex, but when the deal closes the personal satisfaction is tremendous.

In summary, my transactions experience includes two LBOs, an IPO, numerous secondary investment financings and public financings, more than 20 acquisitions and four divestitures. For each, I have provided strategic, financial and negotiations expertise, from initial review, due diligence, planning, preparation and documentation stages through sophisticated deal structuring and financial transactions.

Complementing my transactions experience is equally strong performance as a CFO. For 20 years, I have held full financial, tax, internal audit and administrative leadership responsibility for two billion dollar plus corporations. This facet of my career has been equally challenging and rewarding, providing me the opportunity to participate in complex reorganizations, restructurings, new ventures and other growth-driven corporate development programs.

My contributions to First Meredith have been dramatic. As one of three Management Co-Owners and the CFO, I have worked to transition a highly-leveraged LBO into what is now a multi-billion dollar corporation currently in the final stages of acquisition negotiations with a Fortune 500. We took a company that was in tremendous debt, paid off hundreds of millions in financings, spurred a profitable acquisition program and built a high-profit, high-performance organization.

Now the time has come to look for new executive opportunities. Once the deal closes and I facilitate the final transition, my role will no longer be necessary. As such, I am exploring new paths where I can continue to combine the breadth of my financial, corporate and dealmaking experience.

I would welcome the chance to speak with you about such opportunities and do appreciate both your time and consideration.

Sincerely,

Ronald E. Riley

Enclosure

WILLIAM DUNN
945 Red Desert Circle
Santa Fe, New Mexico 87505
(505) 992-3522

September 23, 2000

David Rosenberg
President
TriStar Video
934 Paramount Drive
Los Angeles, CA 90032

Dear Mr. Rosenberg:

It is unique in today's marketplace to find an individual with a strong blend of financial management, operating management and creative expertise. It has often been my experience that the financial and executive decision-makers in the film and video production industry sit opposed to the creative talents. Objectives vary widely and communication is often strained.

My expertise is in spanning that gap.

While negotiating over $270 million in investment and financing deals for my real estate asset management firm, I also was Executive Producer of a full-length feature film. One moment I was the "deal maker" and advisor to legal counsel on the formation of limited partnerships for specific real estate acquisitions; the next, I was reviewing scripts, selecting acting and creative design talent, and supervising daily film production operations.

That is the value I bring to TriStar. I can "sit on both sides of the fence" to evaluate proposed projects, structure complex financing transactions, manage daily business operations and facilitate cooperative efforts with writers, producers, actors and directors. With more than 20 years of top-flight entrepreneurial and executive management experience, I have demonstrated my ability to bring projects together and deliver results.

My personal interests in film and video production extend back to my teenage years. I am experienced in digital editing and have begun to build an extensive network of industry contacts. Now my goal is to merge my entrepreneurial, financial and creative talents to bring value and strong leadership to a well-established production company.

I would welcome the chance to pursue such opportunities with TriStar and appreciate your time and consideration. Thank you.

Sincerely,

William Dunn

Enclosure

RICHARD FROST
663 Montgomery Street
Nashua, NH 06846
(601) 654-0417

October 3, 2000

Bruce McNaughton
President & CEO
McNaughton Holdings, LLC
934 Olympic Park Circle, Suite 647
Atlanta, GA 30542

Dear Mr. McNaughton:

I am a deal-maker with a unique expertise in corporate development, mergers, acquisitions and corporate financing. My strength lies in my ability to identify prime opportunities and drive forward complex due diligence, transactions and negotiations.

Throughout my tenure with Central Inc., I led the corporation's aggressive expansion program, managing 28 acquisitions and more than $90 million in corporate financings. In cooperation with the president of the company, we created a $110 million national organization from its infancy into what is now one of the largest and most successful organizations within the industry.

Equally notable are my accomplishments in general corporate financial affairs, strategic planning, MIS operations, business process redesign and team building/leadership. Each of these functions has contributed to the growth of the corporation by building a strong infrastructure to support our acquisition and expansion initiatives.

My goal is a top-flight corporate development position with an organization poised for aggressive market growth. I bring to McNaughton Holdings both the transactions and financial expertise critical to profitable, sustained and long-term development.

I look forward to meeting with you to explore opportunities and appreciate your consideration. Thank you.

Sincerely,

Richard Frost

Enclosure

STEVE DARWIN

3448 Flash Run Lane
Dallas, Texas 75111
sdarwin@flash.net

Home: (727) 883-9302
Office: (727) 677-1000
Fax: (727) 677-2001

May 23, 2001

Tom Tucker
Lewiston Group, LLC
724 S. Abraham, Suite B
Chicago, IL 62776

RE: CEO/President/Owner – NETSHARE Job Lead #GM061281

Dear Mr. Tucker:

If your objective is to identify a Senior Executive with substantial merger, acquisition, dealmaking and operating experience, look no further. I bring to your client company more than 20 years' experience as President, CEO & COO, combined with an extensive background in corporate development and transactions.

Let me briefly mention a few relevant highlights of my career:

- Led more than 25 merger and acquisition transactions (from an operational and financial perspective) with top-of-the-line negotiating and dealmaking performance. Further, I then facilitated the seamless integration of these acquisitions into existing holding companies and/or directed them as independent ventures.

- Delivered phenomenal annual revenue and profit returns (up to 400%) within highly competitive markets. Perhaps my greatest achievement was the growth of one division of a $400 million media company – an increase of 287% in revenue and a 639% gain in operating profit.

- Extensive experience in emerging and established technology industries (e.g., software, E-commerce, data warehousing, data storage, office automation). Equally substantial experience in the more "traditional" manufacturing, consumer and business-to-business industries.

- Success leading start-up ventures, turnarounds, high-growth organizations and international expansions.

I am currently working as an Executive Consultant specializing in acquisition analysis and transaction. The challenges associated with such activities have been tremendous, but I am now looking to join a larger investor group. As such, my interest in the advertised position and request for a personal interview. Thank you.

Sincerely,

Steve Darwin

Enclosure

JOHN CARSON

2914 Lake Circle
Lexington, Kentucky 35643
Phone (230) 843-6548
Fax (230) 843-2380
Email jjcarson@inmind.net

May 1, 2001

John Glenn
President
Ceramitec, Inc.
Cincinnati, OH 65432

Dear Mr. Glenn:

With 18 years of senior-level corporate development experience in the materials industry, I bring to Ceramitec a strong record of revenue and earnings growth within highly competitive U.S. and global business markets. Most notably, I:

- Built Bondsil Corporation to over $15 million in revenue and spearheaded the development of customer, partner and co-producer relationships throughout the U.S., Europe and the Pacific Rim.

- Negotiated several acquisitions and international trading partnerships to accelerate Meyer's expansion throughout the U.S., Far East and Australian markets.

- Orchestrated the successful turnaround and return to profitability of Fulcrum through effective leadership of new business start-ups, product licensing programs, global joint ventures and other market-driven development efforts.

- Spearheaded Genstar's aggressive business development, acquisition, joint venture, partnership and marketing programs as the company grew from less than $6 million to over $33 million in revenues.

My greatest contribution to each of these companies — and others — has been my success in identifying and capitalizing upon market opportunities. Whether negotiating a joint venture to penetrate the Japanese market, structuring international co-producer agreements, or managing investment financing for an IPO, I have delivered strong financial results.

I would welcome the opportunity to explore executive-level opportunities and appreciate your time in reviewing my qualifications. Be assured that my experience, network of contacts and product expertise within our industry will add measurable value to Ceramitec.

Sincerely,

John Carson

Enclosure

LESLIE DREW

11 N. Roundrun Drive * Dodson, NJ 08567 * Tel. (976) 676 – 6677
Fax. (976) 676 – 6688 * Ldrew34@worldnet.att.net

January 7, 2001

Dick Armstrong, Managing Director
Investment Trust Ventures
1 New York Avenue
New York, NY 11989

Dear Mr. Armstrong:

I am writing and forwarding my resume in anticipation that you may be interested in a candidate with solid experience in *Corporate Development including mergers, acquisitions, divestitures, restructurings, start-up ventures and long-range business/profit growth.*

A 19-year employee of Bell South, I advanced rapidly through a series of increasingly responsible management positions to my final assignment leading worldwide operations for a start-up venture in the company's growth division. Headquartered in Belgium, I orchestrated the acquisition, integration and launch of a new multi-million dollar global business that, over three years, far exceeded revenue and profit expectations.

As you review my qualifications and career achievements, you'll see a record of consistent success across a diverse range of functions – from managing divestitures to negotiating strategic alliances and co-development partnerships; from leading presentations to investment bankers to conducting high-level strategic and financial analyses to evaluate proposed business ventures and actions; from launching highly profitable new ventures to reorganizing operations to meet cash flow requirements.

Characterized by others as an innovative, decisive and action-driven business leader, I am most proud of my success in positively impacting the bottom-line. Whether through growth or internal realignment, I have consistently improved profitability and supported long-range development. Further, I have outstanding public speaking and presentation skills which have given me a decisively competitive advantage over my peers.

Currently, I am exploring new professional opportunities in the investment banking and corporate development arena, and would welcome a personal interview. As a further testament to my commitment, I am currently enrolled in NYU's Certificate in Investment Banking Program which will be complete by June of this year.

I appreciate your time and consideration, and look forward to speaking with you.

Sincerely,

Leslie Drew

Enclosure

Energy & Environmental Affairs

KeyWords, Action Verbs & High-Impact Phrases to "Nail" Your Cover Letter:

- Environmental & Engineering Project Management

- Regulatory Affairs & Compliance

- Energy Generation & Cogeneration Projects

- Site Remediation & Hazardous Materials Management

- Resource Recovery & Conservation

- Systems & Technologies

- Public, Private & Institutional Funding

- Cost Reduction & Avoidance

- Joint Ventures, Strategic Alliances & Partnerships

- Marketing, Business Development & Revenue Growth

MARIE R. HOBBS
leslie.hobbs@voyager.net
9024 Garden Circle
Dallas, Texas 41835
(201) 694-2958

November 11, 2000

Harry DeCovey
President
Indosuez Development International
600 Anton Boulevard, Suite 2393
Inglewood, CA 90301

Dear Mr. DeCovey:

The challenge during my career with FLAG was to build a sophisticated environmental management organization responsible for regulatory affairs, site remediation, hazardous materials management and legislative advocacy. Today, FLAG boasts of one of the most dynamic environmental organizations in the world, a pioneer in compliance, safety and risk management.

My contributions have been notable and include:

- Over $20 million in revenues and state funding through efforts in containment, cost recovery and cost avoidance.

- Dramatic reduction in the exposure and potential environmental liability of FLAG.

- Participation with other Fortune 500 companies (manufacturing and transportation) in developing a common vision and plan for environmental protection.

- Introduction of quantifiable performance measures to guide environmental initiatives.

Now, at this juncture in my career, I am seeking a top-level environmental management position with a leading manufacturer. The strength of my field experience and regulatory knowledge places me in a uniquely qualified position to make an immediate impact upon your environmental affairs.

I appreciate your time and will follow up next week. Thank you.

Sincerely,

Marie R. Hobbs

Enclosure

FLOYD P. FISHMAN

2394 Michigan Avenue
Chicago, Illinois 60124

Home (847) 255-9188
Office (847) 968-5402
Email 123@net.com

July 23, 2000

Douglas Carter
President
Zulandi Kyocera, Inc.
1055 Oakton Avenue
Chicago, IL 60012

Dear Mr. Carter:

Building asset value and accelerating cash flow are my expertise. With more than 15 years of senior-level development experience in the energy/utility industry, I have negotiated projects worldwide that have generated cumulative earnings of more than $400 million and positioned MG&G as a dominant player in the international development industry.

Starting with a concept in early 1987, the President and I have created one of the most well-respected and fastest growing companies in the industry. To my credit are the significant deals and projects we have negotiated, establishing our presence on five continents and in more than 25 countries.

Not only have I developed successful new ventures, I have repeatedly demonstrated my success in M&A transactions, corporate financing and strategic diversification. I am goal-directed and results-driven with strong and decisive leadership skills. Most important, I am a negotiator, able to facilitate consensus and deliver profit to all partners.

At this point in my career I am seeking new challenges within the power industry and would welcome the chance to pursue any appropriate opportunities with your client companies. I am interested in a senior level operating management position with either domestic and/or international responsibilities. I am open to relocation and would be delighted to discuss compensation requirements at your convenience.

Sincerely,

Floyd P. Fishman

Enclosure

JOHN R. ADAMS

22049 Palm Grass Drive
Boca Raton, Florida 33428

Phone: 561.852.9719   Email: adams11@aol.com   Fax: 561.883.2809

October 12, 2000

Samantha Styer
Oil & Gas Recruiters, Inc.
45 Jersey Pike
Waltham, MA 08937

Dear Ms. Styer:

I am a 12-year employee of Kesson Oil with a career in Sales & Marketing. Although secure in my current position, I am confidentially exploring new professional opportunities in the oil and gas industry, and have enclosed my resume for your review. Highlights of my professional career that may be of particular interest to you include:

- Current leadership of sales, marketing and business development programs for the Florida market ($52 million in annual sales from 175 franchises). Closed 1999 at $6.5 million OVER profit plan.

- Selection for Kesson's Global Leadership Council, an honor bestowed on the top 1% of employees worldwide. Graduated #1 from Kesson's 5-month Technical Sales & Marketing Training Program.

- Delivered a 25% reduction in field/customer support costs while Acting Manager of Business Performance (involving best-in-class practices, benchmarking and business unit revitalization).

- Outstanding communication, presentation, negotiation and customer relationship management skills. Accomplished sales trainer and team leader with an entrepreneurial spirit and solid decision-making and problem-solving skills. Thinks and performs independently.

- Consistently successful in outperforming the competition and winning major accounts.

My goal is a challenging sales, marketing and/or business development position with a company poised for significant growth and expansion. I thrive in challenging, fast-paced and high-stress environments, clearly demonstrated by my performance with Kesson and my years of experience as a paramedic/EMS.

I would welcome the opportunity to speak with you about any current search assignments in the oil and gas industry for a candidate with my qualifications. Be advised that I am open to relocation and that my salary requirements can be discussed at the time of an interview. Thank you.

Sincerely,

John R. Adams

Enclosure

WILLIAM D. SMITH
1915 St. Cloud Drive
Orlando, Florida 33653
(561) 352-6564

February 13, 2001

Jonathan Boman
Chairman of the Board
Innocal Environmental
9345 SW 98th Avenue
Miami, FL 33874

Dear Mr. Boman:

Throughout the past 10 years, I have been a driving force in transitioning Cirrus from a domestic energy company into a diversified multinational corporation with successful ventures throughout Australia, the Far East and Latin America. Challenged by the board to identify and capitalize upon international opportunities, I provided corporate development, financing and negotiations expertise that catapulted Cirrus into a $2 billion organization.

Most notable are my successes in building start-up ventures, orchestrating complex turnarounds of international corporations and accelerating growth within established entities. Further, I have structured and negotiated complex joint ventures and partnerships worldwide to expand market presence, drive revenue growth and strengthen corporate earnings.

My resume highlights specific projects and achievements, ranging from negotiation of international debt financings and foreign hedging programs to creation of innovative marketing and business development strategies. Each has delivered strong and sustainable gains in corporate value — to our customers, our operations and our shareholders.

Now, at this juncture in my career, I am seeking new challenges where I can continue to provide leadership for sophisticated financial transactions, corporate reorganizations and global development projects. I guarantee improved financial results and look forward to exploring opportunities with your organization.

Sincerely,

William D. Smith

Enclosure

Engineering

KeyWords, Action Verbs & High-Impact Phrases to "Nail" Your Cover Letter:

- New Product & Technology Development
- Cross-Functional Team Leadership
- Quality Assurance & TQM Initiatives
- Process Development
- Budget & Cost Improvements
- Sales & Marketing Contributions
- Information Systems & Automation
- Marketing & Resource Management
- Joint Venture & Partnership Projects
- Time-to-Market Improvements

FRANK MILANOVICH
934 Old State Road
Albany, New York 19510
(914) 719-5483

October 24, 2000

William Vanderbilt
The Vanderbilt Group
934 Avenue of the Americas, 12th Floor
New York, New York 10013

Dear Mr. Vanderbilt:

Building organizational value is my expertise. As the Director of Corporate Engineering for Chromitec Corporation and its affiliate company, Boyd Chemical, I pioneered innovative engineering and operating solutions to improve productivity, reduce operating costs, enhance efficiencies and accelerate profit gains.

With more than 20 years experience, I bring to The Vanderbilt Group a strong track record of management and engineering performance:

- Leadership of more than $45 million in total capital improvement projects.

- Management of corporate engineering projects for both existing and start-up facilities in the U.S., Germany, France and The Netherlands.

- Training, development and leadership of 55+ multi-discipline engineering professionals.

- Expertise in all core operating, manufacturing, process and quality management methods.

My goal is a senior-level management position with an organization in need of strong, decisive and proactive engineering leadership. I am open to relocation worldwide, speak five languages fluently and most significantly, have demonstrated my ability to impact positive change.

I look forward to speaking with you regarding appropriate opportunities and thank you in advance for your consideration. My salary requirements are flexible.

Sincerely,

Frank Milanovich

Enclosure

PAUL T. BANYAN

873 Joan Drive
Jasper, WY 83764
(222) 385-3726

January 5, 2001

Bob Bolt, Engineering Manager
Simpl-Mold, Inc.
898 Gray Weigh Station
Jasper, WY 83766

Dear Mr. Bolt:

I am writing at the suggestion of my father-in-law, John Lewis, and would like to submit my resume for consideration for the position of Project Engineer as advertised in last week's Jasper Forum. I bring to the position:

- Nine years of experience in the design and engineering of large-scale industrial and manufacturing facilities, including both new facilities construction and renovation.

- Excellent skills in managing cross-functional design, engineering and project teams.

- Leadership of project scheduling, subcontracting and progress reporting.

- Control of up to $22 million in annual project budgets.

- Introduction of advanced PC technologies to automate engineering capabilities.

I bring to Simpl-Mold combined strengths in both "hands-on" engineering as well as project leadership. In turn, I guarantee my ability to meet project budget and scheduling objectives, deliver improved technologies and support your expanding operations.

Thank you. As requested, my salary requirements are $115,000+.

Sincerely,

Paul T. Banyan

Enclosure

KATHRYN M. HAMBRECHT
1915 Camden Circle
Cherry Hill, New Jersey 09648
Home (609) 970-3245   Office (609) 647-0359
Email kham@jerseyshore.net

December 1, 2000

Robert Carmickle
Director
Nuclear Testing, Inc.
1900 Industrial Way
Roswell, NM 54321

Dear Mr. Carmickle:

I am a well-qualified Environmental Engineer with 12 years' experience directing hazardous waste and site remediation programs nationwide. I bring to the Nuclear Testing broad industry experience, expert regulatory knowledge, and the ability to reduce your environmental costs and limit your exposure.

Highlights of my professional career that may be of particular interest to you include the following:

* Saved my current employer $1 million in potential remediation costs by identifying critical issues negating the value of proposed acquisitions and divestitures.

* Saved a large industrial manufacturer $650,000 in site remediation and hazardous materials disposal costs through well-planned, efficient and timely project management.

* Directed more than 100 Superfund remediation projects for the EPA.

My strengths lie in my ability to manage the entire process — from site review and analysis through planning, budgeting, engineering, field management and regulatory approval. Further, I have extensive experience in environmental training for both executive and operating teams.

Although secure in my current position, I am confidentially exploring new professional challenges and opportunities. Thus my interest in the Nuclear Testing and request for a personal interview. Thank you.

Sincerely,

Kathryn M. Hambrecht

Enclosure

CHRISTIAN LAMBERT
9348 Mississippi Street
Minneapolis, Minnesota 55321
606-535-6533

March 21, 2001

Abbott Laboratories
1401 Sheridan Road
Dept. 39Y, A-1
North Chicago, IL 60064

RE: <u>Environmental Coordinator</u>

Dear Sir/Madam:

With 13 years of professional experience in Environmental Engineering, I bring to Abbott Laboratories an in-depth knowledge of environmental issues, regulations and compliance impacting chemical and industrial manufacturing. The scope of my responsibility has varied widely, from environmental review and analysis of proposed site acquisitions to comprehensive assessment of the waste by-products generated in large manufacturing operations. Highlights of my career include:

- Expertise in resource recovery and conservation.
- Completion of 100+ Superfund projects.
- Extensive knowledge of soil, air and groundwater remediation systems and technologies.
- Design of environmental systems for hazardous waste, hazardous materials, air emissions and wastewater discharges.

Most significant has been my success in resolving long-standing environmental issues, achieving compliance with state and federal regulations, and reducing the costs associated with environmental engineering and remediation. Further, I have worked closely with senior management to guide acquisition, divestiture and product development efforts.

Although currently employed, I am anxious to return to a manufacturing environment and would be delighted to have the opportunity to interview with Abbott Laboratories. I appreciate your confidentiality and look forward to speaking with you. Thank you.

Sincerely,

Christian Lambert

Enclosure

Finance – Corporate

KeyWords, Action Verbs & High-Impact Phrases to "Nail" Your Cover Letter:

- Cost Reduction & Profit Improvement

- Information Systems Development & Implementation

- Investment, Acquisition & Capital Financings

- Corporate Administration

- Cost Accounting & General Accounting Processes

- Streamlining & Reengineering Projects

- Cash Management, Treasury & FX

- Debt Reductions

- IPOs & Secondary Offerings

- High-Profile Contract Negotiations

BERNARD PFEIFER

832 Westend Street   Home   818.438.7971
Watertown, New York 16452   Office 818.867-2010

September 1, 2000

Michael Caufield
Bayside Manufacturing, Inc.
1900 Commercial Way
Bayside, NY 11387

Dear Mr. Caufield:

Corporate finance is no longer just a "numbers" game. As the Senior Financial Manager with Merlena, my responsibilities have extended far beyond finance to include strategic and tactical business planning, marketing, new product development, MIS, sales administration, manufacturing and general operating management within several of the corporation's emerging and high-growth business units. Results have been significant:

- Financial leadership for development and market launch of three major product lines, subsequently generating over $30 million in new revenues to the corporation.
- Reorganization of core business function, delivering a 25% staff reduction with no loss in performance.
- Financial and operating oversight for PC system installations and upgrades to automate field sales and marketing organizations.
- Management of a dynamic $20+ million budgeting process impacting all major operating units throughout the corporation.
- Coordination of large-scale business operating plans with particular emphasis on financial, capital, marketing and organizational development components.

My management style is direct and decisive, yet flexible in responding to the constantly changing demands of my staff, management teams and the marketplace. Most significant is my ability to work across diverse divisions (e.g., sales, marketing, contracts, MIS, product development), linking finance with operations to facilitate expansion, reorganization and operating improvements.

Never satisfied with the "status quo," I earned a reputation throughout Merlena for not only the strength of my financial expertise, but for my ability to communicate and coordinate cooperative efforts through cross-functional business teams. I look forward to speaking with you to further highlight my qualifications and explore your specific financial needs and operating objectives. Thank you.

Sincerely,

Bernard Pfeifer

Enclosure

MARTIN JEFFRIES, MBA, CPA

178 Circle Drive
Tridelphia, Arkansas 56543
Phone: 728-937-2735   Email: martyjeff@voyager.net   Fax: 728-932-3827

October 16, 2000

Michael Slottin
A.T. Kearney, Inc.
1100 Greene Road, Suite 1700
Adelphia, GA 33876

RE: Health Care Finance Executive #NS989

Dear Mr. Slottin:

I am a Senior Finance Executive with extensive experience providing strategic, financial and operational leadership to high-growth healthcare ventures. My expertise can best be summarized as follows:

- 15+ years experience in Corporate Finance / Financial Leadership with a unique expertise in corporate development (emphasis on new ventures, mergers, acquisitions and strategic alliances within the rapidly changing and complex healthcare industry).

- Outstanding qualifications in the planning, staffing and management of complete finance organizations with particular strengths in financial planning and analysis, financial reporting, cash management, internal financial controls, SEC affairs, treasury, accounting, budgeting, and related information technology (including technology transfers).

- Proven success in building and facilitating positive relationships between physicians and other care providers, hospital/health care operating management and executive management teams, investors, Board members, business partners and other stakeholders.

Characterized by others as a strong mentor, team builder and coach, I have aligned myself closely with senior management and executives to provide strategic and financial leadership, identify new opportunities and leverage market position. In turn, my teams and I have launched several new ventures with strong financial, quality and operating results. Further, I have facilitated innovative alliances and partnerships to strengthen performance, expand service offerings and entrench our position as a strong leader in the healthcare market.

I would welcome the opportunity to speak with you regarding your search for a CFO with the privately owned healthcare services provider organization with whom you are currently working. I can assure you that not only do I bring the financial leadership and competencies your client is seeking, but equally strong executive and business leadership talents to accelerate growth and improve financial performance. Thank you.

Sincerely,

Martin Jeffries

Enclosure

DAVID R. KNAPP
121 Denali Road West
Santa Fe, New Mexico 88974
Phone/Fax (555) 989-6543

January 12, 2001

Mike Abbott
Managing Director
Venture Capital Partners, Ltd.
467 Greenland Parkway
Santa Monica, CA 99876

Dear Mr. Abbott:

If you ask any one of my colleagues, employers, Board Directors or clients, they will all tell you the same thing about me – I am a **Financial Turnaround Specialist** with over 20 years of management and leadership experience and a **Columbia University MBA**. They will also comment that virtually everything I have "touched" has experienced positive results – results that are measured in increased revenues, reduced operating costs, expanded market penetration, competitive wins, and improved bottom-line profit and investment results.

My career path has been somewhat unique beginning with more than 15 years of increasingly responsible corporate experience. I came up through the ranks of finance with Keebler, Johnson & Johnson and several other top corporations, culminating in my position as **President & COO** of a $22 million turnaround company that was highly leveraged and over-stocked with no sales organization to market products and recover financial investment. Under my leadership, the company was revitalized, a best-in-class sales and marketing organization was launched and we closed $16 million in new sales within the first year. Other results were equally impressive and included an 8% reduction in operating costs, 22% improvement in production yields and 12% gain in ROI.

It was at that point in 1992 when my career transitioned from corporate to consulting and interim executive assignments. Since that date, I have completed more than 30 engagements across 10 industries – from advanced technology and electronics to consumer products, media, insurance, automotive, health care and more. My more notable clients include Lloyd's of London, McDonnell Douglas, Litton, General Motors, The Monstad Group of Zurich, and Investors of Nigeria Corporation.

To each organization, I have delivered measurable financial and operating results. A few recent and/or notable engagements include:

- **Financial & Operating Turnaround Consultant** to $225 million distribution whose operating income had shrunk over the past three years while sales had continued to increase. Within three weeks, I created and launched a turnaround program to increase operating income $7.1 million ($4 million in hand before the close of the current fiscal year).

- **Financial & Operating Turnaround Consultant** to $200 million manufacturing/fabrication company faced with a tremendous loss in customer base. Within four weeks, created turnaround plan to redesign production planning process and restructure cost accounting system to transition to a more profitable product mix. Projections indicated positive financial results within six months.

- **Interim Chief Financial Officer** for a $50 million electronics manufacturer. Delivered a 60% reduction in administrative and overhead operating costs through redesign of core business processes (e.g., forecasting, cash flow, material control, corporate banking).

- **Operations Turnaround Consultant** to several major US manufacturers. Facilitated design and implementation of MRP, JIT, quality, shop floor control, production scheduling and other performance improvement initiatives. Each delivered measurable results in production yields, product quality, customer satisfaction and bottom-line profitability.

- **Sales & Marketing Turnaround Consultant** to $9 billion health care provider. Redesigned nationwide sales/marketing infrastructure and field organization in response to changing market dynamics and encroaching competition. Projections forecast a 15% improvement in net revenue.

At your request, I would be pleased to provide my resume which includes much greater detail about both my corporate and consulting experience.

My primary expertise is in developing and implementing financial controls for operations that are experiencing under-performance of their assets and resources. My approach is hands-on, a walk-around management style with complete involvement in virtually every operating function within an organization – from strategic planning and financial management to sales, marketing, manufacturing, product development, information technology, staffing, customer management and external corporate affairs.

My interest is in an **Interim CEO, COO or CFO** position where I can create and implement turnaround operating plans able to meet competitive demands, and return strong financial results. While I focus my efforts on the company's revitalization, you can concentrate on recruiting the appropriate industry specialist who will then lead the company after the right operating plans, procedures, systems and actions have been installed.

I would welcome the chance to speak with you to explore such opportunities and do appreciate your time and interest. On a personal note, I am single and currently renting a home. Therefore, immediate relocation and/or travel is easy and perfectly acceptable.

Sincerely,

David R. Knapp

NATHAN R. O'GRADY

985 Market Circle   *   Newbury Falls, MT 88838   *   (998) 324-6431

October 5, 2000

Rick Daly, President
Newtec International
129 Newtec Boulvard
LaGrangeville, NY 12540

Dear Mr. Daly:

As VP Finance, CFO and a member of the Executive Management team of several U.S. corporations, I have earned an excellent reputation for my ability to provide strong and decisive operating leadership in challenging situations. I bring to Newtec International a unique blend of experience in general management, financial management, sales and marketing leadership, strategic planning, team building and technology. Most notably, I:

* Created the strategics, defined the action plans and led the successful turnaround of Gestpak's U.S. sales organization as a member of the executive team. **RESULTS: 20% sales growth and 100%+ profit contribution.**

* Developed integrated systems and financial controls for a start-up satellite communications company (joint venture between White Communications & Express, Inc.). **RESULTS: 50% growth in two years.**

* Automated operations in the U.S., Canada and Mexico for Gestpak and Mobile. **RESULTS: 15% expense reduction and 20% accounts receivable reduction.**

* Led a complex restructuring of corporate debt and balance sheet for Mobile. **RESULTS: Successful $80 million private securities placement, $50 million capital equipment financing arrangement and significant cash flow increase.**

My greatest strength lies in my ability to identify opportunities — for cost savings, revenue growth, quality improvement and increased profitability. Just as significant has been my success in creating the plans to capitalize upon these opportunities and deliver results.

I would welcome the chance to explore senior-level financial opportunities and appreciate your consideration. Be assured that the strength of my financial and operating experience will add measurable value to your organization.

Sincerely,

Nathan O'Grady

Enclosure

ROGER CARPENTER

377 Myerson Drive
Reading, PA 19989

Home: 772.989.8362
Office: 772.343-2000

June 12, 2000

Mark Leyman
President & CEO
Leyman Brothers Manufacturing, Inc.
23 Appleton Way
Appleton, WI 56763

Dear Mr. Leyman:

Managing corporate finance during major turnarounds and change management initiatives is my expertise. I've been at the helm of several successful turnarounds where not only have I restored profitability, but I've delivered significant operating improvements, eliminated millions of dollars in corporate debt, refinanced payment terms and delivered strong annual earnings.

I believe that to lead any effective turnaround, it is essential that the CFO be involved in virtually all operations – from the manufacturing and production to staffing, purchasing, information technology, contracts and so much more. To be truly successful there must be synergy and cooperation between the entire management team. Finance no longer operates in a vacuum; it is an active player throughout the organization.

As you review my qualifications, you will note that my financial skills are excellent and include virtually all core finance, accounting and tax functions. In addition, I have held direct P&L responsibility for several operations, including a $90 million, 150-person organization. I understand how production works and its intimate ties with finance. In addition, I have strong team building, leadership and mentoring skills, evidence of my successes which would not have been possible without the support of my employees.

After nine years with Monarch, I have decided to leave the organization to pursue new executive opportunities. I'm interested in a challenging, fast-paced and performance-driven company in need of strong and decisive financial leadership.

I would welcome the opportunity to speak with you regarding your current staffing needs or any referrals you may have. Thank you.

Sincerely,

Roger Carpenter

Enclosure

90

MARTINA VANDERSLOOT
119 Central Park West, 4D
New York, New York 10025
Home (212) 867-9247
martina.vandersloot@msn.com

February 1, 2001

Human Resources Manager
The Museum of Modern Art
11 West 53 Street
New York, NY 10019

Dear Sir/Madam:

I've had a most unusual financial management career! And, I assume, you're looking for a most unusual and talented Project Director / Deputy Controller.

Let me tell you a bit about myself and my career. With Acction, Inc. since 1984, I have advanced rapidly, earned five major promotions, and am currently spearheading a large-scale project development initiative. More core competencies include:

- 13 years' experience in financial management, financial process, analytical methods and project   management.

- Extensive qualifications in the design, development and introduction of advanced information systems technologies for both in-house and customer use.

- Expert skills in identifying organizational needs, analyzing opportunities, developing reporting protocols and spearheading business development initiatives.

- Excellent accounting, financial management, budgeting, cost management, cost/performance analysis and investment management experience. Familiar with FASB, GAAP and other industry regulations.

- Outstanding oral and written communication skills. Strong qualifications in team building and team leadership.

Although secure in my current position, I am confidentially exploring new professional challenges and opportunities to manage unique projects, programs and business units. As such, my interest in your search for a Project Director / Deputy Controller and request for a personal interview. As requested, my salary has averaged $150,000+ over the past several years. Thank you.

Sincerely,

Martina Vandersloot

Enclosure

PETER FIGLER
1247 Mayberry Road
Encino, California 92876
Email: pfig22@pacbell.net

Home: (426) 974-1235   Fax: (426) 974-1236

April 12, 2000

Mark Petrowski
Finance Recruiters of America
123 Elm Way
Charlotte, NC 28987

Dear Mr. Petrowski:

I am writing and forwarding my resume in anticipation that you may be working with a client company seeking a well-qualified Finance Executive. My experience can be briefly summarized as follows:

- Over **15 years' experience** building best-in-class corporate finance, accounting and tax organizations for start-up ventures, turnarounds and high-growth corporations.

- Solid experience in both **corporate finance and public accounting** (KPMG) with experience in the technology, software, manufacturing, distribution, oil & gas, transportation and construction/real estate industries.

- Consistent success in **improving cash flow, revenues and profits** through design of improved business processes, introduction of sophisticated IT tools and systems, and reduction of corporate tax liabilities.

- **Outstanding IT experience** including several large-scale systems implementations and upgrades, including one that facilitated a better than 34% increase in cash flow for Orizon.

- Success in **partnering finance and operations** to drive performance improvement.

- Excellent **team building/leadership skills** combined with the ability to develop and maintain corporate client relationships within an intensely competitive market.

- Consummate expertise in **corporate taxation**.

Currently, I am exploring new professional challenges and opportunities, and would be delighted to speak with you regarding an appropriate search assignment. Be advised that I am open to relocation and that my recent compensation has averaged $150,000+ per year.

Sincerely,

Peter Figler

Enclosure

MIKE ROBEY

mrobey12345@reno.net
123 Larkspur Circle
Reno, Nevada 82983

Home (892) 773-2839   Office (892) 777-3765

November 28, 2000

Amy Phillips
Phillips Finance Recruiters, Inc.
189 Melbourne Road
Antler, MT 89753

Subject: Mike Robey for CFO

Dear Ms. Phillips :

I would like to submit my name for candidacy for your advertised CFO position with The Mellenbrook Corporation. Briefly summarized, my qualifications include:

- Twenty years of senior-level financial leadership experience with Merck and several of its principal operating companies.
- Expert qualifications across all core accounting and financial practices including financial planning and reporting, tax, treasury, cash management, general and cost accounting, internal audit, credit, budgeting, forecasting, internal controls.
- Negotiation of more than $250 million in corporate financing transactions and participation in over 20 mergers and acquisitions.
- Extensive qualifications in design and implementation of advanced information technologies.
- Management of corporate facilities, real estate, leasing and a massive purchasing program.
- Pioneer in innovative business practices (e.g., outsourcing, workflow and performance efficiencies, corporate ethics).

As the Senior Financial Advisor to top executive and operating management teams, I have provided both the strategic and operating leadership critical to improving financial results, strengthening market position, improving product quality and manufacturability and enhancing our organizational structure. Further, I have delivered more than $50 million in cost savings through the introduction of improved business processes, best practices and standards for financial management, and a portfolio of advanced technology tools.

Characterized by others as creative, intuitive, flexible and decisive, I believe my greatest value is my broad operational and business perspective. Bayer has been an outstanding organization with which to grow and demonstrate my capabilities. Now, I am ready for new challenges and opportunities.

Sincerely,

Mike Robey

Enclosure

ANTONIO GARCIA

2000 Stream Lake Road – Unit 212
Somerset, New Jersey 08734

Residence: 898-873-2289   Email: antgarcia@aol.com   Business: 212-888-9000

February 12, 2001

Roberta Browne, VP - HR
TTT Financial Services Corporation
89 Arnold Lane
Amherst, NJ 03876

Dear Ms. Browne:

Building top-performing financial service organizations is my expertise. Whether challenged to launch a start-up venture, orchestrate an aggressive turnaround and lead a high-growth organization, I have consistently delivered strong financial results. Equally notable is the breadth of my international experience in the Latin American, Asian and Australian markets:

- Nineteen years' experience with **Citizens Trust Bank**, its Brazilian affiliate and its Asian/Pacific region. Introduced advanced IT systems, architectures and applications critical to building new ventures, reengineering non-performing operations and supporting accelerated growth in markets worldwide.

- Impressive senior management career with Voice of America in its US, Latin American, Asian and Australian markets. My most notable achievement was the financial turnaround of Latin American operations, building profits from $4 million to $13 million over five years. Equally significant, I personally negotiated long-term contracts with the four largest banking institutions in Australia, winning against stiff competition because of my personal knowledge and **expertise in both retail and commercial banking**.

- Current leadership as **President/CEO of a "hybrid" technology and financial services organization**, allowing me the opportunity to combine my IT, finance, marketing and general management experience. In less than two years, the company has transitioned from a loosely-operated enterprise into a solid and strategically focused business with tremendous opportunity. Unfortunately, the investors have pulled their funding to pursue other ventures.

My goal is to return to the Financial Services Industry in a senior executive capacity. I am open to a number of opportunities that would allow me to use the diversity of my management skills across various disciplines – operations, sales/marketing, finance and IT. I would anticipate the position to have a strong international focus to capitalize on the wealth of experience abroad and my multi-lingual skills.

I would welcome the chance to speak with you about your senior staffing needs and my potential fit. I do appreciate your consideration and look forward to hearing from you.

Sincerely,

Antonio Garcia

Enclosure

Finance – Investment

KeyWords, Action Verbs & High-Impact Phrases to "Nail" Your Cover Letter:

- Asset & Portfolio Management/Administration

- IPOs, ESOPs, Private Placement & Offerings

- Mergers, Acquisitions & Joint Ventures

- Capital Financings & Debt Management

- Investment Planning & Analysis

- Trading – Stocks, Options, Funds & Commodities

- Foreign Exchange & Currency Hedging

- ROI, ROA & ROE Performance

- Regulatory Reporting & Compliance

- Risk Assessment & Management

GARY G. GRAYSON, JR.

gggjr@ia.com
12 Buffalo Hollow Road
Amesville, IA 56738
Phone: 345-783-9827   Fax: 345-783-7739

September 14, 2000

John Sebastian
Trident Electronics Systems, Inc.
9999 Research Parkway
Cary, NC 28903

Dear Mr. Sebastian:

Identifying business opportunities and developing strategy for new corporate ventures is my expertise. Whether negotiating acquisitions and strategic alliances, structuring capital investments or leading multi-party new ventures, I have consistently delivered strong financial and performance results. My experience spans a broad range of industries including technology, healthcare, oil & gas, real estate, retail, and food and beverage. Most notably, I have:

- Led and/or co-managed more than 10 mergers, acquisitions, joint ventures, strategic alliances and partnerships throughout both the US and foreign markets.

- Restored non-performing business units to achieve profitability through development of strategic opportunities.

- Directed and/or participated in structuring and negotiating transactions valued from less than $1 million to more than $200 million.

- Provided creative and decisive development strategies to optimize market opportunities and drive long-term revenue, profit and market share growth.

The greatest value I bring to your organization is my ability to build relationships between top executives, often with vastly differing objectives and operating requirements. I am a mediator, successful in facilitating positive results, bringing to fruition opportunities never before attempted.

Currently, I am operating a private consulting practice exclusively in corporate development and have managed several unique US/foreign partner projects. Now, I am interested in returning to a corporate position similar to my assignment as Venture Projects Director with Trident Electronics and its affiliates; a position where I can continue to identify, develop and execute new acquisitions, strategic projects, new ventures and other corporate deals.

I would welcome a personal interview at your convenience. Thank you.

Sincerely,

Gary G. Grayson, Jr.

Enclosure

RAFAEL MONTEBON
Rafael.Montebon@overseas.net
2987 Southern Drive
Savannah, Georgia 47552

Phone (651) 967-0788   Fax (651) 967-5947

May 16, 2001

Shawn Carrington
Executive Vice President
Bank of New York
1202 Commerce Avenue
New York, NY 10018

Dear Mr. Carrington:

I am a senior-level Treasury and Trading Executive with 19 years' experience in US, European, Far Eastern and South African markets. Currently, I am exploring new opportunities and would welcome the chance to speak with you directly regarding executive positions with Bank of New York.

For the past nine years, I've lived and worked in the US, representing and managing the investment, trading, marketing and risk management affairs of one of the top 100 banks in the world. I've performed extremely well, taking the organization from a loss position to strong profits with a 100% increase in trading volume. Earlier successes were just as significant:

* Increased trading volume in Japan from *$500 million to $6 billion with 500% increase* in profitability.
* Captured a *150% increase in sales and 300% increase in trading volume* in Singapore.
* Established *new and profitable* South African trading organization.
* *Managed $5 billion* US treasury and trading operation in France.

Each of these positions has not only required strong financial, investment, negotiating and trading qualifications, but a unique expertise in cross-cultural business development and relationship management. I have established a high-profile reputation within each country and led each organization through change, growth and performance improvement.

I look forward to speaking with you regarding your search for a Treasury Vice President, and appreciate your consideration.

Sincerely,

Rafael Montebon

Enclosure

FRANK BARTRUM
19 Cherry Tree Lane
Trenton, New Jersey 04770
(201) 648-1428

March 21, 2001

Thomas Richardson
President
Mitchell Investments, Inc.
2140 Sunshine Boulevard
Melbourne, FL 33551

Dear Mr. Richardson:

The time has come, I've sold my snow shovel, and my wife and I are on our way to Florida. This winter proved to be one of the worst and we're headed for warmer climates.

As such, I'm divesting my financial services company in New York and now looking for a position in investment sales/marketing and portfolio management with a Florida-based organization. Highlights of my professional career include:

• Over 15 years of professional experience in financial services, investment management, marketing and portfolio development.

• Unique expertise in index option investment strategies.

• Development of new portfolio to over $20 million in assets under management.

• Negotiation of competitive wins against major competitors.

• Strong skills in investor development and relationship management.

I am currently travelling between New York and Florida on a routine basis, and would welcome the opportunity for a personal interview on my next visit. As such, I will contact you to schedule a convenient time to explore your need for a strong, decisive and well-qualified investment professional. Thank you.

Sincerely,

Frank Bartrum

Enclosure

JAMES LAWSON

500 Oakmont Court
Lawrence, Illinois 68708

Home (874) 793-3197
Office (874) 778-3402

June 2, 2001

Walter Franklin
President
Schwab Investments
2103 Michigan Avenue, #120
Chicago, IL 60600

Dear Mr. Franklin:

Currently Senior Vice President of Government Bond Trading for Wiley Securities, I have transitioned the organization into one of the top-performing trading companies in the market. By controlling our risk, we increased revenues by 42% within just one year while accelerating market share and strengthening our competitive position.

Now, however, I am confidentially exploring new professional opportunities and would welcome a personal interview with Schwab Investments. I bring to your organization a unique blend of qualifications:

- 15+ years' experience in government bond trading, financing and risk management.
- Expert qualifications in team building, training and organizational leadership.
- Proven success in building and retaining client relationships within extremely competitive and volatile investment markets.
- Strong background in systems and process automation.

Throughout my career — with Wiley, E.F. Hutton and Lehman Brothers — I have strengthened the value and performance of each company's government bond trading organization. This value can easily be measured in terms of growth in market share, risk management and financing.

I would welcome a personal interview at your convenience and appreciate your confidentiality. Thank you.

Sincerely,

James Lawson

Enclosure

GILBERT MITCHELL

gilmitch@hotmail.com

789 Elmhurst Road
San Diego, CA 90766
819-898-4545

July 14, 2000

Andrew Martinson
Managing Director
Investments Unlimited, Inc.
656 42nd Street, Suite 1200
Madison, WI 57637

Dear Mr. Martinson:

Identifying, funding and optimizing corporate investment opportunities is what I do best. Whether launching a start-up venture, facilitating a industry roll-out, acquiring assets through acquisition and joint venture, or divesting non-performing holdings, I have consistently delivered double-digit growth in revenue, ROA and ROI.

My greatest strength is my ability to assess the potential financial value of a specific asset, evaluate its potential fit within an existing portfolio of companies, and then facilitate favorable financing transactions, deals and partnerships. Then, under my leadership, I have built the value of these assets by introducing advanced technologies, redefining markets, improving operations and recruiting talent management teams.

The enclosed resume highlights some of my most notable achievements, projects and transactions. There are many more that I can share with you during an interview to demonstrate the breadth of my experience and performance.

My goal is an executive-level position with responsibility for strategic planning and corporate development including mergers, acquisitions, joint ventures, financings and other transactions. As such, I would welcome the opportunity to speak with you regarding such opportunities and appreciate your consideration of my qualifications.

Thank you.

Sincerely,

Gilbert Mitchell

Enclosure

Food & Beverage

**KeyWords, Action Verbs & High-Impact Phrases
to "Nail" Your Cover Letter:**

- Labor Cost Savings

- Food Cost Controls

- Purchasing & Supplier Negotiations

- Menu Development & Profitable Pricing

- Productivity Improvement

- Guest Relations & Retention

- Staff Training & Development

- Multi-Site Operations Management

- New Site Start-Up

- Special Events

ELVIS P. CASCELLA

771 Ross Drive
Lawrence, Kansas 45434

Home (555) 978-8050
Fax   (555) 978-0155

January 26, 2001

Human Resource Director – Ad #96C
Coca-Cola Foods
P.O. Box 2079
Houston, TX 77252-2079

Dear Sir/Madam:

With more than 15 years' experience in Food Industry sales, marketing and business development programs, I bring to Coca-Cola Foods the exact qualifications you seek for the position of Region Market Manager.

- Expertise in identifying, developing and managing business development programs designed to penetrate emerging markets, accelerate growth within existing markets, and strengthen annual revenue performance.

- Extensive qualifications in the recruitment, training and leadership of both direct sales and broker sales networks.

- Strong strategic planning skills with proven success in translating strategy into tactical action plans.

- Delivery of multi-million dollar revenue growth within challenging and competitive business markets.

- Excellent record of performance in managing and further developing key account relationships with strong presentation, negotiation and sales closing skills.

Most significant is my ability to build and manage cooperative working relationships with my sales teams, distributors and customers. Through these efforts, we have been successful in launching new products, redefining our product mix to meet market demand, and outperforming competition.

After years of sales experience within the food service industry, I was recruited to accelerate a sales and marketing program for a national organization. Within the first year, I delivered significant revenue gains and strengthened our retention by 58%. Although successful, I miss the dynamics of the food service industry and am now pursuing opportunities to return. As such, my interest in your search and request for a personal interview.

Sincerely,

Elvis P. Cascella

Enclosure

HORACE RENE
1006 Avenue de Apartie
Montreal, Quebec H5P 3T1
Phone (514) 478-9825   Fax (514) 478-2148

December 1, 2000

Jacques Levesque
Director
Le Hotelier
1984 Noset Boulevard
Montreal, Quebec H9R 1Q9

Dear Mr. Levesque:

I have recently relocated to Montreal and am contacting you to express my interest in employment opportunities. With 15 years experience in the Food & Beverage industry, I offer:

* Excellent qualifications in the start-up of new F&B outlets, banquet operations and conference centers, as well as the expansion of existing service operations.

* Consistent achievement of all expense budgets and revenue objectives with strong analytical and negotiating skills.

* Demonstrated success in increasing customer satisfaction and retention, improving revenues and outperforming competition.

* Strong skills in recruiting, training and supervising a large service staff.

I have worked for properties around the world, many with exclusive F&B operations. To each, I have provided strong and effective management and improved financial gains. I realize, however, no matter the strength of my experience, relocation to a new country is always a challenge and requires a learning curve. I am ready for such a challenge and anxious to reignite my career.

I am available, of course, at your convenience for an interview and thank you in advance for your consideration.

Sincerely,

Horace Rene

Enclosure

HENRY MARTINEZ
119 Circle Court
Ocean City, New Jersey 19117
(609) 356-8919

November 15, 2000

Director of Operations
Caesar's Palace
2000 Flamingo Road
Las Vegas, NV 76532

Dear Sir/Madam:

I am a well-qualified Food & Beverage Professional with more than 10 years of top-flight management experience. Beginning my career with the Sands Hotel & Casino, I advanced through a series of positions from Cook to Supervisor to my final promotion as Assistant Manager of five operating locations. Subsequently I was recruited to lead a diversity of F&B operations within the entertainment, restaurant, hotel and contract food service industries.

Through my strengths in personnel management, budgeting, administration, quality assurance and purchasing, I have met and/or exceeded all operating challenges — to increase revenues, control costs, improve staff productivity and efficiency, and deliver strong and sustainable results in customer service, satisfaction and retention. I am creative and team-oriented in my leadership style. I expect top performance in myself and my staff, and strive to instill a sense of personal worth and contribution to achieve overall corporate goals.

Now, my goal is to return to the casino industry where I can again lead fast-paced, customer-driven operations. I am in the process of relocating to Las Vegas and would welcome a personal interview to explore management opportunities with Caesar's Palace. I look forward to what I hope is the first of many positive communications.

Sincerely,

Henry Martinez

Enclosure

Government

KeyWords, Action Verbs & High-Impact Phrases to "Nail" Your Cover Letter:

- Finance & Administrative Management

- Increased Budget Appropriations

- Policy & Procedure Development

- Regulatory & Legislative Compliance

- Constituent Development & Relations

- Consensus Building

- Contract Negotiations & Administration

- Public & Private Partnerships

- Municipal Service Operations

- Economic & Business Development Programs

WILLIAM J. FOX
28 Babbling Brook
Hartford, Connecticut 06987
(203) 692-2323
wmfox@government.net

April 29, 2000

Personnel Policies Subcommittee
Legislative Office Building
Room 5100
Hartford, CT 06106-1591

RE: Executive Director Search

Dear Sir/Madam:

Throughout my 14-year career in Municipal & Legislative Management, I have not only demonstrated strong business management qualifications, but the unique ability to build consensus among diverse political and special interest groups to work cooperatively towards common goals. The combination of both has been the foundation for my success and my contributions.

As you review my resume, you will note that I bring a strong portfolio of general management skills to the General Assembly. Most significant is my expertise in finance, budgeting, human resources, contracts, facilities management, administration and information technology. Further, I have been personally accountable for legislative reporting and regulatory compliance for three large municipalities throughout the Eastern U.S.

My greatest value to General Assembly is my professional network. Active in municipal and statewide legislative affairs for the past several years, I have built strong working relationships with legislative and judicial leaders throughout the state. These relationships will inevitably be of significant value in my ability to manage within the Assembly.

I am anxious to interview for the position and will follow up next week. Salary is negotiable. Thank you.

Sincerely,

William J. Fox

Enclosure

MATTHEW P. WEBSTER
20 Clayton Court
San Diego, California 95174

Phone (415) 672-1030   Fax (415) 672-1012

October 20, 2000

Robert Dickstein
President
AT&T, Inc.
1500 Edison Avenue
New York, NY 10010

Dear Mr. Dickstein:

With more than 15 years' experience in the Telecommunications Industry, I bring to AT&T a unique expertise in Right of Way Operations and Government Affairs. Currently, as the Director of Local Government Relations for my company's largest-ever technology deployment, I am leading a highly-visible initiative to win the support of local municipalities to facilitate our projects and further our competitive position within the market.

Previously, during my tenure as Right of Way Manager, I led the management team that structured and negotiated hundreds of easements to support our expansion and regional diversification. This position also required extensive government liaison efforts to meet our immediate and long-term objectives.

My greatest strength lies in my ability to build consensus. I have been recognized throughout my career for consistent success in team building and project success. Further, I have broad technical, engineering and legal qualifications specific to the telecommunications industry (including wireless video and other emerging technologies).

Although secure in my current position, I have decided to pursue new professional challenges and would welcome the opportunity for a personal interview at your convenience. I appreciate your confidentiality and look forward to speaking with you.

Sincerely,

Matthew P. Webster

Enclosure

107

JEFFERY A. CAVANAUGH
1928 Woodland Drive
Charlotte, North Carolina 28213
(704) 523-0609

September 5, 2000

Robert O'Connor
Commissioner, City of Sacramento
P.O. Box 1090
Sacramento, CA 98231-1090

Dear Mr. O'Connor:

For the past 14 years, I have held several increasingly responsible positions as Finance Commissioner / Finance Director for three large municipal government organizations. To each city, I have provided strong and decisive financial leadership, delivered tremendous financial gains, and positioned for long-term and profitable growth.

Now, at this point in my career, I am seeking to transition my experience into a broad-based general management position with a growing and dynamic city government. Thus my interest in your search for a Finance Director and request for a personal interview.

Highlights of my career that may be of particular interest to you include the following:

- Active participation, in cooperation with Mayor, City Council and other government officials, in the planning and leadership of large municipal organizations (servicing up to 80,000 residents).

- Expertise in administrative management, operations planning, departmental operations and inter-departmental coordination.

- Development of policies and standards governing operations, fiscal affairs and technology.

- Strong public speaking and public relations competencies.

- Extensive involvement in high-profile economic and business development programs.

- Leadership of successful public and private funding programs totaling more than $35 million throughout my career.

I am available at your convenience for a personal interview and would be delighted to provide any additional information you may require. Thank you for your time and consideration.

Sincerely,

Jeffery A. Cavanaugh

Enclosure

Health Care

KeyWords, Action Verbs & High-Impact Phrases to "Nail" Your Cover Letter:

- Revenue & Profit Growth

- New Clinical Services & Provider Networks

- New Revenue Generating Programs & Ventures

- Managed Care Programs

- Technology Implementation

- Capital Project Management

- Risk Management

- Regulatory Affairs & Compliance

- Health Care Policy

- Health Care Service Delivery & Administration

ANDREW W. NEWMAN
422 East Lake Drive
Provo, Utah 88764
(902) 873-8725

March 12, 2001

Denise Danielson
President
Global Health Care, Inc.
24 Madison Avenue #1900
New York, NY 10090

Dear Ms. Danielson:

In 1994, I was recruited to join the management team of Health & Homedics to guide strategic planning, business development, sales, marketing and distribution operations for a recent acquisition. The company had identified the home health market as a primary growth vehicle, consummated an acquisition and launched the industry's first successful superstore concept. Today, we boast of a $40 million business built from a concept, a vision and lots of hard work.

The greatest value I bring to Global Health Care are my strengths in sales, marketing and distribution. Throughout my career, I have guided profitable regional and national sales organizations, conceived and developed innovative marketing campaigns, and created a large-scale distribution center supporting over 35 locations. For each, I have created the operating infrastructure, established financial plans and budgets, recruited and trained personnel, and provided the drive and energy to achieve aggressive financial results.

Of particular interest to you, my experience is heavily concentrated in the health care, medical and pharmaceutical industries. As such, my network of contacts – with vendors, health care providers, insurance providers and others in the community – is extensive. Further, my knowledge of health care products and services is extensive.

Currently, I am employed as the Director of Sales & Marketing for Health & Homedics, leading the entire national sales organization. I am secure in my position and only considering new opportunities that offer challenge and reward. As such, if you believe that my qualifications position me well for your Director of National Sales position, I would welcome a personal interview. At that time we can discuss my present salary and current compensation goals.

I appreciate your confidentiality and thank you for your consideration.

Sincerely,

Andrew W. Newman

Enclosure

THOMAS P. WINDSOR
985 Lakeside Drive
Oshkosh, Michigan 63126
Home (616) 343-8274   Office (616) 343-2804

May 10, 2001

Hospital Search Committee
c/o Grant Cooper & Associates, Inc.
795 Office Parkway, Suite 117
St. Louis, MO 63141-7146

Dear Committee Members:

It is with great interest that I submit my resume for consideration as President & CEO of your client's metropolitan health system. I bring to the position a diversity of experience and strong track record of performance in the strategic planning, development, marketing and management of diversified health care service organizations.

Highlights of my professional career include:

- Fourteen years of top-flight executive management experience in the health care services and products industries, including several successful and profitable start-up ventures.

- Delivery of strong revenue and profit growth within extremely competitive markets.

- Strong qualifications in community outreach and public affairs, particularly as they pertain to building managed care networks and service organizations.

- Broad-based general management skills in MIS technology, human resource affairs, training, facilities and materials management, general accounting, financial planning and analysis, budgeting, board presentations and other senior-level operating management functions.

My leadership style is direct and decisive, yet I am flexible in responding to the constantly changing demands of my staff, management team, customers and market. I am familiar with most regulations governing health care practice, and have been the driving force behind several financially and operationally successful organizations.

I look forward to speaking with you to further pursue this opportunity. Compensation requirements can be discussed at the time of our interview. Thank you.

Sincerely,

Thomas P. Windsor

Enclosure

111

CARL WATSON, M.D.
2649 North Wabash Avenue
Chicago, Illinois 60610
Home (312) 480-9809   Office (312) 916-4125

February 4, 2001

James L. Lewis
Lewis & Associates
100 West 49th Street, 15th Floor
New York, NY 10019

Dear Mr. Lewis:

Currently a Director of Memorial West Hospital / Medical School, I am exploring new management opportunities in the emerging health care, managed care, pharmaceutical and biotechnology industries. With more than 15 years of health care management experience, strong clinical qualifications and current attendance in Kellogg's MBA program (expected in 2002), I am seeking the opportunity to combine my skills for a top-level management position.

Beginning my career as a Medical Doctor and Radiologist, I quickly expanded the scope of my responsibility to include a diversity of business management functions — from strategic planning, staffing and budgeting to pioneering programs in technology, quality and performance improvement. In sum, I manage the "business" of medicine.

Notable achievements include recognition by JCAHO for my efforts in quality and regulatory affairs, development of innovative management and professional training programs, publication of research in more than 60 journal articles, and introduction of state-of-the-art information, radiologic and medical systems. I have helped to build a department at Memorial that is not only recognized for its clinical expertise, but just as significantly for its management, financial, technological and quality achievements.

With the addition of my MBA degree, I am now ready to transition my qualifications into the private sector where I can participate in the development, operations and leadership of a successful organization. If you are working with a client company seeking a candidate with my qualifications, I would welcome a personal interview. Please note that I am interested in relocating to New York and that my compensation requirements are flexible. Thank you.

Sincerely,

Carl Watson, M.D.

Enclosure

JERRY JOHNSTON, JR.

---

898 East Monroe Street
Marquis, Indiana 47095

Phone: 239.937-5522
jjohnston999@aol.com

October 30, 2000

Michael R. Peterson
Chairman
Health Care Performance Systems, Inc.
766 E. 42nd Street, Suite 750
McLean, VA 22873

Dear Mr. Peterson:

Building financially-strong health care companies is my expertise. Whether challenged to launch a start-up venture, orchestrate a turnaround, or lead a company through accelerated growth and expansion, I have consistently delivered solid financial performance:

- As **President/CEO** of HealthTech, Inc. (a major player in the health care capital equipment market), I drove revenue growth from $850 million to $1.1 billion.
- As **President/CEO** of RSH (industry leader in health care equipment), I restored organizational stability, halted losses and built revenues from $175 million to $375 million with double-digit profits.

These two achievements are indicative of the caliber of my entire professional career – identify business opportunities, develop strategies, build infrastructures, create products and conquer the market. My performance with both HealthTech and RSH was so significant that these companies have been honored by Fortune Magazine, Selling Power Magazine and Industry Week Magazine.

I pride myself on the diversity of my skills which range from the "big picture" functions of strategic planning, corporate development, acquisitions and international expansion to the daily operations of manufacturing, sales and technical operations. I've held direct P&L responsibility for 10+ years and delivered cost reductions totaling more than $25 million.

However, the time for change has come. After 18 years with the organization, I am confidentially exploring new executive opportunities and would welcome the chance to speak with you.

Sincerely,

Jerry Johnston, Jr.

Enclosure

JAY LESTER, M.D.
541-4th Street
New York, New York 10019
(212) 460-3324
DocJay@md.com

February 28, 2001

Adam Washington
Managing Partner
Healthcare Executives Worldwide
1874 Avenue of the Americas, 43rd Floor
New York, NY 11542

Dear Mr. Washington:

I am a well-qualified Health Care / Hospital Administrator with 16 years of professional experience in the development, budgeting, staffing and management of multi-specialty health care programs and services. Highlights of my professional career include:

- Extensive experience in the introduction of quality assurance, utilization review and internal audit programs that have consistently enhanced the delivery of health care services.

- Establishment of health care policy governing large regional health care and managed care networks throughout the U.S., Canada, South America and Europe.

- Implementation of aggressive cost controls that have reduced annual expenditures with no negative impact on the quality of care or care providers.

- Excellent qualifications managing relationships with Boards of Directors, Finance Directors, major donors, regulators and others involved in health care planning and funding.

- Full management responsibility for all general business functions (e.g., budgeting, physician recruitment, staff training, facilities, provider relations, public relations, insurance administration).

I have most recently travelled throughout the jungles of South America, working with local physicians, nurses and health care administrators to facilitate the development of preventive medicine, nutrition and immunization programs. Now that I have returned to the U.S., I am anxious to again assume an administrative assignment with a hospital, clinic or other health care organization, and would welcome a personal interview to discuss potential opportunities. Thank you.

Sincerely,

Jay Lester, M.D.

Enclosure

ADAM R. ARNOLD
12 Montack Place • Asheville, North Carolina 28897
Voice: (744) 239-2399 • Fax: (744) 788-7654 • Email: ara@ctc.net

February 14, 2001

Andrea Williamson
President & CEO
BioTech Solutions, Inc.
45 Emery Road #909
Tulsa, OK 49837

Dear Ms. Williamson:

I am a well-qualified Marketing Professional with 15+ years' experience. Most notable have been my achievements in new market development, new business development, market research, service/product line expansion and customer relationship management. Through my efforts, I have been successful in driving revenue and profit growth within competitive markets.

Now, at this juncture in my career, I am seeking new professional challenges and opportunities in a senior-level marketing capacity. The value I bring to BioTech includes:

- More than 15 years' experience in marketing within the healthcare and allied industries.
- Ability to quickly and accurately identify market demand.
- Pioneering efforts in new product and new service development.
- Consistent success in customer profiling to drive marketing strategy and action.
- Strong presentation, communication, negotiation and public speaking skills.

Never satisfied with the status quo, I strive to build profitable businesses by clearly understanding the market, the competition and what needs to be done to retain a competitive lead. This is the strength and the track record I bring to your organization. In addition, please note that I have strong general management experience including direct P&L.

I would welcome a personal interview and appreciate your time in reviewing my qualifications. Thank you.

Sincerely,

Adam R. Arnold

Enclosure

Hospitality

KeyWords, Action Verbs & High-Impact Phrases to "Nail" Your Cover Letter:

- Guest Services & Public Relations

- Revenue & Profit Improvement

- Occupancy Increases

- Capital Improvement & Renovation

- Corporate, Association & Group Sales Achievements

- Operating & Labor Cost Reductions

- Quality & Service Awards & Recognition

- Technology Enhancements

- New Property Development & Start-Up

- Amenities Programs

TANYA TISHMAN
123 Booth Road
Raleigh, NC 28883
Phone: 727.832.2356
Email: ttishman@raleigh.net

April 14, 2001

Lewis Manning
President
Hospitality Management, Inc.
23 Dover Dell Place
Dover, DE 09837

Dear Mr. Manning:

With 20+ years' experience in the hospitality industry, I have participated in our industry's massive change and transformation. Between the mergers, acquisitions, joint ventures and other strategic partnerships, our industry is virtually being recreated. Hopefully, when things begin to stabilize, we will see that these changes have been of value and that our industry is stronger and better than ever.

During this period of change and growth, stability must be the #1 objective for any operation. It is essential, despite whatever external organizational changes are underway, that the "operation" – what the public sees – continues to operate at 100% peak performance. And, that is precisely what I do best.

Over the years, I have earned a nationwide reputation for my ability to profitably manage highly-charged, fast-paced and labor-intensive operations. Despite the challenges, I have consistently delivered strong revenue and profit results. Here are a few of my most notable achievements:

- Most recently, I managed several major assets (e.g., LA Hyatt, DC Willard) with combined revenues of $256 million annually. Within the first year, my team and I increased revenues, GOP, EBITDA and RevPAR 8.5%, 12.2%, 15.8% and 13.9%, respectively.

- Led KrossRoads Realty ($150 million hotel management company) through a successful sale at $100 million above the original purchase price. Most significant, we stabilized operations and increased revenues 5% and EBITDA 20% while reducing operating costs by $760,000.

- Delivered a 14% increase in revenues and 59% increase in GOP while managing multi-unit operations for Busterman Hotel Management. While directing operations, I participated in the organization's transition to a REIT and co-managed 12 successful acquisitions.

- Advanced rapidly through a series of increasingly responsible sales management and operating management positions with properties owned by Marriott, Marriott franchisees, Hilton and Hyatt Regency. In all assignments, I delivered double-digit revenue growth within intensely competitive markets.

As you can see, the range of my operating management experience is vast and includes strategic planning, budgeting, human resources, information technology, sales, marketing, customer service, physical plant investment and much more. I am an active proponent of internal change, constantly working to introduce new systems and processes to enhance our performance, productivity and profitability.

When operating a hotel, one is challenged to manage thousands of details. Perhaps more critical is the leader's ability to prioritize those details and focus the team on the few that will make the largest contributions to success – customer satisfaction, employee satisfaction, revenues and profits. This is what I consider to be one of my most vital strengths. I can see the big picture while managing all the details to ensure that my properties are competitive, distinctive and some of the most profitable in the country.

Characterized by others as a "New Age leader," I am collaborative and participative in my leadership style. However, I am also the team leader, able to make difficult decisions, solve complex problems and build employee consensus. I value the efforts and contributions of each employee, but at some point, I become the decision maker and move the entire organization in the "right" direction. Further, I have extensive experience introducing leading edge technologies into our industry, including the development of a website and E-commerce capabilities for Richfield.

I am a graduate of New York State University and a Certified Hotel Administrator (CHA) through the American Hotel/Motel Association. In addition, I am a graduate of Marriott's Advanced Management School (in conjunction with Harvard University).

At this juncture in my career, I am interested in a top-level leadership position with full strategic, operating, sales and P&L responsibility for either a single property or a portfolio of assets. I am equally qualified to manage a portfolio of assets or a high-end destination/resort property, whichever offers the most challenge and most market opportunity.

I've worked long and hard throughout my career, and will continue to do so, but am focusing my search on identifying a unique opportunity – something a bit "different" that offers new challenges and new opportunities to build, grow and prosper.

If you are interested in a candidate with my qualifications, I would welcome an interview so that we can begin to discuss potential opportunities. In turn, I guarantee that the strength of my management performance will add measurable value to your operations. Thank you.

Sincerely,

Tanya Tishman

FRANK NELSON, JR.
425 Armadillo Avenue
Rosemont, Texas 77877
299-432-3927

February 14, 2001

Paul Kirwin
President - Country Inns & Suites
Country Hospitality Worldwide
P.O. Box 59159
Minneapolis, MN 55459-8203

Dear Mr. Kirwin:

Congratulations! I've been watching the development of your new property in Rosemont, Texas and can tell you that the entire community is looking forward to the grand opening. We've needed a property of this type in Rosemont for several years (as I'm sure your demographics indicated) and I know that the project will be extremely profitable if well led.

I'm a local resident of Rosemont with a wealth of business experience worldwide. Having recently relocated permanently to the area, I would welcome the opportunity to interview with you or a member of your staff for the position of General Manager with the local property. Let me tell you why I am the "perfect" candidate (albeit atypical):

- 15+ years of general management experience in facilities development and management, including planning, budgeting, logistics, purchasing, equipment, materials and technology.

- Outstanding communication and people-to-people interaction skills. I am well-known throughout the local market, have extensive contacts throughout both the professional and civic communities, and recently completed a yearlong leadership training course with the City.

- Ability to "get the job done" no matter the circumstance. This was critical throughout my career, often working in environments with stringent deadlines and financial expectations.

- Strong qualifications in training, development and leadership with direct responsibility for hundreds of employees, supervisors and managers, and multi-million dollar budgets.

- In-depth understanding of customer service, customer loyalty and customer retention.

I am available at your convenience for a personal interview and guarantee that the strength of my leadership skills and operating performance will position Rosemont for strong and profitable growth.

Sincerely,

Frank Nelson, Jr.

Enclosure

119

CALVIN HIGHMAN, CHA
1973 South 2500 East
Salt Lake City, Utah 84108
Email: high@net.com
Phone/Fax: (801) 466-6088

April 4, 2001

Larry Jefferson
Executive Vice President
Royal Caribbean Resorts, Inc.
1293 Ocean View Drive
Boca Raton, FL 33532

Dear Mr. Jefferson:

With more than 20 years experience in the Hospitality Industry, I bring to Royal Caribbean a strong record of management performance and achievement in:

* Increasing revenues and bottom-line profits while reducing annual operating, overhead and payroll costs.
* Introducing top-flight quality, service and member retention programs.
* Managing complex financial analysis, budgeting and reporting functions.
* Driving successful sales, marketing and member development programs.

With excellent communications, interpersonal relations, organizational, project management and leadership qualifications, I guarantee that I can far surpass your goals and objectives in your search for a General Manager.

I appreciate your time in reviewing my qualifications and will follow up promptly. My recent salary history is $105,000 plus a full benefits package and a 20% incentive plan.

Sincerely,

Calvin Highman, CHA

Enclosure

Human Resources

KeyWords, Action Verbs & High-Impact Phrases to "Nail" Your Cover Letter:

- Organizational Development

- Benefits & Compensation

- Training & Development

- Cost Reduction & Avoidance

- HRIS Technology

- Recruitment & Selection

- Succession Planning

- Workforce Integration

- Corporate Culture Change

- Performance Improvement

SAMUEL P. REIDER
sam.p.reider@madison.net

7837 S.E. Williams Street
Madison, Wisconsin 82040

Home (602) 232-4015
Office (602) 452-2520

May 19, 2001

George B. Schmidt
President
Industrial Manufacturing, Inc.
199 Mississippi Avenue
St. Louis, MO 60545

Dear Mr. Schmidt:

Human Resources is no longer the traditional personnel function and successful managers have recognized this change. Over the past decade as "corporate America" has redefined itself, human resources has become an increasingly vital component in revenue and profit improvement. We have all come to value the strength and potential of our workforce and its influence over our success.

To meet those challenges, I have created HR organizations that are innovative, results-driven and tied directly to bottom-line performance. These programs have ranged from specific business reengineering initiatives to corporate-wide recruitment, staffing and leadership development programs. In turn, financial results have improved and stability has been returned.

Please also note that I have extremely strong generalist qualifications in all core HR functions with particular strengths in labor negotiations and employee relations. Major projects have included benefits and compensation design, succession plans, EH&S program management, quality training and complete workforce realignment programs.

My goal is a senior-level HR executive assignment with a company in need of strong and decisive organizational leadership. After you've reviewed my resume, I would welcome a personal interview and look forward to meeting with you.

Sincerely,

Samuel P. Reider

Enclosure

ELIZABETH LIVINGSTON

13792 S.E. 78th Place
Mercer Island, Washington 98042
Home (206) 401-3525

June 23, 2000

Robert Moser
Executive Vice President
Talbot, Inc.
3000 West Evergreen, Suite 223
Portland, OR 55323

Dear Mr. Moser:

In 1989 I was recruited as the first-ever Director of Human Resources for a 130-year-old organization. Starting with a workforce of 60 employees and virtually no formal HR policies, I built a top-flight HR organization, introduced innovative training and performance management programs, negotiated self-funded benefit programs and led the organization through a period of rapid growth to more than 250 employees at three operating locations.

In early 1996, I accepted the opportunity to spearhead the reorganization of the complete HR and organizational development function following the merger of two of Canada's most respected and innovative investment firms to form Allied Smith, Inc. To date, I have created a cohesive operating infrastructure and recruited 30+ senior management and professionals to support Allied's market launch throughout the U.S.

These experiences have been tremendous and afforded me the opportunity to create innovative HR and employee relations programs that have consistently strengthened our operating performance. However, due to unforeseen changes within the Allied organization, I am now exploring new professional opportunities where I can continue to provide strong and decisive HR leadership. Thus my interest in Talbot and request for a personal interview.

I appreciate your consideration and will follow up next week to arrange a time for a personal interview. Thank you.

Sincerely,

Elizabeth Livingston

Enclosure

EUGENE S. THOMPSON, CCP

P.O. Box 156
Washington, D.C 21056
Email: est@aol.com

Home (202) 624-1465
Office (202) 783-2210
Fax   (202) 783-3322

August 18, 2000

Jeffry Lawrence, President
Inacomp Technology Manufacturing
122 Kroger Drive
Spokane, WA 99056

Dear Mr. Lawrence:

Strong human resources leadership can have a tremendous impact on corporate and organizational value. By building an effective HR infrastructure, providing strategic HR leadership, and controlling escalating compensation and benefit costs, you can immediately improve the financial performance, productivity and viability of your organization. This is the value I deliver.

An accomplished HR executive with strong qualifications in all core generalist functions, I have been instrumental in strengthening performance through my efforts in:

- Union, Management & Labor Relations
- Domestic & International Staffing
- Employee Training & Development
- Safety Management & Control
- Benefits & Compensation Design

- HRIS Technology
- Quality & Productivity
- Employee Relations
- Regulatory Compliance
- Employee Law & Litigation

I am a proactive business manager, credited with the development of innovative productivity, efficiency, quality and performance management programs with strong bottom-line results. Further, my ability to build cooperation — between union and non-union personnel — between employees and operating management teams — between field and headquarters organizations — has been critical to our overall performance.

Although secure in my current position, I am confidentially exploring new professional challenges and opportunities. Thus my interest in discussing your search for a Corporate Human Resources Director. I appreciate your consideration and look forward to speaking with you in the next few days.

Sincerely,

Eugene S. Thompson, CCP

Enclosure

NELSON M. BRIGHTSEN

176 Renaissance Circle
El Paso, Texas 79936-7176
Voice Mail (915) 388-7853 x250   Residence (915) 857-6392

March 3, 2001

William Shepheard
Chairman of the Board
Emergency Air Conditioning Company
P.O. Box 2496
Norfolk, VA 23501-2496

Dear Mr. Shepheard:

Managing human resource performance issues within large and complex industrial manufacturing organizations is a challenge! There are, of course, all the "typical" HR generalist functions found in any company. But within our industry, there is so much more — union issues, union avoidance issues, safety and quality issues, continuous process improvement and productivity/performance issues.

I have positively met all of these challenges, building HR organizations responsive to both management and worker needs. By facilitating cooperation and commitment to common goals, we have avoided potentially difficult situations and achieved some of the highest productivity ratings in the industry.

Just as critical are my contributions to the bottom-line:

- Currently nearing completion of QS-9000 quality certification process for GAP Systems.
- $4 million in operating cost savings for Signal Resources.
- $1.3 million contribution to cash flow for a multi-site service organization.
- Operating unit turnaround from $10 million loss to $10 million profit.

Currently, and confidentially, I am exploring new career challenges and opportunities in an effort to return to the Mid-Atlantic region. As such, I would welcome a personal interview at your convenience. Thank you.

Sincerely,

Nelson M. Brightsen

Enclosure

FRANCES HACKETT
2305 South Pittsburg Street
Rumsford, Kansas 66673
Phone: (316) 231-1690   /   Email: frn@msn.com

May 23, 2001

William Jones
President
Monsanto Corporation
298 West River Road
St. Louis, MO 65898

Dear Mr. Jones:

I am a well-qualified Training & Development Executive with more than 15 years' experience in program design and delivery. My expertise lies in my ability to identify organizational needs and develop training programs responsive to all levels of personnel throughout an organization. Just as significant are my contributions to improved business performance, productivity, quality and profitability.

Highlights of my career include:

- Participated in the start-up of new professional training organization to enhance the business, technical, legal, IS and professional skills of personnel throughout Smith Rand.

- Development and delivery of more than 57,000 student hours of training and incentive programs that generated solid operating and cost contributions for Signal Enterprises.

- Introduction of cross-functional training programs into Clement's manufacturing organization and capture of over $1.1 million in cost savings.

I am a strong business leader and talented instructor with the ability to impact positive change and improvement. My goal is a senior-level training and development management position with a company seeking strong, decisive and dedicated leadership.

I look forward to meeting with you and thank you in advance for your consideration.

Sincerely,

Frances Hackett

Enclosure

STEVEN T. GIBRALTAR
2877 Wood Spirit
Eden, New York 14057
(716) 992-3879

October 4, 2000

John Billings, President
Billings Manufacturing, Inc.
One Dove Plaza
Orland Park, IL 60462

Dear Mr. Billings:

As markets, products and industries become increasingly competitive, companies are faced with unprecedented financial and operating challenges. To achieve and maintain market dominance, there are certain initiatives a firm can undertake to ensure a competitive advantage. One of those initiatives is to build a strong human resource function, putting in place the personnel and corporate culture essential to further growth and profitability.

As a Senior HR Executive, I have met those challenges and been a key contributor to the sustained growth and financial gain of several organizations. Most notably:

- Industrial Metals Corporation. Member of executive team orchestrating the successful turnaround of the corporation with 143% improvement in revenues and profitability.

- Smithfield Bank. Reengineered 2200-employee workforce and delivered a 46% reduction in annual staffing costs.

- P.J. Arnold Company. Captured $300,000+ in annual benefit cost savings.

The scope of my experience spans the entire HR function — recruitment, staffing, benefits, HRIS, employee relations, training and development, succession planning and performance/productivity improvement. I have equally strong experience in purchasing, quality, contracts, government relations and corporate administration. It is the sum of these that has provided me with the qualifications to initiate action and deliver strong results.

Now, at this point in my career, I am seeking a senior-level HR and administrative management position where I can continue to drive forward critical performance improvement, organizational development and change management initiatives. I look forward to speaking with you to pursue opportunities with Billings Manufacturing and appreciate your consideration. Thank you.

Sincerely,

Steven T. Gilbraltar

Enclosure

KEITH ROTHSAY, SPHR
9021 North Haledon
Newark, New Jersey 07508
(201) 474-3601

October 21, 2000

Thomas Malcolm
Horace Industrial
1232 Cedar Street
Memphis, TN 44551

Dear Mr. Malcolm:

Bringing innovative and decisive human resources leadership has been the foundation for my success throughout the past 10+ years. As the Vice President/Director of Human Resources for the $100 million Crystal Metal Services Company, I have pioneered HR, employee relations and labor relations programs that have been the catalyst for tremendous organizational growth and financial gain. Most notably:

- Negotiated over $500,000 in labor cost savings.

- Reengineered core business processes and saved over $1.2 million in workers' compensation, benefit, administration and MIS costs.

- Led a successful workforce reduction initiative with no lawsuits or arbitration.

- Introduced participative management, quality management, leadership training and other performance-driven initiatives.

After a long and successful career with Crystal, the company has undergone a massive reorganization following its recent acquisition. Currently, I am facilitating the workforce reengineering process while continuing to pursue new professional opportunities. My goal is a senior-level HR management position with a high-growth organization and, as such, I would welcome a personal interview to explore such positions with your organization. Thank you.

Sincerely,

Keith Rothsay, SPHR

Enclosure

WILLIAM PETERMAN

567 Ontario Avenue
Dubois, PA 19877
Email: wmpeter@aol.com

Phone: (876) 781-9376
Fax: (876) 781-3726
Voice Mail: (800) 333-3898

March 4, 2001

Dr. Daniel Markman
South Indiana Community College
One Community College Boulevard
Monroe, IN 47362

Dear Dr. Markman:

If you are seeking a candidate with years of experience in Workforce Planning, Development and Leadership, look no further. I'm right in your backyard!

I bring to SICC a unique blend of management qualifications which briefly include:

- Directing workforce planning and management for 700,000 U.S. Army personnel.
- Leading Headquarters-based personnel, training and leadership development programs.
- Designing manpower planning and staffing models for worldwide implementation.
- Authoring, negotiating and administering large-dollar training contracts (including RFP preparation).
- Developing and justifying funding requests from both government and private sectors.
- Managing partner development and multi-organizational linkages/liaison affairs.

In addition, I completed a 9-month consulting contract with SICC during which time I designed and implemented a complete workforce training program for the local Exxon operation. As such, I am somewhat familiar with the College's administrative and outreach operations, and I have worked in cooperation with your personnel. I would be pleased to provide additional information regarding this engagement and the specific individuals at SICC with whom I interfaced.

I would be delighted to have the opportunity for a personal interview and can, of course, be available at your convenience. I thank you in advance for your time and consideration, and look forward to what I anticipate will be the first of many positive communications.

Sincerely,

William Peterman

Enclosure

Information Systems & Technology

KeyWords, Action Verbs & High-Impact Phrases to "Nail" Your Cover Letter:

- New Media, Internet & Online Technologies

- Client/Server & Database Technology

- Telecommunications Technology

- Process Redesign & Automation

- Software Acquisition & Customization

- User Training & Support

- Operating Cost Reductions

- Technology Outsourcing

- Systems Design & New Technology Development

- Information Systems Technology

HENRY WALTERS
3278 Walnut Circle
Revere, Connecticut 16637
(860) 647-3147

December 1, 2000

Joseph Howard, Senior Vice President
Digital Equipment Corporation
1990 Colonial Avenue, Suite 2383
Boston, MA 01748

Dear Mr. Howard:

Developing innovative technology and networking solutions is my expertise. As the Director of Engineering with Maxwell, Duncan, and several technology start-up ventures, I have provided the strategic, technical and operational leadership critical to our market success.

Highlights of my career that may be of particular interest to you include:

* Currently spearheading the development of world class network systems monitoring and management technologies for deployment worldwide.
* Guided Duncan's development of client/server applications for the manufacturing industry in cooperation with major partners (e.g., Honeywell, GE, TI, Allen Bradley, Fisher).
* Created some of the industry's first-ever network performance management, characterization, testing and analysis tools, providing distinct competitive advantages for both internal and external applications.
* Built and led new engineering and R&D organizations through development, staffing, funding and operations.

My greatest strength lies in my ability to evaluate technology requirements, integrating the personnel and resources critical to systems development and operability. Further, I have excellent qualifications in technical marketing, partner relationships and systems/strategic planning.

Currently I am exploring new engineering management opportunities and would welcome an interview at your convenience. I appreciate your time and look forward to speaking with you.

Sincerely,

Henry Walters

Enclosure

BLAKE ISLEY

13906 1st Street
San Francisco, CA 94102

Phone: (415) 477-3255
Email: bisley@indigo.com

March 15, 2001

Matthew Gilliam
Director of Human Resources
Godsey's Telesystems, Inc.
952 Main Street, Suite 122
Menlo Park, CA 97421

Dear Mr. Gilliam:

Technological excellence and success. It lies in one's ability to merge the strategic with the tactical, to understand the needs and expectations of each organization, and to deliver and support the technologies and applications appropriate to each functional organization.

As **Director of Information Systems & Technology / Assistant CIO** for several organizations, I have provided the technological and organizational leadership that has delivered such success. Under my direction:

- Quincy's global IS function has undergone an evolution and is now operating as a worldwide class organization with advanced information, networking and telecommunications operations with 99% systems availability.

- California Association for the Disabled is now one of the most sophisticated in the nationwide organization with exceptional quality ratings, advanced enterprise and networking technologies, and again, a consistent 99% systems availability.

My role in each organization has been to re-create, rebuild and expand IS competencies through both internal development and external acquisition initiatives. The strength of my personal technology skills is excellent. However, more important have been my contributions to the vision, strategy and long-range development of IS organizations that not only capture new technologies but support rapid changes in operations and business demands.

Now, at this point in my career, I am seeking new professional challenges and opportunities, and would welcome a personal interview at your earliest convenience. Thank you.

Sincerely,

Blake Isley

Enclosure

WILLIAM JONES
1250 Scribe Street
Los Angeles, California 94003
Home (310) 928-4850   Office (310) 226-0500

May 31, 2001

Ralph Machianno
President
Netware, Inc.
12000 West Boulevard, Suite 123
Menlo Park, CA 98323

Dear Mr. Machianno:

When I joined Conrad Computer in 1994, I was challenged to re-create and strengthen the internal worldwide computing function for the corporation. Within less than two years, my team and I:

* Improved system availability to 99.5%.
* Built a proactive partnership between application development and operations.
* Transitioned to UNIX architecture.
* Met/exceeded all budget, quality and performance goals.

Previously, during my 7-year career with ART, Inc., I introduced automated MIS operations, brought troubled projects "back on track" and cost-effectively managed a 150-person datacenter operation. Earlier career experience focused on the design, development and delivery of Tandem systems technology.

The combination of my experience in systems operations, applications development, telecommunications and performance management has allowed me to deliver results despite often complex challenges. My technological capabilities are complemented by strong training and leadership skills and a long-standing commitment to productivity and performance improvement.

Although secure in my position with Conrad, I am confidentially exploring new management opportunities where I can continue to lead a top-flight technology organization through change, refinement and improvement. As such, my interest in Netware, Inc. and request for a personal interview. Thank you.

Sincerely,

William Jones

Enclosure

MARY C. CAMPBELL
300 South Windsor Avenue
New Haven, Connecticut 20316
Home (860) 949-8430   Office (860) 565-7316

October 8, 2000

Lyle Berkstein
Apple Computer
1239 Microchip Road
Silicon Valley, CA 98323

Dear Mr. Berkstein:

I am a well-qualified Information Technology Executive successful in identifying organizational needs and leading the development/implementation of emerging technologies to improve productivity, quality and operating performance. Most recently, I have focused my efforts on introducing document imaging technologies as part of First System's corporate-wide vision for developing and managing departmental client/server systems.

The scope of my responsibility has included the entire project management cycle, from initial needs assessment and technology evaluations through vendor selection, internal systems development, pilot testing, quality review, technical and user documentation, and full-scale implementation. Most notable are my strengths in facilitating cooperation among cross-functional project teams to ensure that all projects are delivered on time, within budget and as per specifications.

The strength of my experience (largely acquired through my years in the banking industry) is easily transferrable across industries. My role as IS project manager is not bound by function, but rather by success in responding to the vastly different operating needs of sales, marketing, finance, purchasing, legal, regulatory affairs, administration and other core business units.

Although secure in my current position, I am confidentially exploring new opportunities. My goal is a top-level IS management position where I can continue to provide strong and effective leadership in technology development and solutions engineering.

I look forward to a personal interview and thank you in advance for your consideration.

Sincerely,

Mary C. Campbell

Enclosure

BRENDA WILLIAMSON

235 Costal Highway
Sunset Beach, Florida 33137-5319
(954) 858-4847

March 13, 2001

John R. Smith, President
Intertechnology Manufacturing
1290 Glenview Drive
Chicago, IL 60610

Dear Mr. Smith:

Aware of the fast-track growth of your organization and the advances in technology you have delivered, I am writing to express my interest in senior-level project management opportunities. Highlights of my professional career include:

- 15 years' experience managing design, engineering and project management teams.

- Outstanding technical, engineering, design, analytical and contract administration qualifications.

- Leadership of up to 50-person cross-functional project teams working cooperatively to achieve common goals and performance objectives.

- Consistent success in delivering projects on time and within budget (many ahead of schedule and well below forecasted costs).

- Negotiation of large-dollar, multi-year design, engineering and service contracts that have strengthened market position and accelerated revenue growth.

The core of my experience is in the utility, construction and food processing industries, each with unique technological, engineering and project management requirements. My goal is to remain within one of these industries where I believe my experience and competencies are of most value.

I would welcome the opportunity to speak with you regarding your current management requirements and appreciate both your time and consideration of my qualifications. Thank you.

Sincerely,

Brenda Williamson

Enclosure

RENE BOLLERSON
rene.bollerson@inmind.com

12 McCarthney Boulevard
Woodbridge, GA 44487

Home: 727.873.2222
Office: 727.653.1000

December 17, 2000

Randi Smith, VP – IT & Systems
Osgood Systems, Inc.
2345 Main Run Trolley Road
Peakland, PA 19876

Dear Ms. Smith :

I am writing to express my interest in senior-level IT management positions and have enclosed my resume for your review. As you will note, I am currently employed as a Vice President of Technology with Alpha Omega. My career with the organization has been notable, advancing from early project management positions through a series of increasingly responsible management assignments to my current position orchestrating Alpha Omega's Y2K program worldwide.

The value I bring to your organization is straightforward:

- Over 15 years' experience directing sophisticated, multi-million dollar technology design, development and engineering projects (ranging from software development to global private networks to secure data communications systems).

- Equally strong general management and leadership experience including direct P&L responsibility.

- Outstanding performance in coordinating technology teams operating at sites worldwide, creating common goals, objectives and standards for performance.

- Personally negotiated with major clients worldwide to present technology solutions and Alpha Omega's competencies, accounting for more than $35 million in new revenues and add-on sales.

- Track record of outstanding "CIO-type" experience managing total projects valued in excess of $2 billion over the past 15 years. Fully accountable for technology strategies, design, engineering, implementation, testing, quality, performance and reliability.

After a long and successful career with Alpha Omega, I have decided to pursue senior management opportunities elsewhere. I am interested in a position offering significant accountability and decision making responsibility with full general management, operating, technical and P&L responsibility for an organization.

In anticipation that you may be interested in a candidate with my qualifications, I have enclosed my resume for your review. Thank you for your time and consideration. I look forward to speaking with you.

Sincerely,

Rene Bollerson

Enclosure

Henry H. Hollingsworth

9789 N. Beach Road #202   (727) 808-6767
Naples Island, FL 35654   hhh3rd@msn.com

August 4, 2000

Larry Lensmith, VP – Technology
Tech Systems, Inc.
45 Maple Road
Mapleton, IA 55637

Dear Mr. Lensmith:

I am a Microsoft Certified Systems Engineer (MCSE) with over 15 years' experience in Information Systems & Technology. My expertise spans two entirely different functions within the IT arena:

- *Systems Operations*. For 12 years, I managed all IT operations for the Emergency Medical Services Division of Lewis County in Southern Florida. During this time, I directed several major hardware and software upgrades to transition into a state-of-the-art Windows environment.

- *Systems Design & Installation*. For the past four years, I have managed an entrepreneurial venture with sole responsibility for the sale of technology consulting services and the design/delivery of customized technologies. Most significantly, I facilitated over 1000 system and device upgrades, built and installed NT systems and networks, and supported over 250 customers.

Additional information that may be of interest to you includes:

- *Outstanding customer relations skills*. I am able to quickly build and maintain positive working relationships with my customers, responding quickly to their technology support needs, and providing them with the technical expertise to independently manage their work functions.

- *Entrepreneurial spirit and drive*. I thrive in challenging and fast-paced environments, relying on myself to make decisions, solve problems and move projects forward. I am an independent thinker, constantly ready to accept new challenges and new opportunities.

- *Staff training and leadership*. As a paramedic, I was responsible for a group of 30, coordinating their schedules, providing training and supervision, and facilitating cooperative team efforts.

I would welcome the opportunity for a personal interview and thank you in advance for your consideration. I guarantee you'll be impressed with the quality and depth of my technical expertise.

Sincerely,

Henry H. Hollingsworth

Enclosure

Insurance

KeyWords, Action Verbs & High-Impact Phrases to "Nail" Your Cover Letter:

- Agency Operations

- Risk Management

- Asset Management & Loss Control

- Business Reorganization & Operations Improvement

- Regulatory Reporting & Compliance

- Premium Processing & Billing Operations

- Key Account Wins & Revenue Performance

- Home Office Operations

- Policy & Claims Administration

- Regional & National Sales Management

MICHAEL SEGAL
5901 Flower Meadows
Chevy Chase, Maryland 22093

Phone (301) 821-7510   Office (301) 583-7092
michael.lane.segal@trip.net

June 12, 2001

David Williams
Chairman & CEO
State Farm Insurance
935 North Michigan Avenue
Chicago, IL 60611

Dear Mr. Williams:

Designing creative insurance coverages and risk management programs for construction wrap-ups, celebrity tours, motion picture productions and other high-profile projects is my expertise.

Working worldwide (emphasis in the U.S., Asia, Australia and Middle East), I have guided presidents, CEOs and other top-flight executives through the complex insurance cycle to ensure that their assets are protected, their exposures limited and their liabilities greatly diminished. It is just this expertise I bring to State Farm.

Complementing my consummate knowledge of the insurance industry and unique insurance coverages, I also bring a unprecedented record of achievement in structuring and negotiating sensitive contractual agreements — for insurance, mergers, acquisitions, joint ventures and other cooperative alliances. Whether working as a CEO, Chairman, Vice President or COO, I have provided the strategic and tactical leadership critical to building agency volumes worldwide.

Now, at this juncture in my career, I am seeking new senior-level management opportunities with an insurance brokerage that prides itself on the quality, strength and performance of its products and services. With more than 20 years of industry experience, I have come to know the major players worldwide. Repeatedly, State Farm has been brought to my attention — recognized for not only the quality of its insurance programs, but the strength and determination of your leadership.

I now look to you for new career opportunities where I can continue to provide decisive leadership under your direction, and look forward to what I anticipate will be the first of many positive communications. Thank you.

Sincerely,

Michael Segal

Enclosure

RAYMOND MARTENSON

222 Racine Drive
Lynchburg, VA 24503

Home: 804-384-8765
Email: raymart@cs.com

November 14, 2000

Bert Myers
Director
AAA Insurance Agents, Inc.
4567 Markland Place
Toledo, OH 44478

Dear Mr. Myers:

Throughout my 18-year career in the sale/marketing of insurance products, programs and coverages, I have clearly demonstrated my ability to:

- Drive premium growth within intensely competitive markets.
- Build, nurture and retain critical customer relationships.
- Outpace and outperform the competition.
- Develop and launch new products.
- Build profitable new markets.
- Recruit, train, develop and lead teams of top producers.

My success rests largely upon my ability to build customer relationships, working one-on-one to identify customer needs, develop appropriate product offerings, and negotiate/close complex transactions. I offer excellent presentation skills, am a confident public speaker and an extremely skilled sales trainer. Further and most significant, I have consistently exceeded premium and volume goals, closed each of the past few years with loss ratios well below industry averages, and continued to deliver strong profit performance.

Please also note that I have several industry credentials and certifications including the CPCU, CPIA, CIC, AAI and ARM. In addition to my sales and marketing qualifications, I also have an extensive background in insurance underwriting and policy rating.

Due to circumstances beyond my control, I have recently left National Grange Mutual (April 1999) and am now exploring new sales and marketing management opportunities within the insurance industry. As such, I would welcome a personal interview to discuss your need for sales and marketing leadership and my potential contributions.

I appreciate your time in reviewing my qualifications and will follow up next week.

Sincerely,

Ray Martenson

Enclosure

ALLEN KINGFISHER
kingfisher@voyager.net
2022 Hilltop Way
Arnold, New York 09837
Home (927) 230-3765   Office (927) 811-9800

June 6, 2001

Barbara Howell
Insurance Recruiters of America, Inc.
2 Mason Way
Kansas City, MO 46763

Dear Ms. Howell:

I am currently the General Auditor for The Premium Insurance Company. After eight years with the organization, I have decided to confidentially explore new opportunities and am contacting a select group of executive recruiters specializing in Corporate Audit and Finance. My resume is enclosed for your review. Highlights of my career include:

- Progressive management career as the Senior Audit Executive for three Fortune 500 corporations, each in vastly differing industries and customer markets.

- Consistent record of achievement in improving bottom line financial results by introducing improved audit strategies, processes, controls and technologies. Key contributor to several successful start-up ventures and large-scale corporate turnarounds.

- Success in positioning Audit as a business partner, not an adversary, with both internal and external audiences. These efforts have been vital to restoring corporate credibility.

- Strong general management qualifications in strategic planning, finance, budgeting, professional staffing, organizational development, quality and performance improvement.

My leadership style is direct and decisive, yet flexible in responding to constantly changing demands. I work well in high-pressure and demanding positions with my objective always focused on creating synergy and consensus to achieve common goals. My background also includes extensive training experience and active leadership in several professional organizations

If you are working with a client corporation seeking a candidate with my qualifications, I would welcome the opportunity to speak with you. Be advised that I am open to relocation and that my current compensation exceeds $400,000 annually. Thank you.

Sincerely,

Allen Kingfisher

Enclosure

THOMAS KEELER
349 Indian Trail Road
Cincinnati, Ohio 45632
(845) 533-6532

November 21, 2000

James Williams
President & CEO
Brennan Insurance, Inc.
9348 River Valley Road
Indianapolis, IN 43562

Dear Mr. Williams:

With 20 years' experience in the Insurance Industry, I bring to your organization a wealth of qualifications in the strategic planning, development and profitable leadership of both agency and Home Office operations. My expertise lies in my ability to identify and capitalize upon market opportunities to increase premium growth, accelerate commission income and outperform competition. Most notably, I:

* Delivered a 32% increase in P&C production for Farm Bureau.

* Led the successful reorganization of Allied's Midwestern Region, driving an 84.% increase in annual premium volume.

* Built Home Life Insurance from start-up to $700,000 in first year revenues.

These achievements are indicative of the quality and caliber of my entire professional career. Whether challenged to launch a new venture, accelerate growth within existing agency operations or lead the successful turnaround of a dormant organization, I have consistently delivered results.

Not only have my numbers been strong, I have repeatedly demonstrated strong management and leadership qualifications and developed other industry professionals now recognized as top producers and managers in their own right. My resume details some of my most significant commendations.

Now, at this point in my career, I am seeking new professional challenges and opportunities where I can continue to provide strong, decisive and market-driven leadership. Thus my interest in your organization and request for a personal interview.

Sincerely,

Thomas Keeler

Enclosure

TROY A. BATESON
67 Mermaid Lane
Long Beach, CA 98763
(321) 967-3654

August 14, 2000

David Viens
President
Action Insurance Agency, Inc.
9800 Roseland Boulevard
Rossiter, CO 89376

Dear Mr. Viens:

Building top-performing commercial insurance organizations is my expertise. Starting with virtually nothing in 1984, I built an agency that grew to over $100 million in annual premium value with outstanding profit results. Now, however, I am in the process of relocating to New York and will be selling my agency. As such, my interest in exploring management opportunities with your organization.

Highlights of my professional career that may be of particular interest to you include the following:

- Expertise across more than 15 insurance products from P&C and D&O to Aircraft Liability and Corporate Surety. The enclosed resume details them all.

- Outstanding sales performance, winning highly competitive, multi-million dollar contracts against major insurance industry players.

- Specialization in risk management and liability analysis to reduce loss exposures.

- Recognized leader in the delivery of insurance advisory and corporate consulting services.

I am currently traveling back and forth between California and Colorado, and would like to meet with you on my next trip down. I'm encouraged by the response that I've already received from your local CA office and would be delighted to have a chance to speak with you.

Thank you for your time and consideration. If I don't hear from you within two weeks, I'll call to follow up and schedule a convenient time.

Sincerely,

Troy A. Bateson

Enclosure

International Marketing & Development

KeyWords, Action Verbs & High-Impact Phrases to "Nail" Your Cover Letter:

- Global Marketing & Business Development

- Sales & Profit Growth

- Market Share Improvements

- Public & Private Partnerships

- Mergers & Acquisitions

- Joint Ventures

- New Market Development & Optimization

- Cross-Cultural Communications & Management

- Multilingual Negotiations

- International Account Relationship Management

CHRIS CHRITTON
892 Washington Avenue
Somersville, Oregon 90938
Phone (809) 333-9960   Fax (809) 333-9870

January 1, 2001

Martin Belgium, Director
Ventures International, LLC
22 Montana Boulevard
Phoenix, AZ 89830

Dear Mr. Belgium:

Born and educated in Australia, I have lived and/or worked around the globe – from Asia to Latin America, from the US to the Philippines. The strength of my cross-cultural experience, combined with my 15+ years of senior management experience, places me in a uniquely qualified position to build and direct profitable international operations.

Highlights of my career that may be of particular interest to you include the following:

- Outstanding record of performance in marketing, sales, new business development and new venture leadership.
- Over 10 years of direct P&L experience for multicultural manufacturing, marketing and business operations.
- Appointment to several US and foreign boards of directors and executive committees.
- Excellent track record in structuring, negotiating and managing multi-country joint ventures, strategic alliances and marketing partnerships.
- Strong financial, analytical, negotiation and project management skills.

My goal is an executive-level position in General Management, Marketing, Global Sales and/or New Business Development where I can continue to drive revenue and profit growth throughout both mature and emerging international markets. Aware of your focus on international expansion, I would be delighted to meet with you to explore your current plans and my potential contributions.

I thank you for your time in reviewing my qualifications and look forward to meeting with you.

Sincerely,

Chris Chritton

Enclosure

IGOR SCHWARTZ
390 Springflower Circle
Alpharetta, Georgia 39089
ivanschw@mindspring.com

Phone: (770) 492-0387

Fax: (770) 492-0898

March 14, 2001

Vladmir Scholwenski
Global Enterprises, Inc.
22 Valencia Avenue
Long Beach, CA 98029

Dear Mr. Scholwenski:

For more than 10 years, I have watched as the former Soviet Union and the entire Eastern European region have struggled to transition to a free market economy, principally in Russia and Ukraine. Unfortunately, what I've witnessed is:

- Eastern European political bureacracies and business environments that have been ineffective in responding to these extraordinary changes.
- Russian and Ukrainian businesses that are burdened with tax regulations, permit regulations and other government-imposed obstacles to their performance and productivity.
- The entire world's inability to productively and profitability enter these markets, principally due to their lack of understanding of the intricacies of doing business within these difficult markets.

Through my efforts, I've acquired substantial expertise working with countries in the midst of transistioning to free markets, and understand the unique challenges they are facing. Further, being of Russian heritage, I can appreciate the tremendous obstacles facing this nation and others, merging my background with my 20+ years of life in the US in a free democracy.

Please also note that I have an extensive network of contacts with honest, credible and progressive leaders in the academic, scientific, educational, military, government, political, business, cultural and civic communities, particularly in Russia and the Ukraine. These individuals have been instrumental in supporting my commercial business efforts throughout the region.

To have the opportunity to participate in establishing policies and programs involving the restructuring of the Eastern European markets would be the most rewarding path for my own professional career. As such, I would welcome a chance to speak with you about opportunities where I could provide cultural, economic and business value.

Sincerely,

Igor Schwartz

Enclosure

IVAN VAN DYKE
#1543 Provincial Villa
35 Dongyong Ku Street
100027 Beijing, PRC
Phone/FAX 86-10-6833227

June 1, 2001

Frank Carson
Executive Vice President - Asia
Merrill Lynch Investments Worldwide
1900 Carlyle Avenue, Suite 259
Los Angeles, CA 98633

Dear Mr. Carson:

I am currently the General Sales & Business Manager for Crosby's operation in Beijing. Within less than two years, we have increased billings by 150%+ and built a strong and high-profile reputation. Further, we have strengthened the market positioning of each of our clients — Bausch & Lomb, Coca-Cola, Wools of New Zealand and numerous others.

Living and working in the Far East for the past five years, I have developed an extensive network of contacts with government, corporate and industrial business leaders throughout the region. This is the value I bring to Merrill Lynch. I know the people, the culture, the economy and the market. Only when you have lived in the region for a period of time can you begin to become part of that culture and a respected business professional within the local marketplace.

My goal is a senior-level management position where I can direct sales, marketing, operations, customer service, administration, human resources and finance of an organization within the Far East — quite similar to the responsibilities I manage today. However, my goal is to affiliate with an organization offering opportunities for professional growth, management and leadership.

Please note that I am conversational in five different languages and have tremendous cross-cultural business experience.

I look forward to speaking with you to pursue opportunities with Merrill Lynch.

Sincerely,

Ivan Van Dyke

Enclosure

ALFAN SWITZER
Elderlinstrasse 427
62980 Munich, Germany

Phone: 06189-873-237   Email: alfan@germany.ce   Fax: 06189-336-92

October 20, 2000

Lance Martin
President & CEO
Horizons Global Partners, Inc.
999 Arnold Way
Amherst, MA 09372

Dear Mr. Martin:

Building organizational value is my expertise – value that is measured in increasing earnings, improved operating and organizational inefficiencies, reduced operating costs and sustained competitive performance. And, I have done this in two distinct settings:

1. As a European Partner & Consultant in a prestigious management consulting firm. In my "management" role, I was credited for leading the successful and profitable start-up of new practice groups, retaining key clients, and managing numerous consulting engagements across a broad range of industries and functional disciplines worldwide.

2. As a Consultant in several consultancies in the US, Europe and South Africa. I have succeeded with multi-million dollar earnings, double-digit cost reductions, and countless operational/organizational improvements to enhance client performance. Further, I have provided strategic and financial leadership for numerous mergers and acquisitions, and their subsequent integration process.

The range of my competencies is broad with particular emphasis in strategic change and growth, new market/new business development, competitive analysis, efficiency improvement, process redesign, management and staffing issues, technology issues and much more. My leadership style is direct and decisive, yet I am flexible in responding to the challenges of working in a multinational organization.

My goal is a top-level management consulting partnership with a well-established firm seeking to expand and/or strengthen its practice throughout the European continent. I assure you that my network of contacts and facility in managing across borders will be of significant value to you. I look forward to pursuing a discussion and thank you in advance for your consideration.

Sincerely,

Alfan Switzer

Enclosure

WILLIAM FREEMAN

282 Cherry Tree Court
Overland Park, Kansas 65323
(602) 547-8954

___

March 7, 2001

Brian Masterson
Managing Partner
Masterson Global Ventures, Inc.
2349 Cross Country Trail
Denver, CO 58763

Dear Mr. Masterson:

I am a well-qualified International Business Development, Sales & Marketing Executive with 19 years' experience in the Advanced Technology Industry. Currently I am exploring new professional opportunities with a company seeking strong and decisive international leadership.

My qualifications include:

- Excellent cross-cultural communications and business development skills.
- Management responsibility for both direct and dealer/distributor sales networks.
- Personal selling and management responsibility for key multinational accounts.
- Success in both high-growth and "restart" international markets.
- Strong technical product knowledge.
- Excellent training and leadership skills.

If you are working with a client company seeking a candidate with my qualifications, I would welcome the opportunity to speak with you. Be advised that I am open to relocation worldwide and that my salary requirements are $150,000+. Thank you.

Sincerely,

William Freeman

Enclosure

BENJAMIN J. ROSS
298 Piney Forest
Summerville, South Carolina 75332
Phone: (802) 339-3980   Fax: (802) 339-4276
Email: benjamin.ross@alltel.net

August 23, 2000

James Van Atta
President
Birch Machinery Company
1200 Executive Suites, Room 123
Detroit, MI 43565

Dear Mr. Van Atta:

When I joined Baxter Industries in 1992, I launched the start-up of their first-ever Mexican operations. Over the next three years, I spearheaded an aggressive market research initiative, authored business and marketing plans, recruited local sales and service talent, established distribution channels, and firmly positioned the corporation for long-term market growth.

Previously in my career, I consulted with several U.S. corporations seeking to enter not only the Latin American markets, but also the U.S. and Asia. To each company, I provided strong support in business development, marketing, cross-cultural communications and project management.

With an MBA (emphasis in International Business) and several years of strong international management experience, I bring to Birch Machinery Company the ability to build opportunity and capture new revenues. My goal is to secure a position where I can utilize the strength of my international exposure while continuing to develop my general management and sales/marketing management qualifications.

I would welcome the opportunity to explore positions with your organization and appreciate your time in reviewing my qualifications. Please note that in addition to the above-referenced experience, I also have strong skills in engineering and technology.

Sincerely,

Benjamin J. Ross

Enclosure

HENRY AARONSON
9384 Blue Jay Way
Portland, Maine 75233
Home (207) 829-9639   Office (207) 594-1700

May 2, 2001

Colin Byrd
Hatha International
1200 Bakersfield Avenue
Des Moines, IA 51531

Dear Mr. Byrd:

Employed with R.T.C.C., Inc. for the past nine years, I have been instrumental in the development, global market expansion and profitability of this international trade and import/export corporation (operations in Israel, The Netherlands, Russia and the U.S.). My role has been to identify and develop international trade opportunities to introduce new products into emerging markets and build new revenue streams. As you review my resume you will note that the value I have brought to the organization can be measured by significant gains in revenue, volume and market presence.

Inherent in my responsibilities has been the negotiation of complex strategic alliances between multinational business partners. My strengths in building profitable ventures and facilitating cooperation among diverse business cultures have been the foundation for the company's success and continued expansion.

Most notable have been my innovative efforts in barter trade management, bringing together vastly different business partners and facilitating transactions to transfer products between cultures, countries and continents. My success in developing and negotiating these partnerships is notable.

In addition to my international trade responsibilities, I have also developed and profitably managed joint venture manufacturing and production operations worldwide to supplement our trade programs and expand our product portfolio. Further, I have built distribution networks to accelerate global market expansion.

Now, at this point in my career, I am seeking new professional challenges and opportunities in international trade and import/export. Thus my interest in Hatha International and request for a personal interview. Thank you.

Sincerely,

Henry Aaronson

Enclosure

Law

KeyWords, Action Verbs & High-Impact Phrases to "Nail" Your Cover Letter:

- Corporate Legal Affairs & Policy

- Litigation & Trial Wins

- Regulatory Compliance

- Legislative Advocacy & Lobbying

- Intellectual Property

- Financial & Contract Transactions

- Budgeting & Cost Reduction

- Joint Ventures, Alliances & Partnerships

- IPOs & Secondary Offerings

- New Venture Formation

SARISTA OSAKA, J.D.
1200 Peachtree Drive, Apt. 724
Atlanta, Georgia 30330
(H) 770.983.2372   (O) 770.232-1000

November 20, 2000

John Barkley, J.D.
Miller Dorman & Associates
22 Sasissa Circle
Tokyo 1873 Japan

Dear Mr. Barkley:

I am a well-qualified Japanese-American Attorney with a specialization in International Corporate Law. Practicing since 1982, I have a wealth of experience in international business transactions, international litigation, joint ventures, mergers and acquisitions, international financing, international taxation, software licensing, real estate, U.S. customs and trade law, and employment and labor law.

Highlights of my career that may be of particular interest to you include:

Japanese Business Culture & Professional Contacts
- A native of Japan, I have an intimate knowledge of the culture, customs, business practices, negotiation strategies and decision-making processes of the Japanese people. This has been vital as I have continued to be an active member of the Japanese community while living in the US for the past 10 years. My network of professional contacts includes executives of major Japanese corporations and the Japanese Chamber of Commerce in Atlanta.

Corporate Client Relationships
- I have been extremely successful in acquiring new clients, particularly Japanese companies doing business in the US. In fact, over the past few years, I have brought several new clients, generating over $200,000 per year in legal fees to my current firm. It is anticipated that each of these clients (including the Consulate General of Japan in Atlanta) will continue to work with me.

Education Credentials
- Earned LL.B. and LL.M. from the prestigious Waseda University Graduate School of Law in Tokyo.

I would welcome the chance to speak with you and thank you in advance for consideration.

Sincerely,

Sarista Osaka

Enclosure

153

JENNIFER YEARWOOD, ESQ.
Yearwood@attorney.net

8751 Ravine Road
Fayetteville, North Carolina 27066
(919) 637-0815

March 11, 2001

George Lutz
President
Prudential Healthcare
1908 Woodland Avenue
Salem, MA 04453

Dear Mr. Lutz:

As Corporate Counsel / General Counsel for several start-up and high-growth corporations, I have provided critical legal, technical, financial, "deal making" and operating expertise. Currently, as Counsel for an emerging HMO in North Carolina, my challenges have included:

* Development of improved contract strategies and negotiating positions.
* Management of complex due diligence reviews for proposed joint ventures and mergers.
* Implementation of PC technology to automate legal affairs and documentation.
* Review/analysis of complex legislative initiatives impacting the HMO's operations.

Prior to joining the HMO, I progressed rapidly through my earlier corporate counsel positions, working in cooperation with senior operating management of several prestigious corporations. Achievements were notable and included:

* Delivering a 40% reduction in overhead costs through internal reengineering and process improvement.
* Directing legal formation and operations start-up of new technology venture.
* Revitalizing one organization's marketing programs and negotiated/closed $50+ million in leasing transactions.
* Spearheading start-up of new corporation and negotiated $20+ million in equity sales.

My role as Corporate Counsel has transcended all core business functions within each organization. In addition to managing planning, corporate development, transactions and litigation, I have functioned as a participating partner in the operations, marketing and financial success of each organization.

My goal is an in-house Corporate Counsel position with an emerging health care provider organization in need of strong, decisive and proactive leadership. As such, my interest is in meeting with you to explore such opportunities with Prudential Healthcare. I appreciate your consideration and look forward to speaking with you. Thank you.

Sincerely,

Jennifer Yearwood, Esq.

Enclosure

ANDREW P. DONNELLY
2063 Leesville Drive
Fairfield, Illinois 60252
(708) 657-7640

June 10, 2001

Calvin Powell
President
Tambasco, Inc.
200 Glenview Avenue
St. Paul, MN 55784

Dear Mr. Powell:

With more than 15 years' experience in Corporate Law, I bring to your organization extensive qualifications in:

- International Law — spanning 131 countries worldwide and involving virtually every type of legal transaction.

- Financial Transactions — structuring, negotiating and administering sophisticated, cross-border financial transactions involving multiple parties and millions of dollars in funds.

- Commercial Transactions — negotiating complex business transactions, contracts, licensee and distributor agreements, mergers, acquisitions and divestitures.

Through strong leadership of worldwide legal affairs, I have been instrumental in the tremendous growth and worldwide diversification of Wallace International, spearheading international growth, structuring "first-ever" legal transactions, and providing the foundation for both strong revenue growth and operating cost reductions.

Now, at this juncture in my career, I am seeking new professional opportunities where I can continue to lead a corporate legal function and guide a top-flight executive management team. If you are seeking a candidate with such qualifications, I would welcome a personal interview and thank you in advance for your time and consideration.

Sincerely,

Andrew P. Donnelly

Enclosure

WALTER J. CALDWELL
5 West Princeton Circle
Staten Island, New York 14203
(718) 473-8840

February 3, 2001

Addison Ratcliff
Managing Partner
Brixton, Maddox & Ratcliff
1010 Madison Avenue, Suite 103
New York, NY 11001

Dear Mr. Ratcliff:

I am currently employed as a Senior Associate Attorney in the Real Estate Practice of Frank & Lester. With the firm for the past seven years, I have been built a successful and profitable practice area, based largely upon my strength and expertise in real estate law.

As you review my qualifications, you will note that I have successfully combined the legal functions of the practice with the equally critical responsibilities of client management and representation. My position is highly visible, requiring constant interaction not only with my clients, but with their business partners, financial advisors, investors and tenants.

Throughout my career, I have managed virtually all "routine" real estate functions in combination with a number of sophisticated and contractually-complex transactions. These projects have required innovation in deal structuring and negotiation, and often necessitated exhaustive legal reviews and documentation.

My goal is to continue to practice real estate law. However, I am confidentially exploring opportunities with other firms and would welcome an interview at your convenience. Thank you.

Sincerely,

Walter J. Caldwell

Enclosure

Logistics

KeyWords, Action Verbs & High-Impact Phrases
to "Nail" Your Cover Letter:

- Distribution & Warehousing Operations

- Integrated Logistics Management

- Productivity & Quality Improvements

- Cost Reduction & Avoidance

- Distribution Channel Development

- Transportation & Fleet Management

- Materials & Resource Management

- Team Building & Leadership

- Process Redesign & Automation

- Order Entry & Fulfillment

ALLEN C. BURNS
104 Oakdale Court
Springfield, Massachusetts 17901
Office (413) 490-1993 • Home (413) 598-9866 • Fax (413) 598-9867

September 6, 2000

Paul Garber
President
Ryder International
2349 Bonneville Industrial Park, Suite 129
Santa Rosa, CA 98774

Dear Mr. Garber:

Success. I believe it lies in one's ability to merge the strategic with the tactical, to understand the market, to control the finances, and to build a strong management team. No one function is accountable for performance. It is the interrelationship of all core operations and the vision of the leadership team.

Success and improved corporate value are what I delivered to each of my employers. Through my expertise in operations and logistics management, I have delivered strong results:

- Revitalized and rebuilt Epic World's operations, transitioning the organization from a small independent company into a $70+ million corporation with worldwide market penetration. To support our huge growth and expansion, I led over $1 million in technology installations to automate and integrate all core operating, logistics, distribution, transportation and support functions.

- Captured a total of more than $7.5 million in operating cost reductions for Odyssey Distribution, negotiated a multi-million dollar outsourcing contract and personally spearheaded an internal technology "revolution."

These achievements reflect the quality and caliber of my professional career. What they do not reflect, however, are the strength of my leadership style, my ability to build consensus across operating units, and my contributions to improved revenues, service and profitability.

Now, at this point in my career, I am seeking new professional challenges and opportunities where I can lead the revitalization and expansion of large-scale logistics, transportation, warehousing and distribution operations. If your goal is improved performance, efficiency and cost savings, we should talk.

Sincerely,

Allen C. Burns

Enclosure

JAMES R. ELLIOTT
8-49, Kamsaki 2-987
Shinagawa-ku, Tokyo 141-986, Japan

Phone/Fax: 92-5-3767-0909   Email: jrelli@hotmail.com

December 10, 2000

Tim Johnson
Vice President of Operations
Ellendorf Manufacturing & Logistics, Inc.
800 Mellen Drive
Pittsburgh, PA 19837

Dear Mr. Johnson:

Building top-performing logistics, supply chain management and customer service/customer care organizations is my expertise. Whether challenged to launch the start-up of a new venture, orchestrate an aggressive turnaround, or lead an organization through accelerated growth, I have consistently delivered strong financial results:

- Reduced $50 million from bottom-line operating costs for operations in Japan.
- Restored profitability with $40 million revenue growth for Indonesian operations.
- Built new European operation from concept to $4+ million in annual revenues.
- Delivered double digit revenue growth in several key US markets.

My operating results are equally solid:

- Created innovative logistics and supply chain management programs to meet diverse operating requirements of major US and international corporations (e.g., Mattel, Procter & Gamble, LA Gear, Nissan, Siemens).
- Developed external outsourcing and partnership opportunities to optimize resources, expedite logistics and enhance quality of service.
- Reconfigured existing operations to optimize internal competencies, lower costs and retain competitive market lead.

As you'll note, my career with Maersk has been solid. Beginning in an entry-level sales capacity, I earned eight promotions to my current international management position. It has been rewarding and a great experience. However, I am now looking to return to the US and am interested in a senior-level operating, logistics and/or supply chain management position. As such, my interest in meeting with you to discuss such opportunities with Ellendorf.

Sincerely,

James R. Elliott

Enclosure

CHARLES T. MONROE, JR.

104 Maple Drive
Baltimore, Maryland 22412
(410) 949-0987
ctmjr@columbia.net

November 4, 2000

Claude R. Johnson
Vice President - Operations
Millview, Inc.
1644 Edmonds Street
Minneapolis, MN 55347

Dear Mr. Johnson:

For the past nine years, I have planned, staffed and directed large-scale, fully-integrated logistics, warehousing, distribution and transportation operations for Ryder Dedicated Logistics throughout North America. The focus of my career has been divided between start-up operations and the aggressive turnaround/repositioning of existing operations. To each, I have delivered strong and sustainable financial results:

*   Built three independent logistics operations for one major customer, from start-up to over $5.5 million in annual revenues to Ryder.

*   Led the successful and profitable turnaround of the Challenge Systems logistics operations, implemented training and productivity improvement programs, restored customer credibility and improved financial performance.

Currently, I am orchestrating a complete revitalization of Ryder's operations in Baltimore, an organization fraught with customer dissatisfaction and poor financial performance. In less than nine months, my team and I have re-captured key accounts, improved revenues and reduced operating costs. The organization is now positioned for strong growth and expansion.

Although my years with Ryder have been a wonderful experience, I am now ready to pursue new professional challenges. Thus my interest in interviewing as Millview's Director of Logistics. As requested, my salary has averaged $95,000 to $125,000 over the past five years.

Sincerely,

Charles T. Monroe, Jr.

Enclosure

Manufacturing

KeyWords, Action Verbs & High-Impact Phrases to "Nail" Your Cover Letter:

- Productivity & Efficiency Improvements

- Cost Savings & Long-Term Avoidance

- Cross-Functional Team Building & Leadership

- Materials Management & MRP Systems

- TQM, Quality Assurance & ISO 9000

- Technology & Manufacturing Automation

- Process Redesign & Workflow Simplification

- New Plant Start-Up

- Capital & Facilities Improvement

- Product Development & Manufacturability

PAMELA CARTER

125 Lester Boulevard
Pine Tree, ME 02763

Phone: 311.382.2288
carter@bellatlantic.net

January 4, 2001

John Terry
Senior Vice President
SCI Manufacturing, Inc.
22 Treetop Avenue
Boston, MA 09372

Dear Mr. Terry:

Building top-performing and profitable manufacturing operations is what I do best. With a focused commitment to process improvement, quality improvement, efficiency and product optimization, I have successfully launched new ventures, revitalized non-performing operations and facilitated growth worldwide. Highlights of my career that may be of particular interest to you include:

- As **Managing Director** with full P&L responsibility for Pyrex Systems (division of Western Technologies, a $200 million steel fabricator), I returned the operation to profitability after four years of losses through an aggressive program of cost reduction and process improvement.

- During my tenure as **Managing Director**, I captured cost savings of $2+ million by redesigning every core business process that touched production – from vendor contracts and product design/engineering to product fulfillment and product serviceability.

- As **Director of Quality Management** for The Terryman Corporation, I led the development of a company-wide quality organization, introduced leading-edge SPC and CCM technologies, and reduced customer problems by 80% within six months.

- Promoted to **Vice President of Production**, I managed an organization with 100+ employees, 3 locations, 800+ product lines and a $40 million operating budget. Results included a $7 million cost savings and 27-day reduction in order fulfillment time.

Please also note that I have substantial experience in new product design/engineering, supply chain management, environmental affairs, union/management negotiations and the entire scope of HR functions. In addition, I currently work with state-of-the-art online and e-commerce technologies

Although secure in my current position, I am exploring new executive management opportunities and would welcome an interview at your convenience. I guarantee that the strength of my experience, track record of performance and high-energy leadership style will add measurable value to your operations.

Sincerely,

Pamela Carter

Enclosure

162

SHIRLEY B. LAWHORN

410 Sandusky Lane
Knoxville, Tennessee 72205

Home: (615) 536-5408   Email: SBL@AOL.COM   Office: (615) 998-0770

May 30, 2001

Kenneth J. Taylor
President & CEO
Stratton Industrial Products, Inc.
908 Baltimore Avenue
Arlington, TX 45332

Dear Mr. Taylor:

Managing large-scale manufacturing operations requires a unique blend of expertise in planning, budgeting, costing, production management, training and staff leadership. It is this core set of competencies I bring to Stratton Industrial Products.

Over the past three years, I have spearheaded an aggressive reorganization and competitive improvement in a unique manufacturing organization operating 118 locations nationwide and employing over 5500 people. My contributions include:

- Significant reduction in operating costs and capital expenditures.

- 40% growth over three years.

- Introduction of TQM, productivity management, materials management, safety and other programs that increased output, quality and customer satisfaction.

- Development of innovative manufacturing and distribution partnerships with major industry players (e.g., 3M, SC Johnson, Staples).

- Negotiation of more than $350 million in government contracts.

I am confidentially exploring new professional challenges and would welcome the opportunity to interview for the position of Vice President of Manufacturing. My salary requirements can be discussed at the time of our interview. Thank you.

Sincerely,

Shirley B. Lawhorn

Enclosure

163

JAMES R. GREGORY
89 Clovis Way Hill
Lumberville, Cleethorpes
N.E. Lincs DN47 OSR, United Kingdom
Home: 011-44-8976-938273   Office: 011-44-8977-237362

June 5, 2001

Bill Baker
International Recruiters Network
11 Michigan Avenue #1200
Chicago, IL 60067

Dear Mr. Baker:

I am currently employed as Director of Production Operations for a large chemical manufacturing facility in the United Kingdom. I progressed rapidly with the organization, from my early engineering career through several increasingly responsible management positions in the US to my current position. In fact, I am currently slated to return to the US this spring for assignment as Production Director in the company's domestic operations.

Prior to accepting the transfer, I have decided to confidentially explore new executive management opportunities. As such, I am contacting a select group of executive recruiters who may be working with companies seeking an individual with my qualifications. Briefly summarized, they include:

- Current leadership of a GMP production organization manufacturing products generating over $500 million in annual revenue – an organization we have transformed into a model for best-in-class multinational operations.

- Innovation in production processes, staffing, quality, productivity and cost management.

- Previous management of the company's domestic contract manufacturing organization involving a 300% increase in number of products and over $3 million in cost savings.

- Strong performance in start-up, turnaround and high-growth operations.

My objective is to join the executive management team of another manufacturer, either in the US or abroad, where I will have direct strategic planning, operating and P&L responsibility. As you review my resume, you will note that my qualifications include virtually all core management functions, from product development through the entire manufacturing process to global distribution.

I would welcome the opportunity to speak with you regarding any current search assignments for a candidate with my qualifications. Be advised that my current annual compensation is $130,000+ and that I am open to relocation worldwide. Thank you.

Sincerely,

James R. Gregory

Enclosure

MAURICE LOVERN
193 Candlers Mountain Road
Little Rock, Arkansas 54321
(227) 325-2778

_____

February 14, 2001

Frank Wright
President
DeWitt, Inc.
9000 West Crescent Square
San Diego, CA 98632

Dear Mr. Wright:

I am a well-qualified Manufacturing Industry Executive successful in building corporate value through my contributions in engineering and production management, quality, performance reengineering, cost control and profit improvement. My expertise lies in my ability to identify core competencies, link with customer demand, and drive forward innovative technology design, manufacturing and delivery programs.

To each start-up venture, turnaround and high-growth company, I provided the strategic and tactical leadership critical to improving financial results. Most notably, I:

* Increased cycle time by 250% and improved product quality by 75% for RON Systems.
* Captured a 35% gain in revenues and 20% gain in profits for another RON facility.
* Implemented state-of-the-art technologies to automate TDR's manufacturing organization.
* Delivered cost reductions averaging 20%+ for Instruments, Inc.
* Spearheaded implementation of ISO 9002, QS9000 and other quality certifications.

Never satisfied with the "status quo," I strive to increase performance through a combined program of process redesign, personnel development and customer relationship improvement. In turn, I have consistently achieved financial and operating results well beyond projections, and positioned each organization for long-term growth and accelerated profitability.

I look forward to interviewing as Vice President of Manufacturing. Be advised that I am secure in my current position and wish to remain confidential in my search. Thank you.

Sincerely,

Maurice Lovern

Enclosure

JONATHAN L. ROBBINS
9 Buckingham Place
Bedford, Massachusetts 09863
(508) 564-6543

May 28, 2000

Paul Overstreet
President
Sylvania, Inc.
901 Randolph Street
Edison, NY 14753

Dear Mr. Overstreet:

When I began my professional career with Tremont Products, I thought it was a "quick stop" in manufacturing. Years later and many positions since, I now serve as the **Vice President of Production & Distribution**. My challenge was to reengineer the entire logistics process. The results:

- $1+ million cost reduction.
- 75% increase in production output.
- $1+ million capital investment to meet customer demand.

My achievements during my tenure with the Personal Products Company were just as significant and included:

- $2+ million in cost savings.
- $40 million in sales volume for start-up manufacturing line.
- 50% reduction in product damage and 60% reduction in workplace safety incidents.

Recognized by my peers for excellence in operations management, team building, work flow optimization and customer satisfaction, I have tackled each new assignment with a keen focus not only on cost reduction, but also process redesign, productivity improvement and performance gain. In turn, financial results have been significant for start-up ventures, turnarounds and high-growth corporations.

Now, at this venture in my career, I am looking to take the "next step." My goal is a senior-level management position where I can continue to provide strong and decisive operating leadership, while expanding the scope of my responsibilities into sales, marketing and finance.

I look forward to speaking with you about such opportunities and appreciate your time and consideration. Thank you.

Sincerely,

Jonathan L. Robbins

Enclosure

KEVIN LAIRD, JR.
28 Granite Street
Littleton, CO 32033
(303) 654-4533

February 21, 2001

Louis Wesley, President
Langley Production Machinery
1213 Long Meadows
Middleburg, OH 43565

Dear Mr. Wesley:

As **General Manager / Vice President of Manufacturing / Operations Manager**, I have consistently delivered results:

- **30% revenue growth, $1+ million cost reduction and ISO 9002 certification** for Goulder Systems.

- Successful turnaround of Tyler Cable with **90% increase in operating profits and $3 million cost reduction.**

- Accelerated product development program that generated **$5+ million in revenues** for Alloy.

- **$2+ million operating cost reduction** for Bletcher's Powermatic Division.

Throughout my career, I have held full P&L responsibility for Production, R&D, Engineering, Quality, Warehousing, Distribution, Accounting, Human Resources and MIS/Manufacturing Automation. In addition, I have directed staffs of 200+, reengineered workforces to cut costs while optimizing productivity, and provided strong management leadership in start-up, turnaround and high-growth organizations.

My greatest strengths lie in my ability to evaluate existing operations and implement the processes, technologies and systems to improve performance, meet customer objectives and increase bottom-line profitability. Now I am looking for a new opportunity where I can continue to provide strong and decisive leadership.

I would welcome a personal interview to explore management opportunities with Langley Production Machinery and thank you in advance for your consideration.

Sincerely,

Kevin Laird, Jr.

Enclosure

GLENN BARTLEY
GlennUK@london.net
18 Hightower Lane
London 2898, United Kingdom
011-44-2893-237837

November 14, 2000

Susan Anderson
Triad Manufacturing, Inc.
2356 Triad Boulevard
Oldham, IL 68273

Dear Ms. Anderson:

Strengthening the value and performance of complex manufacturing organizations is my expertise. Let me demonstrate.

- In 1995, I was promoted to Director of Production Operations in the UK. My challenge was to revitalize a marginal operation. To date, I have reduced annual operating costs by more than $4 million, introduced innovative staffing and quality improvement initiatives, modernized and upgraded the facility, achieved aggressive safety and delivery goals, and rejuvenated virtually the entire workforce.

- In 1990, I was tasked to build and expand the US contract manufacturing organization. Over five years, we experienced a 300% gain in number of outsourced products, negotiated flat pricing with 80% of our top manufacturers and cut over $3 million from our bottom-line.

- Between 1988 and 1989, I directed a multi-purpose manufacturing facility to full capacity by expanding our customer base, delivered significant operating cost reductions and co-led a critical $23 million expansion project.

These achievements are indicative of the quality and caliber of my entire professional career – identify and capitalize upon opportunities to improve manufacturing performance, enhance product quality and strengthen the bottom-line. Perhaps most significant, I have been successful in creating team-based organizations working cooperatively under my leadership to deliver aggressive financial and operating results.

I am slated to return to the US this spring to manage a large domestic production operation on behalf of my current employer. It is a tremendous opportunity. However, before accepting, I have decided to confidentially explore new executive management positions with other top manufacturers. As such, my interest in speaking with you regarding senior-level opportunities with your organization.

I appreciate your consideration and look forward to our discussion.

Sincerely,

Glenn Bartley

Enclosure

LOUISE R. RAGLAND

4779 Mia Mont Way
San Diego, CA 92922

raglr@ix.netcom.com
Home: 927.832.3223

January 10, 2001

Phil Strongman
Adams Bartlett Recruiters
22 Dominion Valley Road
Newark, DE 09237

Dear Mr. Strongman:

I am forwarding my resume in anticipation that you may be working with a company in need of a well-qualified Operations Executive. Highlights of my career include the following:

- **More than 15 years of progressively responsible experience** in high-quality Manufacturing. Current position as VP Operations for advanced technology company.

- Consistently strong performance in **increasing productivity and efficiency ratings**: 15% increase for RTR Electronics ... a 32% increase for a major packaging company (bringing efficiency to a solid 98%) ... a 60% gain in productivity for Tolerant, Inc.

- Equal success in **reducing operating and overhead costs**: 58% for Tolerant ... $2.3 million for a major cosmetics manufacturing company.

- **Advanced technology skills** in manufacturing systems and PC-based business systems.

- **Expert qualifications in human resources**, team building and team leadership with particular success in driving production growth and performance improvement.

I have established an excellent reputation nationwide for my success in operations management and leadership, including recognition in Industry Week as one of "America's Best Plants." In addition, I have authored two books on manufacturing techniques and production optimization.

Are you available for a brief telephone conversation to further discuss my qualifications and any particular search assignments you may have currently? Although my tenure with RTR Electronics has been a tremendous challenge and quite successful, I am anxious to make a positive move forward. Thank you for your time and consideration. I look forward to speaking with you.

Sincerely,

Louise R. Ragland

Enclosure

Marketing

KeyWords, Action Verbs & High-Impact Phrases to "Nail" Your Cover Letter:

- New Product & Technology Launches
- New Market Penetration
- Strategic Alliances & Co-Marketing
- Joint Ventures
- Product Lifecycle Management
- Cross-Functional Team Leadership
- Market, Industry & Trend Analysis
- Competitive Market Intelligence
- Strategic Market Planning & Positioning
- Product Development & Pricing

MARCUS ANDREWS
100 Windsor Place
Evington, Illinois 55463
(217) 355-5453

March 31, 2001

Clyde T. Dorsey – Senior Partner
Capital Investments
2800 President's Avenue, Suite 106
Great Falls, VA 22066-4106

Dear Mr. Dorsey:

I'm looking for a unique executive opportunity where I can provide strong, decisive and market-driven leadership. My goal is not the "status quo," but rather an emerging, high-growth or turnaround organization that requires an individual with vision, and just as significant, the ability to translate that vision into meaningful action.

My career has accelerated based upon my ability to deliver results despite financial, market and organizational challenges. As you review the enclosed resume, you will be introduced to what I consider some of my most significant accomplishments — revenue and profit gains, long-term cost reductions and critical performance reengineering initiatives.

What distinguishes me from other executives are my strengths in:

- Identifying and capitalizing upon market opportunities to drive growth, expansion and diversification.
- Exploiting an organization's core competencies to gain competitive market advantages.
- Creating vital sales, marketing and service organizations unmatched in customer satisfaction and retention.
- Combining all critical management functions — strategic planning, finance, marketing, product launch, administration, executive development and multi-site operations.
- Negotiating favorable partnerships, strategic alliances and joint ventures.

If positive and improved ROI are your objectives, please call.

Sincerely,

Marcus Andrews

Enclosure

THOMAS HUANG

11 Delaware Avenue * Toledo, OH 49382 * Phone: 444.323.9283
thuang234@missionimpossible.com

March 14, 2001

Larry Nelson
Martinson Manufacturing, Inc.
909 Toledo Avenue
Toledo, OH 49322

Dear Mr. Nelson:

Twenty years ago, technology innovations virtually sold themselves. With a bit of advertising here and there, a company was set to launch a new product. Today, however, things have changed dramatically and marketing has become one of the most vital components to any technology venture. With both global competition and new product roll-outs at an all time high, it is no longer enough to just develop a product. What is required is an astute marketer with technological expertise. And, that is precisely who I am.

Working with some of the world's leading technology companies (e.g., Schlumberger, Emerson, AMERCOM), I have led innovative R&D programs with responsibility for marketing, commercialization, joint ventures, partnerships and licensing. Most significant have been my financial results:

- For Emerson, I drove the development of eight new products generating total revenues in excess of $20 million annually.
- For ATMAN, a German-based company, I increased European market sales from $2 million to $10 million.
- For AMERCOM, I developed and commercialized 20 new products and achieved a 70% win rate on competitve contracts.
- For Schlumberger, I reengineered existing product technology and saved over $1.5 million in company operating costs.

These achievements are indicative of the quality and caliber of my entire professional career – identify market opportunities, drive technology development, and create profitable sales and marketing programs. It goes without mentioning that the strength of my hands-on technology skills has been vital to my success in business development and revenue generation.

Since leaving Emerson last year, I have continued to focus my efforts on technology development and global marketing, and would be pleased to share specific engagements with you during an interview. Currently, I am exploring new career opportunities in technology marketing and would be delighted to meet with you.

Sincerely,

Thomas Huang

Enclosure

WARREN A. BAKER
1620 Meridith Court
Omaha, Nebraska 21753
Email: wbaker@yatzman.com
Phone: (402) 331-0657

November 21, 2000

Howard T. Peyton
President
ElectraData, Inc.
3609 Surrey Avenue
Port Jefferson, NY 11777

Dear Mr. Peyton:

Whether challenged to lead an aggressive market expansion into emerging domestic and international market sectors, launch the start-up of a new business unit or introduce innovative market programs to realign a national sales organization, I have achieved measurable results:

- **As Vice President of New Business Development**, spearheaded Yatzman America's successful market launch into the digital consumer products industry delivering $5.2 million in revenues in first month and $150 million potential revenue stream within five years.

- **As General Manager for Occid's Electronic Imaging Department**, led the start-up of new business unit, guided development of more than nine multimedia, information technologies/products, and drove revenues to $11 million within three years.

- **As National Sales Manager with Closman Products**, championed the introduction of quality, productivity and performance improvement initiatives to restructure and realign the sales organization. Gained a significant competitive advantage and captured key accounts nationwide.

My strengths lie in my ability to conceive and implement the strategic action plans to identify new market opportunities, develop state-of-the-art technologies/products and negotiate strategic partnerships to drive global market expansion and revenue/profit growth. Equally notable, are my strong qualifications in general management, P&L management, financial affairs, recruitment and training.

Now, I am seeking a senior-level sales or management position with a high-growth technology development organization where I can continue to provide strong and decisive sales/management leadership. I would welcome a personal interview to explore such an assignment with ElectraData. Thank you for your time and consideration.

Sincerely,

Warren A. Baker

Enclosure

LISA SPRINGER

34 Smith Road
Lewisville, Arkansas 20347

Home: (761) 676-9322
Email: lisaannspring@aol.com

July 1, 2000

Patti Howard, Associate
Heidrick & Struggles, Inc.
300 South Grand Avenue
Suite 2400
Los Angeles, CA 90071-1685

Dear Ms. Howard:

It is with great interest that I forward my resume for consideration as Senior Vice President of Marketing and Development. With more than 17 years' experience in marketing (the past seven of which have been concentrated in new media and cable broadcast), I bring to the position a unique blend of creative, strategic and management talents of significant value to the organization.

Currently, as the Senior Vice President and Group Account Director for Foundation Communications and its principal business units (including emerging online and multimedia technologies), I spearhead a dynamic media marketing organization. My challenge has been to expand and strengthen market presence through the introduction of a diversified portfolio of advertising, business development, promotional and strategic alliance initiatives. Results have been significant and include:

- Capture of an 11% gain in overall primetime cable share.
- Creation of "standardized" programming and scheduling to attract and retain a loyal audience.
- Development of innovative multimedia advertising and promotional strategies.
- Expansion into new media applications.

Just as significant has been my management success in building and leading cross-functional teams, merging the critical functions of marketing, advertising, research, sales, distribution and creative programming. Further, I have instilled a sense of entrepreneurial vision and creativity to drive forward innovative strategies to win competitive positioning and accelerate revenue growth.

Although secure in my current position, I am confidentially exploring new opportunities where I can direct a large-scale marketing initiative on behalf of a cable/broadcast/media organization. Thus my interest in the Game Show Network and your search for a Senior Vice President of Marketing & Development. I look forward to a personal interview. Thank you.

Sincerely,

Lisa Springer

Enclosure

SALLY ALAIN
777 Arbor Place • Phoenix, AZ 89273
Voice: (904) 666-3928 • Fax: (904) 667-3827 • Email: salain@ctc.net

September 22, 2000

Loretta Andrews-Sloan
Vice President of Global Marketing
INTESEC Technologies, Inc.
2 Roman Terrace
Alpharetta, GA 30983

Dear Ms. Andrews-Sloan:

I am a well-qualified Marketing Professional with more than 15 years' experience in the creative design, development and implementation of corporate marketing initiatives. Through my efforts, I have achieved solid performance in revenue, client and profit growth to dominate regional competition. Now I am looking to transfer my skills back into an advanced technology industry where I began my career.

The value I bring to INTESEC is straightforward – the ability to identify market demand, drive product and service development programs, create innovative marketing campaigns and leverage customer relationships to improve retention. And, I have succeeded.

My strongest qualifications include strategic planning, publicity and corporate image campaigns, market research, advertising, promotions, client incentives, personal selling and marketing communications. I am creative, innovative and flexible, yet decisive in managing projects from concept through execution. In addition, please note that I have strong general management experience including direct P&L.

Always working to stay "ahead of the curve," I have most recently forged several innovative Internet and technology-based marketing programs which have successfully transitioned my current employer from regional to national market presence. This effort has been instrumental in strengthening our corporate image and accelerating revenue growth.

Currently I am exploring new challenges and opportunities where I can lead a marketing organization through growth, expansion and improvement. As such, I would welcome a personal interview to discuss your current needs and my potential contributions.

I look forward to speaking with you and thank you for your time and consideration.

Sincerely,

Sally Alain

Enclosure

175

FRANKLIN J. REED
512 Landon Avenue
Cooperton, Maine 35488
(305) 544-1054

March 8, 2001

Kenneth J. Cress
Cress Equity Partners
1900 Madison Avenue, 14th Floor
New York, NY 10015

Dear Mr. Cress :

Throughout my Marketing career, I have provided strong and decisive leadership to challenging start-up, turnaround and high-growth companies. My expertise lies in my ability to identify opportunities, define strategic goals and vision, and lead tactical implementation. Results are significant and include:

- Transitioning a new marketing organization and product line from concept through start-up to over $100 million in annual volume.

- Realigning and expanding third party distribution network, capturing 20% revenue growth and strengthening competitive market position.

- Introducing innovative marketing, business development and promotional strategies that accelerated growth within existing business units and delivered revenues beyond projections.

- Negotiating strategic alliances and partnerships to accelerate market growth.

- Evaluating merger, acquisition and joint ventures opportunities to expand product portfolios and gain competitive advantages.

My industry experience is diverse and includes banking/financial services, consumer products, packaged goods, publishing and health care. My ability to transcend my marketing expertise into vastly different industries clearly demonstrates my flexibility and ease in understanding the unique marketing characteristics of these specific industries and markets.

Now, at this point in my career, I am interested in new professional challenges where I can continue to provide strong and decisive marketing leadership. Knowing that the venture capital community offers unique opportunities, I have focused my search in such a direction and would welcome a personal interview at your earliest convenience. Thank you.

Sincerely,

Franklin J. Reed

Enclosure

Real Estate

KeyWords, Action Verbs & High-Impact Phrases to "Nail" Your Cover Letter:

- Joint Ventures & Partnerships

- Project Development & Construction Management

- Mixed-Use Commercial, Retail, Residential & Investment Properties

- Major Project Highlights

- Contract Negotiations

- Real Estate Workouts & Recovery

- Asset & Portfolio Management

- Regulatory & Government Affairs

- Environmental Management & Remediation

- ROI Analysis & Performance

BART ANGEL

5565 Trolley's Quarter Road
Lexington, VA 22382

Phone: 823-832-2378
Email: bangel@aol.com

August 14, 2000

Randy Grier
Managing Partner
Abrams Law Firm, LLC
9000 Brooks Blvd., Suite 200
Lexington, KY 38293

Dear Mr. Grier:

As we all know, the businesses of real estate and franchising have become increasingly complex over the past decade. Deals that used to take a few weeks now require months and months of planning, financing, negotiation and regulatory approval. We've all become significantly more attuned to potential liabilities, risks and issues relative to asset protection. And, perhaps most important, our clients have placed an even greater amount of trust in our ability to make cogent decisions and negotiate favorable transactions.

I've been through this process hundreds of times – with both real estate and franchise organizations. Through these experiences, I have developed strong skills and a solid professional reputation for my ability as both a Senior Management Executive and Attorney. Now, I am looking to colleagues, such as yourself, to assist me in identifying new challenges, projects and opportunities.

As you review my resume, you will note that throughout my career I have transacted over $4 billion in real estate transactions, negotiated over $1 billion in financings and successfully guided three franchisors through start-up, growth and improved profitability. I believe that these highlights clearly indicate my ability to identify a solid investment, pull all the players together, secure the financings and deliver positive results.

If you are aware of an opportunity for an individual with my background, I would welcome the referral. If you would like additional information about my qualifications and past experiences, please contact me and we can further discuss any particulars you may be interested in.

I do appreciate your time and assistance, and thank you in advance for your consideration.

Sincerely,

Bart Angel

Enclosure

PAUL E. COLLINS

10324 Mistletoe Lane • Baltimore, Maryland 21121 • Phone (410) 599-2285

February 5, 2001

Stephen Mitchell
Managing Partner
Mitchell & Cohen Investments
4455 Oakwood Avenue
Cleveland, OH 44323

Dear Mr. Mitchell:

Recruited by Rieman Management Corporation (a diversified real estate investment and asset management group) in 1987, I was challenged to rebuild the property management function, accelerate leasing through innovative marketing efforts, and capture long-term cost savings to improve the net profitability of the portfolio.

Results were significant:

• 20%+ gain in net earnings with $5 million increase in gross possible income.
• 98.5% occupancy (highest in the company's portfolio of 25 properties).
• $500,000+ reduction in annual operating costs.
• 100% improvement in tenant service and satisfaction.

Concurrent with my financial gains, I orchestrated tremendous improvements in the operational capabilities, efficiency and productivity of an $80 million residential, commercial and recreational facility (one of the largest such properties in the country). Major projects included first-time automation and several system upgrades, improved preventive maintenance programs, enhanced service training for all employees, and full documentation of all operating policies and procedures.

The value I delivered to Rieman Management will sustain the portfolio for years to come. Now, however, I am seeking new professional challenges and opportunities where I can again provide strong and decisive property management and operating leadership.

I look forward to a personal interview for the VP of Investments position and thank you in advance for your consideration. I prefer to discuss my compensation at the time of our interview.

Sincerely,

Paul E. Collins

Enclosure

PAUL B. GERRITY

4556 Fence Post Road
Arnold, NM 89323-2832

Phone: 927.382.3828
Email: pgerr@aol.com

February 2, 2001

Mike Adams
Director
Real Estate Partners, Inc.
22 Diamond Back Trail
Albuquerque, NM 89382

Dear Mr. Adams:

Building top-performing real estate and franchise organizations is my expertise. Whether challenged to launch a start-up venture, turn around a non-performing operation, or lead a company through accelerated growth, I have consistently delivered strong financial results. Most notably, I:

- Closed over $25 million in real estate financings within one year to support the growth of a privately-held real estate development conglomerate.
- Structured, negotiated and closed over $15 million in "big box" leases with Office Max, Office Depot and other major franchisors.
- Recently supported growth from 20 to 50 locations for an emerging national franchisor.

What is most unique about my career track is my success as both a **Senior Management Executive** (e.g., Vice President, Director, General Counsel) and as an **Attorney**, managing large-dollar, complex real estate acquisition, divestiture, finance and franchise transactions. Not only can I direct strategic planning, business development, marketing, government affairs and field construction operations, I am equally effective in directing critical financing and legal matters.

Currently, I am exploring new professional opportunities where I can continue to use the combination of my talents in both the real estate and franchise communities. I thrive on challenge and opportunity, strive to enhance operating results and am never daunted by competition. Further, I have excellent planning, organizational, negotiation, team leadership and business development skills.

I would welcome the opportunity to discuss any current positions where my qualifications would be of value, and thank you in advance for your consideration.

Sincerely,

Paul B. Gerrity

Enclosure

JONATHAN P. SMITH
5032 Northern Peak
Carlsbad, California 98732
(619) 983-9222

February 14, 2001

President
Development Capital Corporation
1000 Rancho del Gato
Santa Fe, NM 87501

Dear Sir/Madam:

Throughout my 20-year Real Estate career, I have built and led successful development, investment finance, property management and brokerage/sales organizations. To each organization, I have provided the strategic, marketing, financial and operating expertise to deliver strong earnings and sustained revenue streams.

As President of MPR Equity, I built the corporation from concept into a well-established real estate investment group that has completed over $100 million in apartment and shopping center development projects. Most notable has been my success in identifying and negotiating innovative financing instruments with U.S., Canadian, German and Japanese investors, bankers and business partners. Further, I have consistently delivered projects on budget despite the "usual complications and crises."

My success in sales, marketing, leasing and asset maximization is equally strong and includes development of one of the largest and most profitable real estate brokerages in the Midwest.

As you review my resume, you will note that my experience has expanded beyond each corporation to include active leadership of county zoning and planning affairs, downtown economic revitalization initiatives, and both commercial and real estate banking. Now, at this point in my career, I am seeking new professional challenges and opportunities within the industry. Thus my interest in Development Capital Corporation and your search for a VP of Development.

Sincerely,

Jonathan P. Smith

Enclosure

DANIEL R. POWELL
700 Lincoln Place
Baltimore, Maryland 21212
410.444.8736   d.powell@voyager.net

October 12, 2000

John Warner, President
Fidelity Capital Ventures
1000 Michigan Avenue
Washington, D.C. 22002

Dear Mr. Warner:

If you are active in real estate development, community development and/or large-scale, mixed-used construction projects, you will be interested in my qualifications.

- 20+ years' experience in real estate development and management in the U.S. and international markets.

- Complete development and management responsibility for over $500 million in projects over the past 10 years.

- Leadership of more than $450 million in project funding and public/private partnership financing programs.

Most significant, however, is my ability to drive projects through complex community, political and governmental channels. By providing a strong community vision and decisive action plan, I have won the support of community, political, business and financial leaders — support critical to project funding, development and profitable sale/leasing.

Please note that my expertise includes single and multifamily residential, commercial retail, commercial office, light industrial, health care facilities, technology centers, large-scale recreational facilities and more.

I would welcome the chance to explore potential opportunities with your investment firm and or any of your principal holdings, and appreciate your time in reviewing my qualifications. Thank you.

Sincerely,

Daniel R. Powell

Enclosure

Retail

KeyWords, Action Verbs & High-Impact Phrases to "Nail" Your Cover Letter:

- Multi-Unit/Multi-Site Operations Management

- Profit & Loss Management/Optimization

- Merchandising & Product Mix

- Customer Service Management

- Special Events Planning & In-Store Promotions

- Loss Prevention & Recovery

- Buying, Warehousing & Distribution

- Sales Training, Teaming & Leadership

- Facilities Development, Management & Renovation

- Franchising & Product Licensing

NEIL HAMMOND
47 Elmhurt Avenue
Madison, WI 57283
(558) 727-3736 / hammer@net.com

June 12, 2001

Danny Michaelson, Vice President
Value Retailers of America, Inc.
2 VRA Boulevard
Boise, ID 89372

Dear Mr. Michaelson:

Building high-profit, high-end consumer products manufacturing and retail operations is my expertise. Whether launching a new multi-site retailer, developing branded products, or coordinating international product manufacturing, I have consistently delivered strong and sustainable financial results. Most notably, I:

- Founded and built a new venture from concept to **$120 million in annual sales** with 10 retail operations, 35 distribution centers and contract manufacturing partnerships with 20 companies throughout Asia.

- Launched a product development company which introduced state-of-art fabrics to the global garment industry and generated over **$70 million in profitable annual sales**.

- Currently, as CEO of an apparel design company, I've built a new market niche, established a firm market hold and am currently generating **double-digit profits**.

Each of these companies has catered to an exclusive and upscale clientele, discriminating in their tastes, and willing to spend significant dollars for the "right" image, the "right" look and the "right" label.

The greatest value I bring to VRA is the depth and diversity of my executive management talent – from strategic planning, marketing and new business development to retail and distribution operations, retail sales, manufacturing and new product design. What's more, I have strong financial, analytical, negotiation and team building skills. I am never satisfied with the status quo, but constantly working to enhance performance, strengthen quality of operations and service, and improve bottom-line profitability.

At this point in my career, I am seeking an executive leadership opportunity with a well-established and prominent retailer who understands the value of the customer relationship and the innovation it takes to win in today's marketplace. As such, there is no organization I would rather be associated with than VRA and would welcome a personal interview at your earliest convenience.

Sincerely,

Neil Hammond

Enclosure

LEONARD ERICSSON
12 Standish Drive
Poughkeepsie, Pennsylvania 19837
(924) 944-3928

May 12, 2001

Susan Gordon-Howell
Executive Vice President
Saks Fifth Avenue
2 Fifth Avenue
New York, NY 10090

Dear Ms. Gordon-Howell:

Throughout the past 12 years, I have built and profitably managed high-volume, multi-site sales and retail operations. My strength lies in my ability to merge all the finite elements of retailing – most critically, sales – with marketing, advertising, merchandising, inventory, personnel, customer service, finance, facilities and the supporting business infrastructures. What makes my qualifications so unique is the fact that I have worked in a number of different retail situations – new ventures, acquisitions, turnarounds and growth operations.

During my tenure with National Stores and two of its principal operating companies, I have repeatedly demonstrated my success by providing strong financial results. In one situation, sales grew to over $40 million; in another, revenues increased at a rate of better than 35% annually. This has been achieved largely as a result of my efforts in providing a strong strategic vision and a business structure to support success.

Currently secure in my position, I am confidentially exploring new management opportunities where I can continue to combine my strengths in sales leadership, retail operations, team building and market growth. I am accustomed to working within highly competitive markets and understand that store image and branding are vital to sustained growth. Further, I am both personally and professionally committed to quality performance and customer satisfaction.

Aware that you are currently seeking a Senior Operations Director to join your management team, I would welcome the opportunity to interview for the position. I guarantee that the depth and quality of my experience will be of measurable value to your operations. Thank you. I appreciate your confidentiality.

Sincerely,

Leonard Ericsson

Enclosure

Sales

KeyWords, Action Verbs & High-Impact Phrases to "Nail" Your Cover Letter:

- Revenue Increases
- Profit Increases
- Market Share Increases
- New Product Launches
- Multi-Channel Distribution Development
- Global Expansion
- Sales Training & Team Leadership
- Key Account Successes
- Sales Force Automation
- Selling Cost Reductions

ELIZABETH HAYES
1221 Barkely Boulevard
Austin, Texas 75388

Phone (531) 626-7836   Fax (531) 626-3826

November 4, 2000

Max Syberson
Venture Capital Investors of NC
23 Barge Avenue
Raleigh, NC 28839

Dear Mr. Syberson:

If you are interested in a top sales and marketing director for one of your technology ventures, please take a moment to consider my qualifications:

- Over 15 years of sales and marketing management responsibility with several of the nation's most prominent technology companies (e.g., Landmark Systems, Applied Data Research, Sterling).

- Consistent record of double digit revenue growth in intensely competitive US and international markets for start-up enterprises, emerging ventures, turnarounds and high-growth corporations.

- Ability to anticipate market demand and opportunity, develop strategic plans, assemble resources and lead tactical field teams responsible for sales, product introduction, key account development and bottom-line revenue/profit growth.

- Unique expertise in negotiating win-win distribution and reseller contracts to expand market penetration and outperform the competition.

I am an accomplished business manager with direct experience in P&L management, team building/team leadership, training, product management, strategic planning and organizational design/development. I thrive in challenging, fast-paced and intense environments where my performance directly impacts the bottom-line. Further, I have solid negotiation, decision making and problem solving skills.

Currently, I am seeking a new senior management opportunity where I can continue to provide strong sales and marketing leadership within the technology industry. Aware of the quality of your portfolio companies, I would be delighted to speak with you about such opportunities. Thank you.

Sincerely,

Elizabeth Hayes

Enclosure

ANDREW T. GRUNERT
1200 Moss Green Path Way
Adelphia, South Carolina 29876
Email: agrunertr@carolina.rr.com

Phone: 803-889-3675   Fax: 800-666-8937

April 1, 2001

Maria Muldoon
President & CEO
Books.com
22 Marmley Avenue
Detroit, MI 45739

Dear Ms. Muldoon:

Building top-performing sales and marketing organizations in today's economy requires a unique blend of leadership, product, personnel and technical talent. We have watched the sales industry undergo phenomenal changes as the Internet and E-commerce have reinvented selling and customer management. The companies that are succeeding are those that have embraced these changes and responded accordingly. And that is perhaps the greatest value I have delivered to my current employer.

When I began with the organization in 1992, I was part of the team challenged to build a start-up venture. As the company grew, so did my responsibilities in all areas of sales and marketing leadership, from strategic planning to account management, acquisition integration, sales team recruitment and training, and so much more. It was then that I began to introduce E-commerce activities into the organization, the single greatest factor in the company's financial and market success.

As you review my qualifications, you will note that I am best described as the "consummate sales professional," able to quickly ascertain what resources, personnel and products will optimize market performance and drive long-term revenue growth. Then, combining that with the latest in technology-based sales tools, my teams and I delivered phenomenal financial results including over $25 million in new product sales over the past 18 months with a $2 million improvement in operating income.

Currently, I am exploring new management opportunities where I can transition my skills into a high-growth, technology-based corporation. My years with BFGoodrich have been tremendous and I will always value the organization. However, I am anxious to move into an assignment with a company in need of strong leadership and poised for solid growth.

Thank you.

Sincerely,

Andrew T. Grunert

Enclosure

DOROTHY A. PATTERSON

14 Riley Lane   864-392-3927
Craig, RI 09870   dpatterson23@aol.com

January 17, 2001

Al Greenbrier
Executive Vice President of Engineering
Axial Telecommunications, Inc.
455 Trail Path Boulevard
Lewisburg, WV 38276

Dear Mr. Greenbrier:

Beginning my professional career as one of the first female engineers ever hired into AT&T, I progressed rapidly through a series of responsible technical, product development, marketing and sales management positions with AT&T, MCI and XCEL (an early-stage telecommunications venture). And, to each organization, I delivered strong and sustainable financial results:

- With MCI for seven years, I closed a $25+ million contract with a Fortune 10 and created the company's national account model. I then restored the Ameritech relationship and negotiated an additional $20 million contract for telecommunications support throughout the Far East.

- With XCEL Telecommunications, I delivered a 122% increase in corporate sales within just one year as I raised $35 million to support product development and market expansion. The latter demonstrates the tremendous value and impact of my sales abilities, negotiating with investors and financiers to "sell" something that did not even yet exist.

- During my 14-year tenure with AT&T, I excelled. I sold their first-ever $100 million telecommunications contract, created a global technical sales support organization and delivered up to 200% of quota within just six months.

My most recent positions in the financial services, energy and professional staffing industries have allowed me to demonstrate the transferability of my sales and marketing skills into new and exciting environments. However, I still firmly believe that the telecommunications industry offers tremendous opportunities and am anxious to return to "where I belong."

I would welcome the chance to speak with you about senior sales and marketing leadership positions with your organization, and thank you in advance for your consideration. I guarantee there has never been a sales situation or challenge that I was not able to meet and conquer. Thank you.

Sincerely,

Dorothy A. Patterson

Enclosure

NICHOLAS HENDERSON

2343 Jefferson Boulevard
Arlington, Virginia 23068

Home (703) 642-4140
Office (703) 859-6991

April 4, 2001

Vice President of Human Resources
XYAN, Inc.
1012 West Ninth Avenue, Suite 100
King of Prussia, PA 19406

Dear Sir/Madam:

As National Market Manager with AT&T, I bring to your organization 11 years of progressively responsible experience in the strategic planning, design and leadership of winning sales, marketing and business development programs. My notable achievements include:

- Design of two service-driven product extensions, including development of all marketing communications and full-scale market launch. **RESULT: $2 million in revenues within first year.**

- Creative concept and deployment of a series of promotional and marketing campaigns for the national introduction of a completely new product line. **RESULT: $3.5 million in monthly revenues within first year.**

- Realignment of pricing and market positioning strategies for AT&T's national account portfolio. **RESULT: Consistent wins over competition AND a measurable improvement in net profitability of each sales transaction.**

Complementing my ability to produce sales dollars are equally strong qualifications in training and leading professional sales teams, providing strategic market vision with appropriate tactical action plans, and responding to the constantly changing demands of the market. I lead by example and provide strong decision making, problem solving and project management skills.

If decisive and action-driven leadership skills are your goals, we should meet. At that time, I would be pleased to provide specific information regarding my salary history and current salary requirements. Be advised that I am currently employed and respect your confidentiality in my search.

Sincerely,

Nicholas Henderson

Enclosure

BRIAN BLOCK
12 Montvue Road #212
Baltimore, Maryland 21204
Phone: 410.938.2838   Email: bblock@raven.net

October 14, 2000

Bill Baxter, President & CEO
Triax Financial Services Corporation
23 Dunbar Street
Baltimore, MD 21230

Dear Mr. Baxter:

A past Senior Vice President with Card Establishment Services (acquired by First Data Corporation in 1985), I had a strong and successful sales, marketing and business development career with this large financial service corporation. Challenged to not only deliver revenue growth within existing markets and customer accounts, I was also tasked with creating and launching a portfolio of new credit card processing and enhancement services. Results were significant and included:

- Captured major contracts with leading corporations and financial institutions (e.g., Media Bank, Hyatt, Ramada, numerous Wall Street investment firms).
- Identified market opportunity, negotiated and closed a $3 million contract with Enterprise.
- Conceived, developed and introduced more than 20 new and innovative products and services to solidify our competitive advantages.
- Architected the organization's first-ever customer care and loyalty programs, resulting in major improvements in long-term customer retention and the sale of profitable, value-added services.

Characterized by others as a "team-based" sales and marketing leader, I owe much of my success to the individuals I have trained and developed. Realizing the intrinsic value of the customer relationship, my focus has been on recruiting individuals successful in this type of environment, committed to delivering actionable solutions and always working to improve the bottom-line. And, we have succeeded within intensely competitive situations.

For the past 18 months, I've managed an exclusive sales and marketing consulting group. Although the challenges have been interesting and my contributions notable, I miss the dynamics of the financial services arena. As such, I've decided to close my practice and return to the industry.

I would welcome a personal interview to explore senior sales and marketing opportunities, and guarantee that the strength of my performance will add measure value to your company, your customers and your new ventures. Thank you for taking the time to review my qualifications. I look forward to speaking with you.

Sincerely,

Brian Block

Enclosure

LEONARD BAXTER

---

122 Palm Spring Boulevard, Miami Springs, FL 33389
Phone: 551.237.2372
Email: leonard.baxter@springs.net

June 22, 2000

Samuel Goodson
Chairman of the Board
Emerson Electric Company
45 Dodge Boulevard
Akron, OH 43827

Dear Mr. Goodson:

Building customer relationships and driving profitable sales growth is my expertise. Whether challenged to launch a start-up venture, facilitate a market turnaround or accelerate revenues within a high-growth, global energy corporation, I have consistently delivered strong financial results.

As you review my resume, you will note that I progressed rapidly to my most recent VP and Senior VP positions, based upon my ability to drive revenues and improve profitability within intensely competitive markets worldwide. I have been recognized for my performance in capturing major accounts, developing and marketing value-added services, facilitating product development teams, penetrating new markets, and most significantly, building top-performing sales teams.

You'll be most interested in my current engagement with one of the world's largest energy companies, its affiliates and joint venture partners. The company had previously retained a Top 6 consulting firm to guide them in repositioning themselves within the market, executing critical Y2K initiatives and managing a massive global customer analysis project. However, nothing had been achieved. It was at that point that I was retained to put all three projects back on track and reclaim the company's market position. And I have succeeded, achieved all financial objectives and positioned the firm for continued market growth.

I have found the energy industry to be demanding and competitive, yet exciting with unlimited opportunity. I believe that the underlying sales, marketing and business development strategies that drive the industry can be significantly enhanced and that under my leadership I can deliver positive results. As such, I would welcome the chance to meet with you to explore your current senior sales and marketing needs, and my potential fit and contribution.

I thank you in advance for time and consideration, and look forward to speaking with you.

Sincerely,

Leonard Baxter

Enclosure

MICHAEL JENKINS
Mike.Jenkins@cars.com

1281 Steel Street
Bethlehem, Pennsylvania 19068

Home (415) 642-4140
Office (415) 649-6991

December 10, 2000

Matthew Kinard
President
SAAB Motor Cars
1293 Century Avenue
Atlanta, GA 30129

Dear Mr. Kinard:

When I recently shopped for a new vehicle, I was at a crossroads. A car enthusiast my entire life, I vacillated between a Volvo and a Saab. Which offered the most for my money, which provided the best in service and which was most effectively merchandised? The answer was clear — it was the Volvo. Do you want to know why?

An accomplished sales executive (currently employed with Xytoc in Pittsburgh), I am perhaps more critical than most. When I decide to invest $20,000 ... $30,000 ... $40,000 in a product, I want to buy from an educated sales professional who understands my needs and my expectations. This was my experience with Volvo.

So ... what can Saab do to more effectively compete? We all know that it is more than just styling and presentation. It is the entire selling and customer management cycle. It is understanding the product and its value, and clearly translating that to each prospective customer through both direct and indirect channels. And this is where I believe I can be of significant value to the Saab sales organization.

Do not misinterpret my intentions. I am not a car salesman and never have any intentions of pursuing that career path. I am, however, a talented, aggressive and determined sales executive who understands the dynamics of selling, product management, merchandising and customer loyalty. It is this expertise I wish to bring to Saab and through which I guarantee to deliver results.

I would welcome the chance to meet with you to explore senior-level sales and market management opportunities with Saab, and share my personal experience as an "on-the-street" consumer. I'm sure you'll be surprised by my feedback and encouraged by my recommendations.

Sincerely,

Michael Jenkins

Enclosure

Senior Management

KeyWords, Action Verbs & High-Impact Phrases to "Nail" Your Cover Letter:

- Strategic Planning, Vision & Direction

- Domestic & International Business

- Start-Up, Turnaround & High-Growth Companies

- Revenue & Profit Growth

- New Product, Service & Technology Development

- Corporate Culture Change

- IPOs, Joint Ventures, Alliances & Partnerships

- Cross-Functional Team Building & Leadership

- Tactical Planning & Operations Management

- Productivity, Efficiency & Quality Improvement

BRYCE R. BURTON

2500 Santa Monica Blvd. #222
Santa Monica, California 93872

Phone: (310) 681-3829
Fax: (310) 681-3726

December 30, 2000

Phillip Carson
Rowcson Manufacturing
900 Oleson Boulevard
Montgomery, AL 39283

Dear Mr. Carson:

Building corporate value is my expertise. Whether challenged to launch a start-up, orchestrate an aggressive turnaround or accelerate growth, I have consistently delivered strong financial results. The value I bring Roweson can best be summarized as follows:

* More than 10 years of direct P&L responsibility across diverse industries and market sectors.
* Strong, decisive and profitable leadership of global sales and marketing organizations.
* Keen financial, negotiating and strategic planning performance.
* Consistent and measurable gains in operations, quality and efficiency productivity.
* Outstanding record of leadership in the consumer products and management consulting industries.

To each organization, my teams and I have delivered strong and sustainable operating, market and financial advantages critical to long-term growth, profitability and competitive performance. Most notably, I:

* Increased sales 9.6%, reduced headcount 45%, shortened leadtimes 60% and improved quality performance 300% for a $120 million company.
* Orchestrated successful turnaround and return to profitability of Stockton Fabrics. Cost reductions surpassed $2 million, account base increased 15% and annualized cash flow improved $1.2 million, while launching the most successful new product introduction in the company's history.
* Accelerated market growth of The Miller Group of Companies in a highly competitive and volatile market, increasing revenues 45% within the first year and delivering equally significant reductions in operating costs and corporate debt.

My goal is a top-level management position with an organization seeking to achieve market dominance as well as aggressive revenue and profit projections. I am most interested in interviewing for the position of Vice President of Operations where I will provide the strategic and tactical leadership critical to success in today's fast-moving environment. I look forward to meeting with you and the other principals.

Sincerely,

Bryce R. Burton

Enclosure

MARTIN M. RAYMOND
122 Calcutta Street
Edmondton, Oklahoma 54738
(616) 297-8935

July 15, 2000

George G. Miller, Jr.
President / CEO
Grambling Manufacturing & Distribution
8000 Wallabee Road
McKeesport, PA 19387

Dear Mr. Miller:

As a fellow CEO, I've most likely dealt with many of the same issues that you have – reducing costs, optimizing operations, improving staff competencies and, ultimately, strengthening the bottom-line. My particular achievements have been in the transportation industry where, time after time, I have provided both the strategies and action plans to improve performance. This has included start-up ventures, turnarounds and high-growth organizations.

Most recently, on a contract assignment with a $1.7 billion consumer products company, I evaluated a new acquisition they had made in Poland and, within just 22 days, gave them a game plan to consolidate their transportation operations and cut their costs by 15%. During my tenure with Prism (a transportation roll-up venture), I restructured/integrated 10 transportation companies and delivered one year savings in excess of $6 million.

These are the types of projects I would like to continue pursuing. Obviously, because of my background, I am most comfortable working with other top executives. However, I am equally effective in building an immediate rapport with operations personnel, winning their trust and confidence to move projects forward without any perceived threat.

Please note that I have a Harvard MBA, providing me with an intensely strong academic and theoretical background in Management, Business Administration and Organizational Leadership.

I would welcome the chance to spend some time with you – either in person or over the telephone – to discuss your transportation and distribution operations, their strengths and weaknesses as you perceive them, and any particular challenges you are currently facing. Let's see if there isn't an opportunity to reduce your costs, improve operations and strengthen profitability.

Sincerely,

Martin M. Raymond

Enclosure

JOHN WELLINGTON
87544 Spring Garden
Placentia, California 98551
(311) 888-8841

July 23, 2000

Alexander Larness
President & CEO
IO-Lab Technologies
1200 Washington Way
Menlo Park, CA 98441

Dear Mr. Larness:

I am a successful entrepreneur who has developed, financed and built eight new ventures throughout my career. Combined revenues have exceeded $35 million annually with my current project forecasted to generate $45 million in first year sales. The diversity of my industry experience ranges from private tennis and racquetball clubs to state-of-the-art technologies.

So ... why do I want a job?

I'm looking for stability and a change in life-style. The years of entrepreneurial ventures have been personally and professionally rewarding. However, the toll on my family has been significant. Now, at age 45, I am interested in channeling my skills in a new direction where I can provide senior operating leadership.

If you are seeking an individual who can make an immediate and positive impact upon your operations, revenue stream and profit margins, we should talk. I desire a position in a dynamic environment that offers flexibility, challenge and opportunity.

Sincerely,

John Wellington

Enclosure

LARRY BLOOMFIELD

12 Gator Road
Boca Raton, Florida 33486

Home (407) 541-2514   Fax (407) 541-7783   Office (305) 985-1005

April 1, 2001

Philip Newfield
PNC Investments
342 The Marsh
Hilton Head, SC 64774

Dear Mr. Newfield:

In 1983 I had an idea for a new business venture. Thirteen years later, that idea has been transformed into a $6+ million corporation with 24 operating locations throughout the Miami metro region. Growth has been steady and progressive; earnings consistently stronger year after year.

My role as President has included all operating functions of the entire organization — strategic planning, sales, marketing, purchasing, distribution, human resources, PC technology and corporate finance/accounting. I am particularly strong in the areas of real estate leasing and legal affairs, and have personally managed complex contracts, agreements and corporate law transactions.

Based upon my achievements, I was featured in the September 1995 edition of **Forbes Magazine**, citing my expertise in market development, business management and profitability. Now, however, I have decided to sell the corporation and am interested in a senior-level operating management position where I can provide strong, decisive and effective leadership.

If you are seeking a candidate with my qualifications, experience and track record, I would welcome a personal interview. Thank you for taking the time to review my qualifications.

Sincerely,

Larry Bloomfield

Enclosure

MARTIN I. MAXWELL

247 Odess Lane
Amherst, MA 01887

Phone: 972-938-2736
martin.i.maxwell@worldnet.att.net

March 14, 2001

Ari Mestapoulos
Chief Executive Officer
Global Plastics, Inc.
6000 Market Street
Philadelphia, PA 19382

Dear Mr. Mestapoulos :

As a well-qualified Vice President & General Manager, there are five things I do best:

- **Identify and develop new business opportunities.** In my current position as the #1 Management Executive for Orion's US operations, I have tripled sales and profits by capturing new business opportunities – new sales, new products, new partnerships, new markets and more. Not only have I identified these opportunities, I have built the operations and infrastructures to support them and provide a truly competitive market advantage.

- **Build profitable new customer markets.** As International Sales Manager for GM's $200 million EVC Technology Division, I led a successful International expansion program, increased European sales 100% and entered the Japanese market with $500,000 in initial sales orders.

- **Spearhead successful new product development programs.** Currently, as VP/GM with Orion, I have led 11 new product development initiatives, from product and market planning through design and manufacture to market launch. These products now generate $75 million in annual sales.

- **Revitalize non-performing manufacturing operations.** With more than 15 years of senior-level manufacturing and operations management experience, I have been the catalyst for dramatic technological, quality, productivity and product performance.

- **Make money.** If you boil it down to the basics, making money is my expertise. Over the course of my career, I have generated combined revenues of more than $450 million while cutting $200+ million in operating costs. Profits have risen as much as 82% per year.

I would welcome a personal interview at your earliest convenience. Thank you.

Sincerely,

Martin I. Maxwell

Enclosure

TERRENCE MICHAELSON
472 Ivy Link Way
Danville, Ohio 44837
Email: tmichaelson@cs.net

Residence: 513-727-3876   Office: 513-980-4000

May 1, 2000

Lewis Bragg
President & COO
Bragg-Hubert Industries, Inc.
750 N. Huron Road, #200
Lakeland, MN 57362

Dear Mr. Bragg:

Success. I believe that it lies in one's ability to merge the strategic with the tactical, to understand the market and the competition, to effectively control the finances, and to build a strong, productive and committed workforce. No one function is accountable for performance. It is the integration of it all and the combined strength of the management team.

Success and corporate value are what I have delivered throughout my career working with start-ups, turnarounds, high-growth companies and multinational corporations. To each, I have provided the strategic and tactical leadership critical to revenue growth, cost reduction and profit improvement. This has been accomplished primarily through my efforts in leading organizational development initiatives, rebuilding non-performing operations, introducing best-in-class business processes, negotiating mergers and acquisitions, and challenging my workforce to produce.

I consider myself a broad-based general management executive with experience in all core operating functions, top-flight negotiation and problem solving skills, and the ability to make difficult decisions. Working in cooperation with other senior executives, I have established a reputation for my energy, drive and results. Now I am seeking a new career opportunity that will not only challenge my abilities but allow me to lead an organization to its next level of performance.

Let me also note that one of my greatest talents is my ability to build relationships within and outside an organization. This includes senior executives, operating management teams, professional staffs, support staffs, attorneys, auditors, regulators, bankers and investors.

If you are currently seeking an executive management candidate with my qualifications, I would welcome the opportunity for a personal interview and thank you in advance for your consideration.

Sincerely,

Terrence Michaelson

Enclosure

200

DENNIS JAMISON
Route 7 Box 350
Allentown, Pennsylvania 17571
Home (717) 781-7257   Fax (717) 781-5731

May 15, 2001

Samuel Spencer
Chairman
Total Energy, Inc.
23 Cumberland Highway
Portland, OR 41214

Dear Mr. Spencer:

What value do I bring to Total Energy? The answers are clearcut:

* 18 years of strong leadership experience as **President/COO, Managing Director** and **Vice President of Marketing & Business Development.**
* Broad-based experience across diverse product, service and technology industries.
* Success in merging the strategic with the tactical, delivering long-term gains in revenues and profits, outpacing the competition and dominating the marketplace.

To each organization, I have provided strong leadership with measurable results:

* **100% revenue growth** as CEO of Bridle Incorporated.
* **30% growth in market share** and **20% profit increase** as Vice President with Morrisman Industries.
* **25% growth in national distribution** as Vice President with Pacific Green Industries.
* Three amazing "bottom-line" turnaround and business restructuring initiatives.

Characterized by others as visionary, decisive and charismatic, I possess keen instincts and strategies to quickly effect change and improvement. My management style is participative, high-energy, results-driven and "hands-on." Further, my technical qualifications in both manufacturing automation and PC/MIS technology are strong.

Although active in my consulting practice, I am interested in a unique opportunity to return to a larger organization with a solid business infrastructure and a recognizable need for strong and decisive leadership. I look forward to pursuing such opportunities with Total Energy and thank you for your consideration. A resume will follow as per your request.

Sincerely,

Dennis Jamison

CHRISTOPHER FRANKLIN
259 Court Street
Greenwich, Connecticut 06495
Home (203) 738-8704   Office (202) 789-7548

March 10, 2001

Anthony Arnold, President & CEO
Top Cat Apparel
2888 Island View
Garden City, NY 11542

Dear Mr. Arnold:

High-growth companies require leadership talent that is broad in perspective, merging all core functional disciplines to achieve common goals and deliver aggressive performance results.

In my career, I have done just that. With more than 15 years of senior-level management experience, I personally directed virtually all operating, strategic, marketing and financial functions. Most significantly, I delivered strong performance in earnings, cost reduction, process improvement and long-range business development.

High-growth companies also require visionary leadership. It is not enough to manage the day-to-day operations. Rather, it is critical that the leadership team provide direction, action and success.

My achievements clearly reflect my ability to deliver:

- In my current turnaround general management assignment, I am creating and implementing strategic and tactical plans to build revenues by 10%-15% over the next year.

- Previously, as General Manager of Accounting and IS organizations, I captured $13 million in cost reductions, implemented new technology and improved quality ratings to above 97%.

- In my entrepreneurial venture, I transitioned a concept into a fully-operational business, negotiated seed financing and achieved profitability in the first year.

Perhaps most significant, high-growth companies demand excellence and require leadership able to strengthen the value of the corporation, its products, its technology and its customer service.

Currently, I am involved in an interim management situation and am exploring new career challenges. Thus my interest in meeting with you to explore such opportunities where I can provide aggressive and decisive leadership, action and results. I look forward to your call.

Sincerely,

Christopher Franklin

Enclosure

LAWRENCE SWANSON
38 Desert Road
Phoenix, Arizona 78481
LarryS@aol.com   Phone: (602) 313-0208

October 2, 2000

Lester Lobdell
President
Maddox, Inc.
1900 Wabash Avenue, Suite 120
Chicago, IL 60842

Dear Mr. Lobdell:

At age 34, I've risen through the ranks of several large corporations, starting with a career in Engineering and Technology, transitioning into Finance and, most recently, focusing on Marketing and International Business Development. The sum of these experiences has now prepared me for a position in General Management where I can integrate these functions and provide strong and decisive leadership.

* As a Marketing & Business Development Manager, I am currently spearheading United's aggressive entry into emerging Southeast Asian markets and creating innovative manufacturing and marketing alliances.

* As a Financial Professional, I provided high-level planning and analytical support to United and several of their operating subsidiaries to facilitate reengineering and organizational change initiatives.

* As an Engineering Professional, I was promoted to a leadership position within one year and directed several sophisticated technology development and implementation projects.

Equally strong are my planning, organizational, problem solving and communication skills. I thrive in fast-paced, technologically-sophisticated environments that require innovative leadership and decisive action. Now, I am ready to meet new challenges and deliver strong results.

I would welcome an interview at your convenience and appreciate your time and assistance.

Sincerely,

Lawrence Swanson

Enclosure

GEORGE RICHARDSON
1007 Mountain View Road
Charlotte, North Carolina 27710

Home: 919-783-4922

Office: 919-797-9100

March 15, 2001

Yvonne McMasters
President
Overhead Manufacturing
1900 Parker Road
Syracuse, NY 11441

Dear Ms. McMasters:

My skill set is quite unique. I'm an Attorney, CPA and most importantly, Senior Executive, successful in combining core business functions to provide strong, decisive and profitable leadership. The scope of my experience is broad, spanning countless industries worldwide. Most notable is my success in corporate development, M&A transactions, corporate finance/recapitalization and international trade. Highlights are included on the enclosed resume.

My operations, transactions and projects have impacted major companies worldwide — Metromedia, Mitsubishi, Bank of America, GATX, Howard Hughes Medical Institute, Pennzoil, PaineWebber, AEA Investors and others. In turn, I bring to your organization the wealth of experience I have gained through these efforts and a demonstrated record of financial and operating achievement.

Currently, I am exploring unique and dynamic executive opportunities where I can continue to provide integrated operating, legal and financial leadership. Your firm was personally recommended and, as such, I am enclosing a resume for your review. I look forward to hearing from you and do appreciate your time.

Sincerely,

George Richardson

Enclosure

Technology Company Management

KeyWords, Action Verbs & High-Impact Phrases to "Nail" Your Cover Letter:

- New Technology Development

- New Technology Market Launch

- Revenue & Profit Growth

- IPOs, Joint Ventures & Strategic Partnerships

- Integrated System Solutions

- Competitive Wins

- Capital Financing & Venture Capital/Institutional Investment

- High-Growth Ventures

- International Expansion & Distribution

- Technology Industry Honors & Awards

DAVID BUCKLEY

12 Montpelier Avenue
Charlotte, NC 29837
dbuckley@flash.net

Home: (203) 922-3877
Office: (203) 383-1000
Fax: (203) 383-9089

May 23, 2001

Dirk Dickson
Ronald Lehman Associates, Inc.
PO Box 673
Murray, PA 19098

RE: **President – US Operations –Job Lead #GM0398**

Dear Mr. Dickson:

I believe that I have precisely the qualifications as stated in your posting for the above-referenced position. Briefly highlighted, they include:

- More than 20 years' experience with high-growth technology companies in the financial services, software, networking, office automation, data storage and E-commerce industries.

- Combined expertise as both President/CEO and CFO, providing me with a unique skill set ranging from strategic planning and organizational design, to multinational sales and business operations, to corporate finance and investment management.

- Management of complex financial transactions, contracts, acquisitions, joint ventures and corporate sales. Launched start-up of professional investor relations organization.

- Record of consistent revenue and profit growth in each and every assignment. During my tenure as CEO of a $400 million group of media companies, I delivered phenomenal financial results including a 287% revenue increase and 639% operating profit increase for one division.

Most notably, as President & COO of Geyer, I managed the entire US operation. Challenged to reverse a downward trend, I built the organization from $10 million to $60+ million in revenues with multi-million dollar profits. I facilitated the acquisition of product technologies from Canada, Japan and Europe into the US economy, redesigned the product management and distribution system, and provided strategic leadership.

I would welcome the opportunity to speak with you and appreciate your consideration. Thank you.

Sincerely,

David Buckley

Enclosure

MITCHELL BINGHAMPTON
mbing@delmgt.com

477 West Elkwood Drive
Wilmington, DE 19987

Home: 302.789.8784
Office: 302.788.7800

January 5, 2001

Art Johnson, Managing Partner
Investors International, Inc.
25 Santa Monica Boulevard
Santa Monica, CA 93882

Dear Mr. Johnson:

I am forwarding my resume in anticipation that you may be working with a company in need of a well-qualified President/CEO. Highlights of my career that may be of particular interest to you include:

- Built new venture from start-up into a 300-employee corporation distributing $4+ billion in customer products annually.
- Delivered annual growth averaging 35% with 35% return on capital and 50% year-over-year return to shareholders.
- Structured and negotiated two successful gobal acquisitions.
- Invested $35+ million to build a best-in-class IT organization to support the corporation's dramatic growth and nationwide expansion.

Additional qualifications include:

- 10+ years of direct P&L and operating management responsibility.
- Outstanding performance in marketing, sales and new business development (with particular emphasis on major account relationships).
- Equal strong operating and financial performance in turnarounds and revitalizations.

My experience lies in the product, service and distribution industries, and clearly demonstrates my ability to deliver strong financial results across diverse markets. I thrive in challenging, fast-paced and results-driven organizations where teams work cooperatively to achieve aggressive business goals.

I would welcome the opportunity to speak with you regarding your current search. I am open to relocation and that I would anticipate compensation in the $175,000 to $200,000 range. Thank you.

Sincerely,

Mitchell Binghampton

Enclosure

GARY R. JORDAN

1934 South Flower Road
Garden City, New York 11737
Gary.R.Jordan@spacenet.net

Home   516.873.2836
Business 516.791.4747
www.garyjordan.com

October 3, 2000

Roger Booker
Booker Executive Recruiters
1200 Park Avenue, Suite 122
New York, NY 10010

Dear Mr. Booker:

The changes in Information Technology are evolving at a unprecedented rate. Never before have we experienced such a phenomenon or so many challenges. As an MIS Director, I am routinely faced with these challenges and the need to evaluate specific technologies and their ability to meet our operating requirements. This is where I have excelled.

During the past 10+ years, I have spearheaded the acquisition and development of emerging technologies to meet current organizational needs while providing the flexibility for change as technologies continue to evolve. Most recently, I directed the integration of object oriented, networking, Internet, multimedia and other technologies that have strengthened internal operating capabilities, reduced costs and improved service levels.

With a unique blend of MIS and general management experience, I have positioned each technology organization as a key partner to the operating management team, responding to their specific needs and recommending proactive systems solutions. In turn, each organization is now recognized as a pioneer in information technologies, respected by their peer organizations and commended for their ability to produce.

Starting my career in the for-profit business sector, I advanced rapidly. Most recently, I transitioned my experience into non-profits, providing them with competitive technologies to drive performance improvement. Now, I am anxious to return to a for-profit corporation where greater opportunities exist for both technological and professional advancement.

If you are working with a client company in need of strong, decisive and proactive MIS leadership, I would welcome the opportunity to explore the position. Be advised that I am open to relocation and that my recent compensation has averaged $145,000 annually. Thank you.

Sincerely,

Gary Jordan

Enclosure

DENNIS L. CARTERET

121 Grand Avenue * Elmtree, MA 02765 * (713) 982-3876 * DennisL24@aol.com

May 24, 2001

Joseph Barnes
Managing Director
IT Investment Trust
29 Marshall Boulevard
Boston, MA 02930

Dear Mr. Barnes:

Building successful and profitable Internet and E-commerce ventures is my expertise. Highlights include:

- Currently launching the start-up of a B2B and B2C venture in partnership with AOL, Pillsbury.com, Mrs. Fields and other major players. Structured and negotiated innovative funding and marketing alliances to advance a high-profile "go to market" campaign. ***Projecting first year profitable revenues of $12 million***.

- Negotiated Board funding, wrote business plan, negotiated multi-million dollar advertising campaign and orchestrated the operations start-up of a new .com venture (subsidiary of well-established manufacturer). ***Delivered first year revenues of $2.5 million***.

I bring to your organization years of senior leadership experience with bottom-line P&L responsibility for virtually all core business functions – from strategic planning, investment funding and new business development to operations, marketing, branding, logistics, finance, HR and information technology. My management style is direct and decisive, yet I am flexible to responding to constantly changing organizational, competitive, market, staff and technology demands.

Currently, I am exploring new executive opportunities with a high-tech organization poised for aggressive and significant growth. Aware of the quality of your organization and your commitment to market expansion, I would welcome a personal interview and can guarantee that the quality and depth of my experience will add measurable value to your organization.

Thank you.

Sincerely,

Dennis L. Carteret

Enclosure

JORDAN JASPER

211 Fox Runn Drive
Milwaukee, WI 52174

Phone: 772-373-7608
Fax: 772-373-6422
Email: jjasper@msn.com

January 21, 2001

Sam Billings, President
Grocery.com
2 Main Plaza Drive
Billings, MT 89372

Dear Mr. Billings:

Consumer product and service companies today are faced with unprecedented competition. With the emergence of E-commerce technologies, the opportunities for customer communication are phenomenal. Today, more than ever, a company must understand "who" their customers are – their lifestyles, preferences, buying trends and much more. This is the value I bring to your organization.

Briefly summarized, my expertise includes the following:

- **Developing a clear strategic path and vision**. Planning, leadership and communications are the foundation for any successful company, and this is perhaps my greatest worth to your organization. I provide a clear direction, build cooperative working relationships across diverse functional organizations, and create the processes that deliver action and results.

- **Identifying & capturing customer markets.** Through a comprehensive program of customer research, analysis, profiling and segmentation, I can readily identify target markets and customers. Using that data, I then create the products, business processes, sales and distribution channels to reach those customers and drive revenue growth.

- **Optimizing multi-channel distribution strategies**. My success in creating multi-channel programs is currently generating strong performance across many consumer categories. I know how to determine what channels are appropriate for each segment, how to penetrate those channels and how to integrate E-commerce to complement more traditional channels.

- **Leading corporate financial affairs**. As a CFO and in all of my executive management positions, I have planned, structured and managed critical finance functions, ranging from capital financing to cash flow management, budgeting and financial planning/analysis.

Currently, I am interested in a new and exciting executive opportunity where I can leverage my consumer industry, strategic planning, business development, leadership and financial expertise to foster profitable growth. I would be delighted to discuss such opportunities with you. Thank you.

Sincerely,

Jordan Jasper

MOHAD E. KASMER
121 Greengate Lodge Road
Arnold, MD 22837

Home: 410.893.8797
m.kasmer@prodigy.net

Office: 703.222.1100
Fax: 703.222.1112

March 23, 2001

Bill Elliott
Elliott Partners, Ltd.
222 Wisconsin Avenue, NW
Arlington, VA 22209

Dear Mr. Elliott:

As President and CEO of three technology ventures, I guided each company to achieve unprecedented financial results:

- Increased Meredith Technology Services' valuation tenfold in less than two years and structured/ negotiated the profitable sale of the corporation just two months ago.

- Built RSK Systems' revenues tenfold, grew E-Business portfolio of new products and services to 50% of total revenue, and increased company valuation 500%.

- Transitioned Lavender Technologies from product concept to market launch and successful $10 million private placement.

Just as significant is the breadth of my experience in mergers, acquisitions, divestitures, joint ventures, strategic alliances and other corporate development initiatives. In total, I have participated in more than 35 corporate transactions of this nature and been directly involved in raising over $300 million to fund growth, expansion and product development. Further, I have extensive experience throughout both US and international markets, including fluency in two foreign languages. This has afforded me a uniquely competitive advantage in managing international expansion and technology introductions.

My goal is an executive management position with a technology company poised for dramatic growth, either through internal development, reorganization, turnaround or acquisition. Aware of the quality of the companies in your portfolio, I would be delighted to meet with you to explore such opportunities and my potential contributions. Thank you.

Sincerely,

Mohad E. Kasmer

Enclosure

STAN SHERMAN
122 Murray Place
Dogwood, New York 11929
Email: stan.sherman@moon.com

Home (516) 823-1989   Office: (516) 866-9300 x192

January 11, 2001

Greg Billson
President
Advanced Technology Devices
One Technology Drive
Raleigh, NC 29808

Dear Mr. Billson:

I am currently employed as a Vice President with eCommerce Technologies, a high-growth vendor of Internet tools and interactive solutions. With the company for a little over two years now, I have been a driving force in eCommerce's tremendous growth with a better than eight-fold increase in revenues. My personal contributions have been notable and include:

- Recruiting the "right" people, putting the "right" internal technologies in place, correctly defining our customers' technology and solutions requirements, and building a top-performing Professional Services and Quality Assurance organization to support it all.
- Developing a solid infrastructure to optimize existing resources and control cost structures while supporting dramatic growth.
- Guiding the development, commercialization and market launch of state-of-the-art technologies.

One of the greatest values I bring to Advanced Technology Devices is my diversity of experience, from the small entrepreneurial environment of eCommerce to the large corporate structure of IBM. Regardless of the organization, I have repeatedly demonstrated my ability to drive forward sound business plans with the support of both top management and my business teams.

Following a recent acquisition of eCommerce, I am now confidentially exploring new professional challenges and opportunities. As such, I would welcome the chance to speak with you regarding Advanced Technology's current operations and need for strong, decisive and competent senior ledership.

To facilitate our discussion, I have enclosed my resume for your review and will follow up with you next week. Thank you in advance for your time and consideration.

Sincerely,

Stan Sherman

Enclosure

ANDREA CARGILL

222 Smith Mont Drive
Greentree, WA 98099

Phone: 630.989.6767
andreaca@atlantic.net

February 11, 2001

Jason Armstrong
MultiLink Technologies, Inc.
122 Mason Drive
Ames, IA 56767

Dear Mr. Armstrong

Interested in a candidate with years of experience building, managing and optimizing advanced technology companies and products? A candidate who has delivered more than $12 million in total cost savings while contributing to more than $100 million in new revenues?

That is precisely the experience I bring to your organization. As Vice President and Director, responsible for Operations, Production and Quality, I have been a key player in the development and delivery of innovative technologies throughout diverse B2B and B2C markets. Most significant is my strength in managing the entire process – from strategic planning for new business development through product design/engineering to the integration of labor, technologies and operations through to final customer delivery (and the continued management of that customer relationship).

My career has included both the development of new technologies as well as the redesign and performance optimization of existing technologies. In addition, I have managed huge migration projects, including one for Thomson in which we converted 60,000 customers in just three months.

Just as critical has been my success in process redesign, quality and performance improvement. To each and every organization, I have delivered measurable gains in operational efficiencies while reducing costs, optimizing performance, improving service delivery and strengthening bottom-line profitability.

Currently, as Vice President with TimberTech, I have built a fully-functional, online member community within just three months. With 6000 users to date, we are anticipating revenues of better than $2 million within our first year. However, I am confidentially exploring new executive management opportunities that will better suit my leadership style and my professional goals.

I would welcome a personal interview at your convenience and thank you in advance for your time.

Sincerely,

Andrea Cargill

Enclosure

WINSTON R. RALEIGH
winston.r.raleigh@msn.com
89 Graves Mill Court
Jonestown, FL 33909
813.985.8925

September 12, 2000

Drew Margate, EVP – Technology Development
Marvel.com
122 E. 95th Street, NW
Washington, DC 20036

Dear Mr. Margate:

Currently, as Vice President with Strident E-Technologies, I have built a new online member community that is achieving phenomenal success. Starting with a concept and a few great ideas, I created, tested and launched a new site in just 150 days with a staff of only eight. Three weeks and 6000+ members later, we were soaring. Our projections indicate growth to 20,000 members by year-end with a conservative 50% increase in 2001.

My team and I have orchestrated the entire operation, from content development and aggregation to production, world class quality initiatives, user acceptance and online member support. We've created a portfolio of innovative online promotions, consumer savings plans, sweepstakes and other marketing programs, and the entire fulfillment support organization. Currently, I am focusing on integrating what we have created with the company's core operations. It has been an exciting opportunity.

Just as valuable and intense was my experience with The Ryerson Corporation. I progressed from Product Manager responsible for the corporation's largest product line to Quality Manager spearheading an entire quality management organization. In my final position as Vice President, I rebuilt an entire organization with 800+ informational products (CD-ROM, print and online) and delivered cost savings of more than $7 million.

I thrive in a challenging, fast-paced organization where the goal is to create, deliver and retain the customer relationship. My communication, negotiation, problem-solving and project management skills are solid. Further, I am an outstanding team leader, able to build consensus across diverse organizations.

Currently, I am confidentially exploring new executive management opportunities and would welcome a personal interview for the position of Vice President of Operations. I am confident that the strength of my experience, track record of performance, and knowledge of the information-based online market will add measurable value to your organization.

Thank you.

Sincerely,

Winston R. Raleigh

Enclosure

RON QUINCY
2442 Evergreen Way
Minot, South Dakota 56244
raq@worldnet.att.net

Phone: 581.233.7867

Fax: 581.233.6658

November 21, 2000

KPMG Recruiting Center
8200 Brookriver Drive, Suite 400
Dallas, TX 75247

RE: **KNOWLEDGE MANAGEMENT- DIRECTOR (Code 2298700)**

Dear Hiring Manager:

I would like to submit my credentials for the above-referenced position:

- **Nineteen-year career** in Corporate Intelligence, Knowledge Management and Information Protection (with recent experience in the protection of Corporate Internet Intelligence).

- Built and currently manage a highly-successful **"knowledge/intelligence" consulting practice** with major corporate clients throughout the US and Far East.

- Solid experience across a **broad range of consulting specializations** including strategy development, organization and redesign, performance improvement and e-commerce.

- Expert qualifications in **client relationship development**, management and retention. Skilled negotiator with excellent public speaking, communication and team leadership skills.

- Extensive experience leading project teams in the design, development and delivery of advanced technologies (e.g., **information systems, Internet intelligence and security, systems architecture, data warehousing/data mining, AI, DSS**).

- **Well-respected in the industry**. Featured on NBC Dateline, quoted in Larry Kahner's *Competitive Intelligence* and honored by Society of Competitive Intelligence Professionals.

I would welcome the opportunity to interview for the above-referenced position and can guarantee you that the sum of my experience meets, and often exceeds, your qualifications. I look forward to our first interview, and thank you in advance for your time and consideration.

Sincerely,

Ron Quincy

Enclosure

215

4

Special Letters That Make
a Difference

THIS CHAPTER IS DEVOTED TO THREE TYPES OF JOB SEARCH letters:

- Venture Capital Letters
- Networking Letters
- Interview Follow-Up Letters

These letters are differentiated from all of the other sample letters in this book because they are not what one would consider a "traditional" cover letter. They are either written to a unique audience (such as venture capital firms) or for a unique reason (other than as a strategy to get in the door for an interview). As such, the key points of each of these three letters need to be clearly defined so that you will understand:

- When to use these letters
- How to use these letters
- The messages that each of these letters must communicate
- The true purpose of each of these letters
- The unique features of each of these letters

As we move through this chapter, you'll first find an introductory page to each type of letter that defines the information above. Following are several samples of

216

each that you can use to get ideas regarding content, format, and presentation of these letters. Let the samples serve as the foundation when you begin to write your own networking, venture capital, and follow-up letters.

Venture Capital Letters

Purpose: When writing letters to venture capital firms for employment either with the VC group or with one of their portfolio companies, your #1 objective is a contact (phone or email) from the firm in anticipation of an interview. Therefore, just as in a "traditional" cover letter, you must emphasize your notable career achievements, project highlights, financial expertise and experience in dealmaking (e.g., joint ventures, mergers, acquisitions, financings, partnerships). Be sure that you don't just highlight anything from your career, but focus on the skills, qualifications, and accomplishments that are most related to those that would be needed by a venture capital group. It is generally recommended that only senior-level professionals apply directly to VC groups. The firm itself hires the top management of their investment holdings. All others are hired directly by a particular company owned by the group. Therefore, those letters should be written to the companies and not to the VC firm.

Tone: The tone of the letter should be upscale and distinctive, written for a high-level audience of well-qualified, senior-level investment and management professionals. It is not a casual note. Rather, it should be written in a formal tone (assuming that you do not personally know the individuals to whom you are writing).

Unique Features:

- ALWAYS communicate success, achievement and performance.

- ALWAYS communicate that you are a senior-level professional or executive.

- ALWAYS communicate the value (knowledge and experience) you bring to the firm.

- ALWAYS "drop" names that you think may be of value in getting you in the door for an interview.

- ALWAYS communicate any information you may have about the VC firm, its portfolio of holdings and the portfolio's performance to demonstrate your knowledge of the organization.

- ALWAYS communicate your knowledge that is relevant to their products, services and/or technologies.

- ALWAYS ask for an interview.

- NEVER discuss compensation unless it has been asked for.

ROBERT T. ROUNDTREE
192 Leaf Road
Mapletown, NY 13378
Home: (315) 289-7388   Email: rtr33@aol.com   Work: (315) 788-0500

May 25, 2001

Arnold Baxter
Managing Director
Baxter Partner Ventures, LLC
1800 Sand Hill Drive, Suite 222
Menlo Park, CA 98277

Dear Mr. Baxter:

Recruited to Maxim Technology Corporation in 1979, I am one of the five senior executives responsible for the dramatic growth of the company, from a $7 million privately-held government contractor into a $100+ million NYSE high tech systems organization with operating subsidiaries worldwide. My contributions have been diverse with an intense focus on mergers, acquisitions, divestitures, joint ventures, technology partnerships and other strategic corporate development initiatives.

Highlights of my career that may be of particular interest to you include the following:

*   Structuring, negotiating and transacting over 10 M&A transactions to acquire the technology, talent and organizational infrastructure to support PAR's dramatic growth and expansion.

*   Leading the company's 1998 IPO and its subsequent secondary offerings as well as its transition from NASDAQ to the NYSE as growth continued at an unprecedented rate.

*   Negotiating complex, multi-million dollar technology sales and partnership agreements with major systems and software companies nationwide (including Microsoft, Hughes, IBM and Unisys). Personally credited with negotiating over $50 million in agreements.

*   Creating and managing a high-profile investor relations and corporate communications initiative targeted to rating agencies, major media and shareholders nationwide.

Currently, I am seeking the opportunity to transition my experience into either an M&A or venture capital firm where I can continue to plan, strategize, negotiate and execute favorable transactions. Thus my interest in meeting with you to explore such opportunities with your organization. Thank you.

Sincerely,

Robert T. Roundtree

DUANE R. MASTERS

787 Clearwater Drive   Home: 561-298-3855
Miami, FL 33898   Cell: 444-989-1090

December 1, 2000

Nancy Dollins
Executive Managing Director
Dollins New Ventures, LLC
22 Madison Avenue, Suite 1202
New York, NY 10094

Dear Ms. Dollins:

My greatest professional successes have focused on my ability to increase the value of corporate assets and holdings. In my current position, my contributions have resulted in:

- 20% growth in corporate assets and valuation.
- 30% ROI on all new venture projects.
- 50% increase in website traffic and e-commerce revenues.

This has been accomplished through my combined expertise in new business development, strategic planning for growth, acquisition negotiation/management and new venture start-up. I am particularly effective in evaluating proposed opportunities to evaluate their financial potential and their "fit" within the existing corporate asset portfolio.

Equally notable is my strong corporate legal experience. Prior to joining my current employer, I worked for a prestigious law firm in New York City. During my 11-year tenure with the firm, I:

- Structured and negotiated $400 million in corporate legal, financial, acquisition and asset-based transactions for clients across more than 15 industries.
- Launched the firm's first-ever business/client development effort with unprecedented success.
- Demonstrated top-flight negotiation skills in challenging and complex business relationships.

Currently, I am confidentially exploring new professional opportunities within the venture capital community where I believe the combination of my legal, business development, e-commerce and general management expertise is of greatest value. Aware of the quality of your investments and the strength of your leadership team, I would welcome the opportunity for a personal interview. Thank you.

Sincerely,

Duane R. Masters

Enclosure

ERIC GRACESON
ericgraceson@msn.com

424 E. Cathcart Lane
Lansing, MI 48978

Home: 412.344-7823
Office: 412.677-9808

August 12, 2000

Lane Carson, Chief Executive Officer
Carson Investments, Inc.
892 Lansing Mountain Drive
Lansing, MI 48766

Dear Mr. Carson:

I am writing and forwarding my resume in anticipation that you may be "in the market" for a well-qualified President, CEO and Senior Operating Executive. Highlights of my professional career that may be of particular interest to you include:

- Built new venture from start-up into a 300-employee corporation distributing $4+ billion in customer products annually.
- Delivered annual growth averaging 35% with 35% return on capital and 50% year-over-year return to shareholders.
- Invested $35+ million to build a best-in-class IT organization to support the corporation's dramatic growth and nationwide expansion.

Additional qualifications include:

- 10+ years of direct P&L and operating management responsibility.
- Outstanding performance in marketing, sales and new business development (with particular emphasis on major account relationships).
- Equal strong operating and financial performance in turnarounds and revitalizations.

My experience lies principally in the product, service and distribution industries, and clearly demonstrates my ability to deliver strong financial results across diverse customer markets. I thrive in challenging, fast-paced and results-driven organizations where teams work cooperatively to achieve aggressive business goals. Aware of the quality of your portfolio, I am certain such an environment does exist.

I would welcome the opportunity to speak with you regarding your current and anticipated executive staffing needs, and can guarantee that the quality of my leadership and management performance will have a significantly positive impact on your operations. Thank you for your time and I'll forward a resume at your request.

Sincerely,

Eric Graceson

JAMES R. JEFFERSON

299 S. Seneca Street
Racine, Washington 98299

Phone: 530-887-3345   Email: jrj234@aol.com   Fax: 530-909-7766

March 22, 2001

Stan Davis, Managing Executive
Pinnacle Ventures, Inc.
90 Long Meadow Drive
Charlottesville, VA 22890

Dear Mr. Davis:

Let me present the following for your investment consideration:

- Existing joint venture opportunity in China for the development of a manufacturing operation to supply concrete throughout the entire country. Business plan, marketing plan and all financials are complete. Partners are in place and the project has begun preliminary phases. Current status requires additional financing (preferably from the US or Chinese investment community). Conservative projections indicate achieving annual sales of $350 million within first five years with long-term market potential at more than $1 billion.

Currently, I serve as Chairman of the Board of the US venture partner – Crane Transnational, Inc. My core responsibilities include full leadership of the entire joint venture project, direct negotiations with Chinese business partners and government officials, road show and investment presentations, and the entire business/operating development function. Upon investment, I plan to continue in my role as the senior executive responsible for the creation, growth and success of this venture.

A brief mention of my qualifications includes a 12-year management career with SEC Corporation, including nine years as President of core business divisions. My success in these positions focused primarily on operating turnarounds, market revitalizations, organizational development and worldwide sales/marketing. I was then recruited to Cranfield Machine, Inc. as President & CEO.

I would welcome the opportunity to meet with you to present the specifics of the Crane Transnational venture. Please let me know how you wish to proceed, what specific information you would be interested in reviewing, and when we can schedule an appointment. Thank you.

Sincerely,

Jim Jefferson

Enclosure

FELIX GRABOWSKI

212 Mountain Range Drive
Encino, California 94229

Home: (408) 776-6723   Email: grabow@pacbell.net   Fax: (408) 776-9062

August 15, 2000

Martin Moore
Moore Brothers Investments, Inc.
698 Carson Boulevard
Carson City, NV 89765

Dear Mr. Moore:

Delivering strong ROI, ROA, ROE and profit results is my expertise. Whether directing corporate finance for a high-growth corporation, turnaround business or start-up enterprise, I have consistently provided the strategic financial leadership critical to operating success.

Of particular interest to you will be my past four years as KPMG's Senior Manager to Aaron Corporation. In this capacity, I worked hand-in-hand with senior executives to execute dramatic changes in corporate tax and finance worldwide. My first initiative was to revitalize the organization, introduce profit- processes and create a culture that fostered shared decision making. Results were dramatic:

- 35% reduction in staff turnover (equivalent to a savings of more than $3 million annually).
- Implementation of $150,000 IT project projected to increase cash flow $2 million per year.
- Creation of a best practices organization with consistently solid financial returns.

Just as significant was my experience with Devine, Inc., an early stage technology company. My challenge was to create a sophisticated financial infrastructure to support the corporation's growth and expansion. And, I succeeded. Over a 3- year period, I developed, implemented and directed a world class finance, accounting and tax organization that provided the control and leadership critical to sustained profitability. What's more, through my efforts, I uncovered $1 million in misappropriated funds.

Please also note that I have broad-based industry experience including, but not limited to, technology, software, manufacturing, distribution, transportation, oil & gas and construction/real estate. These experiences clearly demonstrate my ability to transfer my skills from one industry to another.

I would be delighted to speak with you about such positions with one of your portfolio companies. I guarantee that the wealth of my financial expertise, combined with strong strategic, organizational and leadership skills, will add measurable value to your operations. I look forward to your call. Thank you.

Sincerely,

Felix Grabowski

Enclosure

MARTIN R. FELSON

92 Narrow Bridge Lane
Annandale, Virginia 22788
Phone: 703-429-8797   Email: m.r.felson@aol.com

November 3, 2000

Lex Kravitz
Kravitz Family Ventures, LLC
2 Alexander Street, Suite 122
Chicago, IL 60666-9032

Dear Mr. Kravitz:

You'll be interested in my qualifications if you are:

- Interested in penetrating in the Latin American investment market or expanding your presence.
- Looking to strengthen your expertise in the agricultural, forestry and/or high-technology markets.
- In need of a qualified executive with strong merger, acquisition and partnership experience.
- Seeking an individual with experience in investment finance, dealmaking and capital financing.

This is precisely the experience I bring to your firm.

- Throughout my professional career, I have worked extensively in both US and Latin American markets, most recently in a venture founded by Michael Rothschild. I am bicultural and bilingual (Spanish & English), allowing me to perform equally well on both continents.
- My investment and business management career expands from one end of the "industry" spectrum to another with 10+ years in high tech and 10+ years in agricultural, forestry and other commercial commodities.
- I have personally structured and negotiated more than 50 mergers, acquisitions, partnerships, alliances, distributorships, reseller agreements and other corporate transactions.
- For the past four years, I have worked as a Senior Executive with OPIC and more recently, with a private equity investment firm. Through these experiences, I have sharpened my experience in financing, portfolio management, market and commodity analysis, and risk management.

Currently, I am exploring new professional opportunities and would welcome a personal interview at your earliest convenience. Thank you.

Sincerely,

Martin R. Felson

Enclosure

Networking Letters

Purpose: When writing letters to your network of contacts, you want to encourage them to initiate action on your behalf, either by giving you contact names of prospective employers or making a personal introduction on your behalf. It is critical when writing these letters that you make it clear you are asking for help, not a job. People are almost always willing to help, but they may not be quite as willing to give you a job.

Tone: The tone of the letter should be professional, yet casual, but will depend entirely on how well you know each individual to whom you write. When you're communicating with someone you've known well for the past 20 years, the style of the letter is easy and conversational. However, when you're writing to the president of a company you briefly met at a meeting several months ago and have never spoken with again, the letter should be more formal in tone and content.

Unique Features:

- ALWAYS ask for your contact's help and assistance.

- ALWAYS communicate the type(s) of positions you are seeking.

- ALWAYS communicate the specific industry(ies) that are of interest, if appropriate.

- ALWAYS ask for referrals, recommendations, and leads.

- ALWAYS include some personal information about yourself or your contact, family, activities, interesting projects, and the like.

- ALWAYS thank them and offer to do the same for them whenever they may be in need.

- NEVER write a traditional, formal cover letter that focuses on your overall career track and notable accomplishments, although you may certainly include a few select highlights.

- NEVER discuss compensation requirements or salary history.

- NEVER ask directly for a job.

RANDALL STOKES
288 Smithtown Road
Hartsford, CT 09809
Home: (203) 633-9098   Work: (203) 788-2200
Email: rstokes23@msn.com

January 24, 2001

John Wiley
233 Millston Way
Darby, CT 09022

Dear John:

After 19 years with RTC Technology, I have decided to resign my position and seek opportunities elsewhere. I will always look back with fond memories of the success we have achieved and the tremendous impact we have had upon technology markets, products and performance.

Let me take just a moment to familiarize you with some of the most notable accomplishments of the organization. As you may be aware, when I joined RTC the company was a specialty R&D contractor to the Federal Government with annual revenues of approximately $7 million. Through my efforts and those of the other four members of the executive team, we transitioned the company into what is now a $100+ million NYSE high tech systems company with operating subsidiaries worldwide.

My personal contributions have been twofold. As General Counsel, I am credited with creating the entire corporate legal, business affairs and risk management organization. During my employment, I structured and negotiated hundreds of mergers, acquisitions, divestitures, intellectual property agreements, joint ventures, technology sales agreements and more. Further, I created the corporation's investor relations function, designed the corporate communications program and personally managed external business relations.

As a General Manager, I held full P&L, operating and marketing responsibility for the $48 million Medical Systems Division. It was during this period that I launched several next generation technology products, created a global distribution organization, and delivered a 25% contribution to bottom-line profits.

Now that the time has come to move on, I am anxious to identify new executive opportunities where I can utilize the combination of my legal and general management skills to provide strong, decisive and actionable leadership to another technology venture. In anticipation that you may be aware of an organization seeking an individual with my skill set and track record of performance, I have taken the liberty of enclosing my resume.

Any assistance you can offer would be most appreciated. I thank you for this effort and those in the past. If there is ever anything I can do for you, please do not hesitate to contact me.

Sincerely,

Randall Stokes

MARTY LINKHORNE
martylink@mi.net

22 Mink Run Lane * Warrenton, MI 23567 * (H) 413-336-7899 * (W) 413-599-2000

September 23, 2000

Larry Mayerson
Adelphia Enterprises
123 Main Street, Suite 22
Dearborn, MI 56776

Dear Larry:

It's been a while since we've spoken and I apologize for not being more diligent in keeping in touch. But you know the routine … work, more work, wife, kids, house … the list goes on and on. My intentions are always good, it's just that time flies by these days!

And, of course, I'm now getting in touch because I could use your help. I've decided to leave Dell after five years and am interested in finding a new senior management opportunity with another high-tech company. Between my experience with IBM and now with Dell, I believe that technology is where I belong and where I'm of most value to an organization.

My years with both companies have been outstanding and given me tremendous opportunities, well beyond my early beginnings in engineering. In fact, I'm now managing a global supply chain development initiative as well as OEM operations worldwide for HP. Previously, I managed over $250 million in after market sales programs, directed over $45 million in new facilities development projects, and was a key driver in the company's successful and profitable E-Commerce launch.

To ensure that I'd be competitive in the market, I enrolled in graduate school in 1999 and will be receiving my MBA this June. With everything else in my life, school has been a tremendous commitment and a valuable learning experience. However, I'm delighted that it's over!

I would appreciate any recommendations, referrals or contacts you could provide to me that might get me in the "right" doors. I've enclosed a copy of my resume just to give you a bit more factual information about my background and will give you a call next week. Any suggestions you may have would be wonderful. Thank you. I owe you one!

Sincerely,

Marty Linkhorne

Enclosure

MILT LARSON
22 Elmhurst Lane
Wayne, MO 60990
(451) 897-3765

March 2, 2001

Drew Appleton
Miller-Dodge Brothers, Inc.
699 Watson Boulevard
Williamson, MO 60899

Dear Drew:

Life is great! Since taking advantage of an early retirement opportunity from the US Research Service, I've had time to spend with family and friends, thoroughly enjoyed my eldest daughter's wedding, and have actually been able to have a full conversation with my wife. I don't think that had happened since somewhere in the mid 1980's!

After years and years of an intense work schedule, unending deadlines, and complex financial and organizational transactions, I can now breathe again! I've also had the opportunity to reflect a bit on my career and those that contributed so significantly to my personal and professional success. Undoubtedly, you are one of those who, through your efforts, spurred my achievement and strengthened my performance.

Retirement is an "odd bird." Although I am enjoying myself, I miss the business relationships and intellectual challenges associated with ESOPs, privatizations and other sophisticated financial transactions. I also miss having the opportunity to mentor and develop other top-notch finance professionals, sharing my management expertise to complement their "technical" qualifications.

To meet that need and give back to those who have so freely given to me, I am now offering my services on a "project" or "consulting" basis to a select group of individuals and organizations. And, the best part, is that I do not expect any compensation, other than associated travel costs as applicable. I'm pleased to have the opportunity to contribute and am delighted to find myself in the most unique position of being able to do so.

I'll follow up within you in a week or two and hope you realize that this offer comes from my heart, and not my pocket! You know me, and you know that I operate at the highest level of professional and ethical standards. The best to you and your family. I'll talk to you soon.

Very truly yours,

Milt Larson

SAM DUDLEY
samdudley@aol.com

P.O. Box 229
Greenville, MA 02459

Phone: (508) 662-7867
Fax: (508) 662-7868

January 10, 2001

Kit Kramer
902 Mellon Road
Menson, MA 02876

Dear Kit:

I'm looking for a really unique professional opportunity and I need your help. Specifically, I'm interested in senior-level consulting and interim executive assignments, Board of Director appointments and, perhaps, another full-time President/CEO position. Most important, I am NOT looking for the "typical" job. What I want is a new challenge, a new project, a new venture, a turnaround or any one of a number of other opportunities where the focus is on building something new or reenergizing what already exists.

To refresh your memory just a bit, I've included a copy of my resume which highlights the strength of my experience in the manufacturing, distribution and aftermarket products industries. Let me also highlight a few key points of particular interest:

- As the President/CEO of R2C, I built a start-up venture from concept into a $220 million company with four locations, 50 employees and annual profit margins averaging 32%.

- Established a global distribution network with 150 domestic and 100 international partners. Total combined revenues from both distribution channels exceeded $150 million annually.

- Created a multi-site offshore manufacturing operation which reduced cost of goods by as much as 50% annually. In addition, led project team in developing and bringing to market 10 new product lines (over $75 million in combined revenues over 10 years).

Critical to my career has been my ability to build relationships – with customers, distributors, bankers, investors, business partners, employees and others. As trite as it may sound, I really am a "people person" with strong communication skills and a dynamic presentation style.

Now, after two years of golf, my handicap is the best it's ever been and I'm delighted! Unfortunately, I'm bored and miss the challenges I was so accustomed to in the past. The break has been revitalizing, but I'm now ready to move forward.

If you are aware of a company or consulting group that could benefit from my experience, I would welcome the contact information and your referral. I'll follow up with you in about a week or so to see if you have any recommendations. Thanks so much for your assistance and I'm happy to return the favor whenever you need it.

Sincerely,

Sam Dudley

Enclosure

ALEX ALLENTON
22 Roche Drive
Elmhurst, New Jersey 09877
Phone: 908-208-9080 / Fax: 908-208-9188

August 25, 2000

Ray Nelson
22 Heathcliff Lane
Rochester, NY 19008

Dear Ray:

When I reflect back on my career at J&J, it's hard to believe that I left more than eight years ago. Seems like only yesterday! Despite all the transition, what a great company it was and what a tremendous learning ground for so many of us.

As you're aware, I resigned my position with J&J to assume a VP of Finance position with a high-growth communications company. Our growth was phenomenal, building Thompson from $18 million in annual revenues to more than $120 million with 28 distinct operating companies/divisions. In fact, after just five years, I was promoted to the #1 finance position in the company's largest and most profitable operating division.

Then, in 1998, I was enticed to join an early-stage merchant banking group in need of strong financial and operating leadership. I thought this would be a tremendous opportunity and, in many ways, it has been. Over the past two years, I orchestrated a major acquisition and its complete reorganization and have recently launched the start-up of a new high-tech venture. Our long-term goal is an IPO; however, there have been so many changes within the investor group that I have begun to question their long-term commitment.

As such, I'm contacting a select group of my colleagues to inquire if you are aware of any executive opportunities for a candidate with my qualifications. I'm interested in a position that will combine my financial and operating expertise, and would consider a start-up venture, a rapid turnaround situation or a high-growth company. I need a new challenge!

I would appreciate any ideas, recommendations or referrals that you could offer and will, in the future, be delighted to do the same for you if the situation ever arises.

I've enclosed a copy of my resume and will follow up with you shortly to get your feedback. Thanks so much.

Sincerely,

Alex Allenton

Enclosure

STEVEN R. MADISON
87 Birchtree Road
Chicago, Illinois 60090-2290
(847) 312-9833

May 4, 2001

Dan Bitton
Vice President
Tokida Pharmaceutical
1 Tokida Drive, MS 229
Martinsville, IL 60822

Dear Mr. Bitton:

Bruce Williams, a long-time business associate and friend, recommended I contact you directly. I understand that Tokida is interested in bringing aboard a Senior Executive to manage East Coast sales, marketing and business development efforts. Bruce personally knows my sales background – with Phillips (where we worked together), Arnold Drug and Bristol – and thought that this would be a great opportunity for all of us.

Let me take just a moment to highlight a few of my most significant career achievements:

Sales Revenue & Profit Growth

Throughout my entire career, I have been directly responsible for the strategic planning, development and leadership of top-performing sales, marketing and business development organizations. Most notably, I:

- Built a new sales organization for Phillips from start-up to $70 million in annual sales, increased national account sales by 19%, established multiple product distribution channels and delivered annual profit margins of 25%+.

- Captured a 27% increase in sales for Bristol's key account division and won a National Sales & Marketing Award for creative concept/strategic development.

- Delivered record profits (27%) and maintained double digit profits for six consecutive years for DHL Worldwide Express. Instrumental in driving total company sales growth from $35 million to $200+ million over 10 years.

- Increased TeleTrac's net revenues by 38%, reclaimed market position and restored financial health.

Sales Recruitment, Training & Team Leadership
One of my greatest challenges has been to recruit, train, develop and manage teams of top-sales producers (ranging in size from 11 to 89). And I have excelled:

- Built two of Phillip's most successful sales teams that delivered 20%+ growth and double digit profits within an intensely competitive market.

- Conceived, developed and launched a national employee recognition program that increased sales productivity 18% and sales efficiencies 14%.

Market Knowledge
I know the East Coast market and have extensive contacts with top-level executives at major corporations throughout virtually every industry, including pharmaceutical, biomedical and other core health care markets.

- Throughout my career, I have managed and closed sales with more than 100 pharmaceutical and health care companies and institutions throughout the US, with particular concentrations in the East Coast and Midwest US markets. Most critical, my contacts are with top-level decision makers and their direct reporting staffs.

Strategic Planning & Organizational Leadership
As you'll note on my enclosed resume, not only am I a well-qualified sales executive, I have substantial management experience. As such, I bring to Tokida a strong set of executive leadership skills that are valuable in virtually any circumstance.

- Most related to your needs are my strengths in strategic planning – evaluating the opportunities, defining the vision, creating the roadmap and leading the field team. Equally important, is my performance in building and managing strong organizations. Without a strong infrastructure and well-qualified staff, no organization can succeed. My ability to build, develop and win support has been critical to the financial success of each company for whom I have worked.

I would welcome the chance to meet with you. Bruce excited me about the potential with Tokida, your plans for an IPO and your strong leadership team. And that's precisely the type of opportunity I'm interested in – a company positioned for solid growth in the US market. Thank you for your time and your consideration. I look forward to speaking with you.

Sincerely,

Steven R. Madison

Enclosure

LOUIS BILTMAN

22 Montague Road   (237) 847-2897
Alamo, AZ 87507   bilt222@earthlink.net

_____

September 22, 2000

John Davies
89 Lexington Avenue
Marshall, TX 78998

Dear John:

It's been some time since we've spoken, and I hope you do not think it too presumptuous, but I wanted to update you on the latest opportunity my career has presented to me.

Most of my friends and colleagues know me as "Lou, the HR Guy." And, indeed, that is who I was for years and years. It was a tremendously rewarding career path that I now look back on with pride and self-satisfaction. But, at this point in my life, I was ready for new challenges and new opportunities. However, I still wanted to keep my hands in the "HR pot." It's what I do best.

Then, the perfect opportunity presented itself – an opportunity allowing me to leverage my past HR experience in a new direction – executive recruitment. So, now, I'm "Lou, the Executive Recruiter," specializing in the recruitment, selection and placement of senior-level executives for emerging technology companies.

Having made this transition only within the past few weeks, I am just beginning to launch my recruiting efforts and am really excited about the potential. Having worked closely with recruiters throughout my career (from the HR "side of the table"), I completely understand the dynamics of this unique relationship. What's more, I know and appreciate the needs and expectations of my clients' companies.

I hope that if, in the future, you have any executive staffing requirements, you will consider contacting me and letting me work with you to find the "perfect" candidate.

Thanks for your attention and your support. I'll follow up within the next few weeks, if you don't mind.

Your colleague,

Lou Biltman

TONY MILLER

tmiller@nextel.net
233 Alexandria Way
Alexandria, VA 22209-9088
(703) 899-6735

February 2, 2001

Tonya Masterson
Director
Masterson Recruiters, Inc.
299 Valley Boulevard
Silver Spring, MD 20901

Dear Tonya:

I wanted to drop you a quick note to let you know that I've accepted a new opportunity and to thank you for the assistance and support you've offered throughout my career.

On January 1, I joined Atlantis Consulting, a retained search firm specializing in the placement of senior executive talents for the .com industry. This is a new direction for me and I'm really excited about the potential. Plus, with more than 15 years' senior-level corporate experience, I have a unique perspective of the needs and expectations of my clients.

Most important, I want to let you know that if you are ever engaged in a search for a senior-level corporate HR executive, I would still welcome your consideration. I have accepted the position with Atlantis to broaden my perspective and to learn, but my heart and soul belong in corporate HR.

I've enclosed a copy of my resume just to be sure you've got an updated version.

Again, thank you for everything. I hope to hear from you when just the "perfect" opportunity comes across your desk.

Sincerely,

Tony Miller

Enclosure

Interview Follow-Up Letters

Purpose: When writing interview follow-up letters, you obviously want to thank the individual who interviewed you for his/her time and the opportunity. *More importantly*, you want to use your interview follow-up letter as a marketing tool to further highlight the skills, experiences, qualifications, and successes of your career that are directly in line with their needs. Now that you've had an interview with the company, you will be much clearer as to their needs and expectations. You can also use your follow-up letters to respond to, and overcome, any potential concerns about your employment that were addressed during the interview. These types of letters are often referred to as "tier-two follow-up letters."

Tone: The tone of the letter should be professional, yet friendly, as you have already had the opportunity to meet and communicate with the individual to whom you are writing. Remember, it is not a "cold-call" letter; it is a follow-up. Be decisive and straightforward in communicating the value you would bring to the organization, its mission, and its bottom line.

Unique Features:

- ALWAYS begin by thanking the interviewer for the opportunity.

- ALWAYS remember that you are writing a marketing letter, so be sure to highlight information that is directly relevant to their needs.

- ALWAYS respond favorably to any objections that may have been raised during the interview.

- ALWAYS communicate energy, interest, and enthusiasm about the position.

- ALWAYS ask how to proceed, what the next step is, and when you should expect to hear from them again.

- ALWAYS ask for the job.

- NEVER just write a letter that says "Thanks for the interview." Instead, write "Thanks for the interview and this is why I'm so great and so right for your organization."

- NEVER discuss compensation requirements or salary history unless requested to do so.

BOYD CARY
10293 Cedar Street
New Orlean, Louisiana 78874
(661) 654-8723

September 12, 2000

Charles Taylor, President
PYD Technologies
120 Robert Trent Avenue
Columbia, SC 27104

Dear Charles:

First of all, thank you. I really enjoyed our conversation the other day and am completely enamored with the tremendous success you have bought to PYD. There are but a handful of companies that have experienced such aggressive growth and can predict strong and sustained profitability over the years to come.

I would like to be a part of the PYD team — in whatever capacity you feel most appropriate and of most value. I realize, of course, that you already have an HR Director who has successfully managed the function throughout the course of the company's development. It is not my intention to compete with Leslie Smith, but rather to complement her efforts and bring new HR leadership to the organization.

Let me highlight what I consider to be my most valuable and substantiative assets:

I have met the challenges of accelerated recruitment:

- In 1993, I launched a recruitment initiative to replace 50% of the total workforce in a 900-person organization. This was accomplished within just six months and was the key driver in that organization's successful repositioning.

- In 1985, when hired as the first-ever HR executive for a growth organization, I created the entire recruitment, selection and placement function. Over the next two years, I hired more than 50 employees to staff all core operating departments.

- Between 1984 and 1986, I spearheaded the recruitment and selection of technical, professional and management personnel. This was a massive effort during which time I interviewed over 300 prospective candidates throughout the U.S. and Europe.

I have met the challenges of employee retention:

- During my employment with Helms Financial, we were staffing at an unprecedented rate. The faster an organization grows, the more critical the focus must become. Costs associated with recruitment can be significant and must be controlled. Following implementation of a market based research study, I was able to reduce Helm's turnover 35%, saving over $350,000 in annual costs.

238

I have met the challenges of international human resource leadership:

- Throughout my tenure with Laxton Data, I led the organization's International Employment & Employee Relations function. This was a tremendous experience during which time I developed strong qualifications in both domestic and expatriate recruitment, compensation, benefits administration and relocation. Further, I demonstrated my proficiency in cross-cultural communications and business management. I traveled extensively and am comfortable in diverse situations.

I have met the challenges of growth and organizational change through internal development and acquisition:

- Each of the organizations in which I have been employed have faced unique operating and leadership challenges. These situations have been diverse and included high-growth, turnaround and internal reorganization. Each has focused on improved performance and accelerated market/profit growth through development of its human resources and management competencies. To meet these challenges, I have created innovative, market-driven organizational structures integrating pioneering strategies in competency-based recruitment and performance.

- Most recently, I orchestrated the workforce integration of two acquisitions into core business operations. This required a comprehensive analysis of staffing requirements, evaluation of the skills and competencies of the acquired employees, and accurate placement throughout the organization. The integration was successful and all personnel are now fully acclimated and at peak performance.

I hope that the above information demonstrates the value I bring to PYD — today and in the future. You will also find that my abilities to lead and motivate are strong and have always been the foundation for my personal success.

I look forward to speaking with you and would welcome the opportunity to meet Mr. Williams. Again, thank you for your time and your interest. I wish you continued success in your efforts.

Sincerely,

Boyd Cary

QUINCY ANDERSON
946 Cedar Lane
Nashua, New Hampshire 14532
(619) 554-7512

September 14, 2000

Mr. Steven Wexler
President
Princeton Equity Services
190 Wabash Avenue, Suite 120
Chicago, IL 60661

Dear Steve:

Since leaving our meeting last Thursday, I have thought at great length about our discussion, the tremendous opportunity that appears to be present in the Chicago market, and the value I bring to the organization. As such, I would like to take a moment of your time to address several key points.

First and foremost, I am a "dealmaker" and marketer, able to identify and capture opportunities that have driven strong revenue and asset performance. I tackle each new project with a two-pronged focus: (1) negotiate the best possible transaction that, as trite as it may sound, truly is a "win-win" deal for all partners; and (2) create strategic and tactical marketing programs that consistently create value, dominance and earnings.

My efforts can easily be measured by gains in the value of real estate holdings and improved project cash flows. Full financial documentation can be disclosed (without conceding the confidentiality of Maxxen Properties). I have maximized the value of each asset under management and transitioned "average" properties into "top" performers.

You're right. I have never worked in the Chicago market. However, I have demonstrated my ability to build presence within other new markets nationwide (e.g., Atlanta, Southern California). Further, I have an extensive network of contacts across the country, many of whom are well connected in Chicago and will be of significant value in facilitating the start of my own regional network.

I have always been fortunate in that networking is a natural process for me. I am able to quickly ascertain who it is that I must establish a relationship with, identify the appropriate channels to do so, and quickly begin the process. In turn, despite often unfamiliar territories and personalities, I have quickly established myself in key markets nationwide. I am not daunted by challenge, but rather motivated to succeed and beat the odds.

I hope that you and I have the opportunity to continue our discussions and certainly appreciate the amount of time you spent with me last week. I guarantee that I can not only meet your expectations, but clearly exceed them.

Sincerely,

Quincy Anderson

Enclosure

MARSHALL BARBOUR
1298 Fletcher's Mill Lane
Kansas City, Missouri 60553
(564) 144-0433
marshall@mo.net

July 1, 2000

Solomon Ritchie
Telcox, Inc.
1209 Camino Real
San Diego, CA 93542

Dear Sol:

I've just returned from Mexico City earlier today and wanted to immediately get back in touch with you. I remain very interested and enthusiastic about the CFO position with Telcox, Inc., and believe that the strength of my experience in corporate finance, investor relations and administration will be of significant value to the organization. Knowing that the interest in this position by other well-qualified financial executives is significant, I guarantee that there is no other applicant that will provide the same caliber of decisive leadership.

The task that you face in creating a competitive mindset and culture within the organization is a daunting one. It is with this understanding that I appreciate your need to identify a candidate with extensive experience in corporate governance and financial engineering. In response to those needs, let me note that I have great confidence in my ability to work cooperatively with talented individuals, many with often "strong" personalities.

Further, in my current position, I am spearheading the development of strategic initiatives to drive shareholder value. This effort requires constant communications with the investment community to disseminate information regarding the process and components of our value creation model. Accordingly, I have developed a strong skill set in the intricacies of capital structure, treasury techniques and EVA principles. This, in tandem with my "hands-on" business experience, has allowed me to effectively market our theme throughout the Wall Street community.

I have been characterized by others as an innovator and change agent, constantly striving to enhance corporate value throughout all core business units. I have always been sought out as a sounding board by senior management, a fact that is evidenced by my rapid advancement within the IBM organization. It is this drive and initiative that I bring to Telcox, Inc..

In closing, I wish to thank you for your time, support and consideration. I believe that you and I will be able to build a strong partnership and deliver results critical to the company's long-term success.

I look forward to further discussions on this outstanding opportunity.

Very truly yours,

Marshall Barbour

WILLIAM HENDERSON
120 Port Street
Lakeside, Minnesota 55441
(312) 323-5487

July 12, 2000

Steven Donovan, President
Toshiba International
1209 Marietta Street
Los Angeles, CA 90045

Dear Steve:

Last month's unveiling of Toshiba's new corporate structure clearly indicates that the "dust is beginning to settle" and it's time to get "back to business." Not only do I appreciate your tremendous commitment of time and energy to this project, but also the enormous effort involved in restructuring a management team the caliber of which will lead Sony through its next stage of growth and technology excellence. Congratulations! It's been a lot of work from which I hope you feel both personal and professional satisfaction.

When we last spoke, you indicated there would be an opportunity for me with Toshiba and I'm still anticipating that position. In the interim, I have continued to move my search ahead and am at various interviewing stages with several corporations. Although several of these opportunities are exciting, none offer the potential that is clearly evident with Toshiba. As such, I need your help in clarifying the time frame of my opportunity with the organization.

Let's not reiterate the achievements of my past career. You already know. What I will share with you is what I have learned throughout my career ... that success lies in one's ability to merge the strategic with the tactical, to understand the markets, to know the competition and to build a strong management team. No one function can be accountable for performance. It is the integration of everything and the strength of the leadership team.

I thrive in challenging, high-energy and high-performance organizations, much like the "new" Toshiba. Further, I remain highly committed to the challenges and opportunities that await me with Toshiba Pictures Entertainment, and anxiously look forward to your call. Let me assure you that the strength of my leadership experience and track record of profitable performance within the technology industry will indeed be an asset to the new Toshiba management team.

Sincerely,

William Henderson

HAROLD WATSON
1200 Pearl Street
Jamaica, New York 11441
(516) 554-3321

September 26, 2000

Arthur Fordstone
Elmira Iron Works
12 Iron Drive
Elmira, NY 17909

Dear Arthur:

To follow-up from our phone conversation regarding your search for a Vice President of Human Resources, I'd like to first of all thank you for your interest in my candidacy. I enjoyed our conversation and believe there may be an excellent "fit" for my qualifications with your client's needs. I'd also like to take this opportunity to highlight a few relevant qualifications.

Organizational Development

- Recognized as a pioneer in organizational design, development and improvement, I have spearheaded innovative programs, plans and processes that have consistently improved productivity, efficiency, quality, cost containment and overall performance. I am a driver and a team builder, successful in rallying support to achieve financial and operating goals.
- Within XATAX, I have orchestrated and implemented a series of strategic organizational development initiatives including process mapping, benchmarking, TQM, and aggressive joint venture and partnership programs.

Training & Development

- The cornerstone of my career has been training and development. From 1980 through 1994, although charged with a diversity of HR functions, my principal focus was the design, development and delivery of training programs for technology, manufacturing, engineering and support personnel. My successes include programs that have been implemented widely throughout various corporations including Ameritech, Bell Laboratories and Siemens.
- Recently, I was the principal in the development of XATAX's first internal MBA program. Not only did I develop overall strategy and training objectives, I also authored a majority of the curriculum, designed instructional tools and actually taught various program components.

Staffing & Recruitment

- I actively participated in the recruitment, interviewing and selection of personnel for multilevel managerial, professional and support positions. As a result of team efforts, I have been fortunate to build a number of top-performing organizations recognized for excellence in personnel performance, technical competencies and leadership capabilities.
- During my three-year tenure with Green's German operations, I led the recruitment and staffing affairs to build an international training organization. This included selection of technical, managerial, instructional, administrative and support personnel.

Compensation & Benefits

- An integral member of management team, I was responsible for the design, development and administration of benefit programs and multilevel salary and compensation plans. Inherent in this responsibility are a portfolio of functions including market analysis, vendor review, price negotiations, plan design, employee communications and program administration.
- A recent project was the development of a comprehensive benefit and compensation strategy for the entire organization. Working in cooperation with a team of HR, administrative, finance and operating executives, we carved out a new strategy which, upon full implementation, will save XATAX significant dollars and provide all employees with improved benefit coverages.

Employee Relations, Health & Safety

- Building positive and proactive Employee Relations has been one of the most personally rewarding aspects of my career. In each organization, I have positioned myself as an ally to the workforce, maintaining an "open door" policy, driving consistent and positive advances in the cooperation between employees and management.
- Throughout my career at Fujitsu, Bell Laboratories and Siemens, I led the design and managed the "hands-on" implementation of a number of employee safety training programs. Each resulted in measurable decreases in employee accidents and workplace incidents.

HRIS Technologies

- For 14 years, I championed the design, development, documentation and delivery of leading-edge training systems technologies for my employers. Created programs which strengthened operating infrastructures, improved staff capabilities and facilitated significant improvements in productivity, quality, efficiency and bottom-line profitability.
- My experience includes a host of other PC applications designed for compensation and benefits administration, employee database management, labor forecasting, manpower analysis and other internal HR functions. Other technology skills are noted on my resume.

I trust that the above gives you a more detailed overview of my career and the value I bring to another organization. My goal is a senior-level HR management position that requires hands-on leadership of all employee affairs. I thank you for your time and consideration, and look forward to further pursuing this opportunity.

Sincerely,

Harold Watson

Enclosure

DAVID JOHNSON
1024 Miller Park Avenue
Baltimore, Maryland 22110

Home (410) 757-7981

Email d.j.24@aol.com

July 9, 2000

Fortunat F. Mueller-Maerki
Egon Zehnder International
55 East 59th Street
New York, NY 10022

Dear Mr. Mueller-Maerki:

Thank you for this opportunity with Abrams Corporation. Since our first interview, and in anticipation of our second meeting on July 30, I have given considerable thought to the position, the expectations of the European parent company and the challenges inherent in the assignment. To that end, I would like to bring several key points to the forefront.

- I am accustomed to change and growth, a critical factor as outlined in the job description for this position. Most recently, during my tenure as President / CEO of Advantage Corporation, I led the organization through tremendous transition with annual growth of more than 24%.

- My expertise in sales, marketing, new business development and key account management has been a critical foundation for the profitable growth of both Advantage and General Corp. For each, I spearheaded the design and delivery of customer development and management programs that consistently accelerated growth and improved financial performance.

- With 11 years' experience in the plastics industry, I know the market, the players and the competition. This will provide Abrams with a tremendous competitive advantage throughout the Americas market.

On a more personal note, I have been characterized as a decisive business leader, able to envision, energize and deliver results. I look forward to meeting with you at the end of the month and would be delighted to provide any additional information. Thank you.

Sincerely,

David Johnson

Appendix

Job Search, Career Management, Coaching, Counseling, Cover Letter, & Other Career Resources

Following is a list of the professional members of the Career Masters Institute, a prestigious professional association whose members work with job seekers worldwide to help them plan and manage successful search campaigns. You will note that these individuals have earned a number of certifications and credentials. For your reference, the most common are referenced below:

CAC – Certified Accredited Consultant
CBC – Certified Behavioral Consultant
CCM – Credentialed Career Master
CEIP – Certified Employment Interview Professional
CHRE – Certified Human Resources Executive
CIPC – Certified International Personnel Consultant
CPC – Certified Personnel Consultant
CPRW – Certified Professional Resume Writer
IJCTC or JCTC – International Job & Career Transition Coach
LPC – Licensed Professional Counselor
NBCC – National Board Certified Counselor
NCC – National Certified Counselor
NCCC – National Certified Career Counselor
NCRW – National Certified Resume Writer
PCC – Professional Certified Coach

ALABAMA

Don Orlando, MBA, CPRW, JCTC, CCM
The McLean Group
640 South McDonough Street
Montgomery, AL 36104
334-264-2020
yourcareercoach@aol.com

Neal Parker
R.L. Stevens & Associates, Inc.
103 Aragorn Circle
Daphne, AL 36526
334-626-8235
nparker@rlstevens.com

Teresa Pearson, CPRW, JCTC
Pearson's Resume Output
16 Castle Way
Rucker, AL 36362
334-503-4314
pearsonresume@snowhill.com

ALASKA

Ann Flister, CPRW
Best Impression
360 E. International Airport Road, #6
Anchorage, AK 99518
907-561-9311
aflister@customcpu.com

ARIZONA

Kathryn Baker
American Career Executives
2400 E. Arizona Biltmore Circle, #2250
Phoenix, AZ 85016
602-381-1667
lbaugh@amcareer.com

Kathryn Bourne, CPRW, JCTC
CareerConnections
5210 E. Pima Street, Suite 200
Tucson, AZ 85712
520-323-2964
Ccmentor@aol.com
www.BestFitResumes.com

Patricia Cash, CPRW
Resumes For Results
PO Box 2806
Prescott, AZ 86302
520-778-1578
patticash@hotmail.com

Fred Coon
Arizona Career Marketing Group
14451 South 8th Street
Phoenix, AZ 85048-4440
480-283-6234
azcmg1@home.com
www.azcareermarketing.com

ARKANSAS

Stephanie Meehan
EdiType Business Services
623 W. Dickson Street
Fayetteville, AR 72701
501-442-9037
editype@dicksonstreet.com

Wanda McLaughlin, CPRW
Execuwrite
314 N. Los Feliz Drive
Chandler, AZ 85226
480-732-7966
wanda@execu-write.com
www.execuwrite.com

CALIFORNIA

Georgia Adamson CPRW, JCTC, CCM
Adept Business Services
180 W. Rincon Avenue
Campbell, CA 95008-2824
408-866-6859
georgiaa@bignet.net
www.ADynamicResume.com

Deborah Bates, MA, RPCC
JOB ONE
2545 Main Street
Susanville, CA 96130
530-257-2568
deborah@snowcrest.net

Julia Bauer, JCTC
eCoach2000
351 Staysail Court
Foster City, CA 94404
650-286-1460
julia@eCoach2000.com
www.eCoach2000.com

Kent Black
Kent Black & Associates
21 Lodge Lane
San Rafael, CA 94901
(800) 588-4145
kbconsult@aol.com

Randy Block, JCTC
Block & Associates
PO Box 5357
Larkspur, CA 94977
415-383-6471
randsrch@aol.com

Nita Busby, CPRW, CAC
Resumes, Etc.
438 E. Katella, Suite F
Orange, CA 92867
714-633-2783
resumes100@aol.com
www.resumesetc.net

Susan Luff Chritton
Pathways/Right Management Consultants
3227 Sweet Drive
Lafayette, CA 94549
510-283-8578
slc4pways@aol.com

Nancy Davis
Grossmont College
8800 Grossmont College Drive
El Cajun, CA 92020
619-644-7615
nancy.davis@gcccd.net

Christine Edick, CPRW, JCTC
Action Resumes
307 E. Chapman Avenue
Orange, CA 92866
714-639-0942
christine@actionresumes.com
actionresumes.com

Lynn Eischen CPRW
Eischen's Professional Resume Service
3258 W. Spruce
Fresno, CA 93711
(559) 435-3538
4resume@csufresno.edu
http://cvip.fresno.com/~ce082

Roleta Fowler Vasquez, CPRW
Wordbusters Word Processing, Resume & Writing Srvcs.
433 Quail Court, Fillmore, CA 93105
(805) 524-3493
resumes@jetlink.net
www.wbresumes.com

Darrell Gurney, CPC
Hunter Arts Publishing
12658 Washington Blvd., #104
Los Angeles, CA 90066
310-821-6303
publisher@hunterarts.com
www.hunterarts.com

Leatha Jones
Write Connection Career Services
PO Box 351, Vallejo
CA 94590
707-649-1400
Leatha@writeconnection.net
www.writeconnection.net

Shannon Jordan
Career Directions/UC San Diego
6925 Lusk Boulevard
San Diego, CA 92121
858-882-8014
shannonA@ucsd.edu
www.extension.ucsd.edu/careers

Nancy Karvonen, CPRW, IJCTC, CCM
A Better Word & Resume
771 Adare Way
Galt, CA 95632
209-744-8203
careers@aresumecoach.com
www.aresumecoach.com

Cindy King
King Business Services
505 West Olive Avenue, Suite 635
Sunnyvale, CA 94086
408-733-5163
ck@kingbservices.com

Dick Knowdell, NCCC, CCMF
Career Planning & Adult Dev Network
4965 Sierra Road
San Jose, CA 95132
408-441-9100
knowdell@best.com

Myriam-Rose Kohn, CPRW, JCTC, CCM
JEDA Enterprises
27201 Tourney Road, Suite 201
Valencia, CA 91355
661-253-0801
myriam-rose@jedaenterprises.com
www.jedaenterprises.com

Denise Larkin
ResumeRighter.com
1027 Clarendon Crescent
Oakland, CA 94610
510-834-9355
denise@resumerighter.com
www.resumerighter.com

Jenny Loveland
Rural Human Services, Inc.
286 "M" Street, Suite "A"
Crescent City, CA 95531
707-464-7441
jloveland@ncen.org

Laura Lyon
Executive Image Resumes
1185 Sandstone Lane
San Jose, CA 95132
408-926-2232
Laura@MyExecutiveImage.com
www.MyExecutiveImage.com

Carole Martin
The Interview Coach
1609 Fountain Springs Circle
Danville, CA 94526
925-933-6208
carole@interviewcoach.com

Dianne Millsap, JCTC
Executive Resume
3841 Carnegie Drive
Oceanside, CA 92056
888-344-7378
Di4Resume@aol.com
www.Di4Resume.com

Phil Mostovoy
Rural Human Services, Inc.
286 "M" Street, Suite "A"
Crescent City, CA 95531
707-464-7441
pmostovoy@ncen.org

Alicia Naiman
CareerProShop.com
4532 Olivegate Drive
Fair Oaks, CA 95628
916-966-5520
careerproinfo@onebox.com
www.CareerProShop.com

Ken Naas
Within Reach!
1060 Adlar Court
Chico, CA 95926
(530) 893-0867
withinreachkn@hotmail.com

Gloria Nelson, CPRW
Resume Works - EASS
333 N. Palm Canyon, Suite 208
Palm Springs, CA 92262
760-322-3465
gjnelson@eass.com
www.eass.com

Anita Radosevic,h CPRW, JCTC
Anita's Business & Career Services
315 W. Pine Street, Suite #5
Lodi, CA 95240
209-368-4444
abcservice@lodinet.com
www.abcresumes.com (in process)

Cricket Rubino
Claremont Executive Services
830 Claremont Drive
Morgan Hill, CA 95037
408-778-7211
crubino@ix.netcom.com
www.claremontservices.com

Walter Schuette, CPRW, JCTC, CEIP
Schuette & Associates, Inc.
931 South Mission Road, Suite B
Fallbrook, CA 92028
800-200-1884
tvwresume@aol.com
www.thevillagewordsmith.com

Katherine Simmons
NETSHARE.com
2 Commercial Boulevard, #200
Novato, CA 94949
415-883-1700
kathy@netshare.com
www.netshare.com

Makini Siwatu, CPRW, JCTC
Accent on Words
405 El Camino Real, #631
Menlo Park, CA 94025-5240
650-323-6823
accentwrds@aol.com

Rebecca Smith, JCTC
Rebecca Smith's eResumes & Resources
40087 Mission Blvd., Suite 306
Fremont, CA 94539
510-623-0768
rsmith@eresumes.com

Gina Snyder
RICS Associates
131 El Camino Real
Vallejo, CA 94590
707-643-8937
ginas@concentric.net

Sheryl Steinruck
Rural Human Services, Inc.
286 "M" Street, Suite "A"
Crescent City, CA 95531
707-464-7441
ssteinruck@ncen.org

Pauline Thaler, CPRW
Best Foot Forward
1218 Carlotta Avenue
Berkeley, CA 94707
510-528-5563
thaler@teleport.com

Dennis Turner
Rural Human Services, Inc.
286 "M Street, Suite "A"
Crescent City, CA 95531
707-464-7441
daturner@ncen.org

Vivian Van Lier, CPRW, JCTC
Advantage Resume & Career Services
6701 Murietta Avenue
Valley Glen, CA 91405
818-994-6655
vvanlier@aol.com

Susan Whitcomb, NCRW, CPRW
Alpha Omega Career Services
757 East Hampton Way
Fresno, CA 93704
559-2227474
susan@careerwriter.com
www.careerwriter.com

Barbara Woods
Rural Human Services, Inc.
286 "M" Street, Suite "A"
Crescent City, CA 95531
707-464-7441
bwoods@ncen.org

COLORADO

Kathy Black, MBA, JCTC
Career Recipes
1960 Denver West Drive, #611
Golden, CO 80401
303-679-1519
kathyjane@careerrecipes.com
www.careerrecipes.com

Nancy Valentine, JCTC
New Career Strategies
2404 Sheffield Circle, East
Fort Collins, CO 80526
970-472-8288
nancy@careerdesign.com

CONNECTICUT

Nancy Collamer
Jobsandmoms.com
29 Hassake Road
Old Greenwich, CT 06870
203-698-3160
ncollamer@aol.com
www.jobsandmoms.com

Catherine Eckert, CPRW
Creative Office Services
24 Timber Lane, PO Box 573
Windsor, CT 06095
860-688-6970
CCECPRW@aol.com

Elie Klachkin, MS, JCTC
Impex Services, Inc.
89 Tunxis Hill Road
Fairfield, CT 06432
203-335-5627
elie@resuMMe.com
www.resuMMe.com

Jan Melnik, CPRW
Absolute Advantage
PO Box 718
Durham, CT 06422
860-349-0256
CompSPJan@aol.com
www.janmelnik.com

Debra O'Reilly, CPRW, JCTC
ResumeWriter.com
16 Terryville Avenue
Bristol, CT 06010
860-583-7500
debra@resumewriter.com
www.resumewriter.com

DISTRICT OF COLUMBIA (WASHINGTON, DC)

Jay Gloede, JCTC
Environmental Protection Agency
401 M Street SW
Washington, DC 20460
202-260-5086
gloede.jay@epa.gov

FLORIDA

Anita Babcock, JCTC
B.O.S.S. Resumes & Career Focus Center
9500 Koger Blvd. N., Suite 222
St. Petersburg, FL 33702
727-577-1737
BOSS1FL@aol.com

Marva Creary
Business Operation Support Services
11985 N.W. 12 Street
Pembroke Pines, FL 33026
954-435-8492
marvelous@skybiz.com

Laura DeCarlo, CCM, CPRW, JCTC
A Competitive Edge Career Service
1665 Clover Circle
Melbourne, FL 32935
800-715-3442
getanedge@aol.com
www.acompetiveedge.com

Cathy Fahrman, CPRW
Heider's Resume Center
10014 North Dale Mabry Highway, #101
Tampa, FL 33618
813-262-0011
hssheider@aol.com
http://broswer.to/heidersresumecent

Art Frank, MBA
Resumes "R" Us
334 Eastlake Drive, Suite 200
Palm Harbor, FL 34685
727-787-6885
AF1134@aol.com

Gail Frank, NCRW, JCTC, MA, CEIP
Frankly Speaking: Resumes That Work!
10409 Greendale Drive
Tampa, FL 33626
813-926-1353
gailfrank@post.harvard.edu
www.callfranklyspeaking.com

Susan Garrett
Visual Media Technologies, Inc.
16332 Gulf Boulevard
Redington Beach, FL 33708
727-399-9838
vmti1@tampabay.rr.com
www.yourdigitaledge.com

Wayne Gonyea
Gonyea Career Marketing, Inc.
1810 Arturus Lane
New Port Richey, FL 34655-4930
800-532-9733
online@resumexpress.com
http://resumexpress.com

Rene' Hart, CPRW
Resumes For Success!
5537 N. Socrum Loop Road, #116
Lakeland, FL 33809
863-859-2439
renehart@resumesforsuccess.com
www.ResumesForSuccess.com

Beverly Harvey, CPRW, JCTC, CCM
Beverly Harvey Resume & Career Srvc
P.O. Box 750
Pierson, FL 32180
904-749-3111
beverly@harveycareers.com
www.harveycareers.com

Jim Kitt
EmployMax.com
2907 West Bay Drive
Bellaire Bluffs, FL 33770
727-499-9444
JTKITT@employmax.com
www.employmax.com

Cindy Kraft, CPRW, JCTC, CCM
Executive Essentials
PO Box 336
Valrico, FL 33595
813-655-0658
careermaster@exec-essentials.com
www.exec-essentials.com

Lisa LeVerrier Stein, MA, MS, CPRW, JCTC
Competitive Advantage Resumes & Career Coaching
433 Plaza Real, Suite 275
Boca Raton, FL 33432
954-571-7236
gethired@earthlink.net
www.jobcoaching.com, www.legalresumes.com

Diane McGoldrick, CPRW, JCTC
Business Services
2803 W. Busch Blvd., #103
Tampa, FL 33618
813-935-2700
mcgoldrk@ix.netcom.com

Shelley Nachum
Career Development Services
4801 S. University Drive, Suite 201
Fort Lauderdale, FL 33328
866-737-7767
Shelley@ExpertResumes.com
www.expertresumes.com

Jim O'Hara
Recourse Communications
1655 Palm Beach Lakes Blvd., #600
West Palm Beach, FL 33401
561-686-6800
johara@rcimedia.com
BestJobsUSA.com

Vito Santoro
Visual Media Technologies, Inc.
1059 Kingsway Lane
Tarpon Springs, FL 34689
727-938-1690
vms@yourdigitaledge.com
www.yourdigitaledge.com

Myra Solomon, IJCTC
Career Edge
260 Crandon Boulevard, #32-113
Key Biscayne, FL 33149-1540
305-606-4358
ACareerEdge@aol.com

Jean West, CPRW, JCTC
Impact Resume & Career Services
207 10th Avenue
Indian Rocks, FL 33785
727-596-2534
Resumes@TampaBay.RR.com
www.ImpactResumes.com

Lea Ann Williams
Executive Maker.com
9013 Deercress Court
Jacksonville, FL 32256
904-519-8516
LeaAnnW@aol.com
www.executivemaker.com

GEORGIA

Julianne Franke
Career Development & Resume Center
4055 Highway 29, Suite 475
Lilburn, GA 30047
770-381-9407
jfranke836@aol.com

Gwen Harrison, CPRW, NCRW
Advanced Resumes & Career Strategies
384 Bullsboro Drive, #344
Newnan, GA 30263
877-353-0025
cmi@advancedresumes.com
www.advancedresumes.com

Don Skipper, M.S., M.M.A.S., CCM
R.L. Stevens & Associates, Inc.
PO Box 49491
Atlanta, GA 30359
770-399-5757
dskipper@rlstevens.com
www.interviewing.com

IOWA

Elizabeth Axnix, CCM, CPRW, IJCTC
Quality Word Processing
329 E. Court Street
Iowa City, IA 52240-4914
800-359-7822
axnix@earthlink.net

Marcy Johnson, CPRW, CEIP
First Impression Resume & Job Readiness
11805 US Hwy. 69
Story City, IA 50248
515-733-4998
firstimpression@storycity.net
www.resume-job-readiness.com

ILLINOIS

Ann Brody
Career Solutions
1145 Franklin Avenue
River Forest, IL 60305
708-771-6848
ABHighland@aol.com

Jeff Brown, J.D.
Jeffrey Grant Brown, P.C.
105 W. Adams Street, #3000
Chicago, IL 60603
312-789-9700
brownlaw@primenet.com
www.jbrownlaw.com

Jack Chapman
Lucrative Careers, Inc.
511 Maple Avenue
Wilmette, IL 60091
847-251-4727
jkchapman@aol.com
members.aol.com/payraises

Siegfried Heck
All Word Services
924 E. Old Willow Road, Suite 102
Prospect Heights, IL 60070
847-215-7517
siegfried@ameritech.net

Cathleen Hunt, CPRW
Write Works
6630 North Northwest Highway
Chicago, IL 60631
773-774-4420
cmhunt@attglobal.net

Sally McIntosh, NCRW, CPRW, JCTC
McIntosh resumes.com / Advantage Resumes
35 Westfair Drive
Jacksonville, IL 62650
217-245-0752
sallysjm@aol.com
www.reswriter.com / www.mcintoshresumes.com

Jeff Williams
Bizstarters.com, LLC
415 E. Golf Road, Suite 110
Arlington Heights, IL 60005
847-593-5305
cms@postal.interaccess.com
www.bizstarters.com

INDIANA

Deloris Duff, CPRW, IJCTC
Document Developers
5030 Guion Road
Indianapolis, IN 46254
317-297-4661
deesdocs@earthlink.net

Mary Ann Finch Vandivier
Resume Counselor.com
40 S. 4th Street
Zionsville, IN 46077
317-873-3189
resumewriter@resumecounselor.com
www.resumecounselor.com

Linda Wood
Roche Diagnostics
9115 Hague Road, Bldg. A
Indianapolis, IN 46250
317-576-4990
linda.wood@roche.com
www.roche.com

KANSAS

Kristie Cook, CPRW, JCTC
Absolutely Write
913 N. Sumac
Olathe, KS 66061
913-269-3519
kriscook@absolutely-write.com
www.absolutely-write.com

Jacqui Barrett Dodson, CPRW
Career Trend
7501 College Blvd., Suite 175
Overland Park, KS 66210
913-451-1313
dodson@careertrend.net
www.careertrend.net

Leslie Griffen
CSG Partners, Inc.
7101 College Boulevard, Suite 740
Overland Park, KS 66210-1891
913-469-6660
Lgriffen@csgpartners.com

Patricia Miller, CPRW, JCTC
P.S. Agency, Inc.
250 N. Rock Road, #300C
Wichita, KS 67206
316-686-6529
patmiller@feist.com

Rudolph Smith, Jr.
Career Success
8814 W. 64th Place, #206
Merriam, KS 66202
913-722-1994
thaisun@swbell.net
www.webnow.com/careersuccess

James Walker, M.S.
Resource Consultants, Inc.
2919 Northwood Drive
Milford, KS 66514
785-239-2278
answergrape@hotmail.com

KENTUCKY

Debbie Ellis, CPRW
Career Concepts
103 Patrick Henry Court
Danville, KY 40422
859-236-4001
info@resumeprofessional.com
www.resumeprofessional.com

Amy Whitmer
Envision Resume Services
PO Box 7523
Louisville, KY 40257
502-473-1780
amy@envision-resumes.com
www.envision-resumes.com

LOUISIANA

Laurie Roy, CPRW, IJCTC
Just Your Type, Inc.
1006 E. St. Mary Blvd.
Lafayette, LA 70503
800-225-8688
laurie@justyourtype.com
www.justyourtype.com

MAINE

Trudy Haines, CPRW
HainesService/LetterPerfect
647 Main Street
Lewiston, ME 04240
207-783-8973
HainesSue@aol.com

Rolande LaPointe, CPC, CIPC, CPRW, IJCTC, CCM
RO-LAN Associates, Inc.
725 Sabattus Street
Lewiston, ME 04240
207-784-1010
RLapointe@aol.com

MARYLAND

Wendy Adams, B.S., CC
LearnShare
1000 Scott Street
Baltimore, MD 21230
410-728-2060
learnshare@aol.com
www.LearningShare.com

Diane Burns, CPRW, IJCTC, CCM
Career Marketing Techniques
5219 Thunder Hill Road
Columbia, MD 21045
410-884-0213
dianecprw@aol.com
www.polishedresumes.com

Vincent DeSanti
Pinnacle Career Resources, Inc.
10632 Little Patuxent Parkway, Suite 300B
Columbia, MD 21044
410-740-4111
PinnCareer@aol.com

Lisa Dolce, JCTC
Pinnacle Career Resources, Inc.
10632 Little Patuxent Pkwy., Suite 300B
Columbia, MD 21044
410-740-4111
PinnCareer@aol.com

Sherry Kolbe, Certified Job & Career Coach
Resume Consultants
212 Washington Avenue
Towson, MD 21204
410-823-9568
resumeconsult@hotmail.com

Dottie Perlman, NCC, PCC
Insight Associates, LLP
11611 LeHavre Drive
Potomac, MD 20854
301-294-0133
dottie@insight1.com
www.insight1.com

Marshall Wellisch
Job Searchers, Inc.
7676 New Hampshire Avenue
Silver Spring, MD 20783
301-445-2466
mwellis@toad.net

MASSACHUSETTS

Bernice Antifonario, M.A.
Antion Associates, Inc.
885 Main Street, #10A
Tewksbury, MA 01876
978-858-0637
Antion1@aol.com
www.antion-associates.com

Lea Cabeen
Corp. for Business Work & Learning
38 Broad Street
Newburyport, MA 01950
617-727-8158
lcabeen@mediaone.net

Pam Connolly, JCTC
A Fine Line
8 Pratt Street
Reading, MA 01867
781-944-5482
pamafl@aol.com

Joan Cousins, M.S.
CareerFocus
1480 West Street
Pittsfield, MA 01201
413-443-1154
jhcousins@aol.com

Beate Hait, CPRW, NCRW
Word Processing Plus
80 Wingate Road
Holliston, MA 01746
508-429-1813
beateh1@aol.com
www.ibssn.com/resumes

Larry Linden, Ph.D.
R.L. Stevens Inc.
115 Pine Street
Clinton, MA 01510
978-368-1458
llinden@rlstevens.com
www.interviewing.com

Bonnie Worthley
53 Howard Street
Haverhill, MA 01830
978-372-8125
Bszar@aol.com

Stephen Youd, MA, JCTC
Winning Percentage Careers
385 Court Street, Suite 311
Plymouth, MA 02360
508-746-3282
WPCareers@aol.com
www.career.baweb.com

MICHIGAN

Janet Beckstrom
Word Crafter
1717 Montclair Avenue
Flint, MI 48503
800-351-9818
wordcrafter@voyager.net

Leora Druckman
Facilitated Futures
1738 Waverly Road
Ann Arbor, MI 48103
734-369-2580
leorad@aol.com

Roberta Floyd
21395 Virginia Drive
Southfield, MI 48076
248-357-2426
rafloyd@earthlink.net

Joyce Fortier, MBA, CPRW, JCTC, CCM
Create Your Career
23871 W. Lebost
Novi, MI 48375
248-478-5662
careerist@aol.com
www.careerist.com

Maria Hebda, CPRW
Career Solutions, LLC
2216 Northfield, Trenton
MI 48183
734-676-9170
careers@writingresumes.com
www.writingresumes.com

Lorie Lebert, CPRW, JCTC
Resumes For Results, LLC
PO Box 267
Novi, MI 48376
248-380-6101
Lorie@DoMyResume.com
www.DoMyResume.com

Rich Porter
CareerWise Communications LLC
332 Magellan Court
Portage, MI 49002-7000
616-321-0183
rtporter@worldnet.att.net

Beverlee Rydel
TR Desktop Publishing
46813 Fox Run Drive
Macomb, MI 48044
810-228-8780
bevrydel@aol.com

Deborah Schuster, CPRW
The Lettersmith
PO Box 202
Newport, MI 48166
734-586-3335
lettersmith@foxberry.net
www.thelettersmith.com

Kathleen Tedsen
TR Desktop Publishing
46813 Fox Run Drive
Macomb, MI 48044
810-228-8780
trdesktop@cswebmail.com

Peggy Weeks
CompuPage
3914 W. Michigan Avenue
Battle Creek, MI 49017
616-964-7533
pweeks@voyager.net

Tammi Wheelock
Data Tamer Resume Service
9 Bonita Drive, Battle Creek
MI 49014-4315
616-964-6355
tammi@datatamer.net
www.datatamer.net

MINNESOTA

David Jones, CPC, CMF, MBA
Personnel Decisions, International
6600 France Avenue South, Suite 501
Minneapolis, MN 55435-1804
952-915-7602
davidj@pdi-corp.com

Mary Kay Kernan, M.A.
University of St. ,Thomas
1000 LaSalle Avenue
Minneapolis, MN 55403-2005
651-962-4763
mkkernan@stthomas.edu
www.stthomas.edu

Barb Poole, CPRW
Electronic Ink
1812 Red Fox Road
St. Cloud, MN 56301
320-253-0975
eink@astound.net

Linda Wunner, CPRW, IJCTC
A+ Career & Resume Design / Linda's PageWorks
4891 Miller Trunk Highway, #208
Duluth, MN 55811
218-723-1995
linda@successfulresumes.com
www.successfulresumes.com

MISSISSIPPI

John Stevens
Ghostwriter Editorial Services
6045 Ferncreek Drive
Jackson, MS 39211
601-957-1479
JJSTVNS@cs.com
www.ghostwriter-resume.com

MISSOURI

E. Robert Jones
University of Missouri - Columbia
W1025 EBE
Columbia, MO 65211
573-882-4487
JonesER@missouri.edu

Meg Montford, CCM, CPRW
Abilities Enhanced
PO Box 9667
Kansas City, MO 64134
816-767-1196
meg@abilitiesenhanced.com
www.abilitiesenhanced.com

Karen Silins
A+ Career & Office Pro
9719 Woodland Lane
Kansas City, MO 64131
816-942-3019
apluscareer@aol.com

Robin Smith
Family Support Center
750 Arnold Avenue
Whiteman AFB, MO 65305
660-687-7132
robin.smith2@whiteman.af.mil

Gina Taylor, CPRW
Gina Taylor & Associates, Inc.
1111 W. 77th Terrace
Kansas City, MO 64114
816-523-9100
GinaResume@aol.com
www.GinaTaylor.com

John David Walters, Ph.D.
Charter Institute of Training & Staff Development
1301 N.E. 74th Terrace
Gladstone, MO 64118
816-468-7276
careercrafters@hotmail.com

MONTANA

Laura West
Agape Career Services
20695 E. Mullan Road
Clinton, MT 59825
888-685-3507
agape@blackfoot.net
www.AgapeCareerServices.com

David West
Agape Career Services
20695 E. Mullan Road
Clinton, MT 59825
866-245-6248
agjob4u@blackfoot.net
www.agapecareerservices.com

NORTH CAROLINA

Douglas Allen
10309 John's Towne Drive
Charlotte, NC 28210
704-541-5370
doug@dougallen.com
www.dougallen.com

Alice Braxton, CPRW
Accutype Resume & Secretarial Services
635C Chapel Hill Road
Burlington, NC 27215
336-227-9091
accutype@netpath.net

Dayna Feist, CPRW, JCTC
Gatehouse Business Services
265 Charlotte Street
Asheville, NC 28801
828-254-7893
gatehous@aol.com

Doug Morrison, CPRW
Career Planners
2915 Providence Road, Suite 250
Charlotte, NC 28211
704-365-0773
pwresume@mindspring.com

John O'Connor
CareerPro Resumes
3344 Hillsborough Street, Suite 300B
Raleigh, NC 27607
919-821-2418
careerpro2@aol.com
www.careerproresumes.com

Vanessa Satterfield, CPRW
A Notable Resume
PO Box 37, Clayton
NC 27520-0037
919-550-8884
anotable1@aol.com

NEBRASKA

Renata Anderson
Typing Pro
4012 N. 94th Street
Omaha, NE 68134
402-573-1014
renata@radiks.net

Bridget Ann Weide
Image Building Communications
6818 Grover Street, Suite 302
Omaha, NE 68106
402-393-4600
RWDigest@aol.com
www.ResumeWritersDigest.com

NEVADA

Cindy Fass
Comprehensive Resume Srvcs.
5300 Spring Mtn. Road, 212-D
Las Vegas, NV 89146
702-222-9411
crsinvegas@aol.com

NEW HAMPSHIRE

Michelle Dumas, CPRW, NCRW
Distinctive Documents
146 Blackwater Road
Somersworth, NH 03878
603-742-3983
resumes@distinctiveweb.com
www.distinctiveweb.com

NEW JERSEY

Vivian Belen, NCRW, CPRW, JCTC
The Job Search Specialist
1102 Bellair Avenue
Fair Lawn, NJ 07410
201-797-2883
vivian@jobsearchspecialist.com
www.jobsearchspecialist.com

Neil Cunningham
ACT Associates
519 Fairfield Avenue
Ridgewood, NJ 07450
201-493-1316
neilc@nis.net
www.actresumes.com

Sally Dougan
Bert Davis Consultants
25 McCatharn Road, Lebanon, NJ 08833
212-838-4000
saldougan@aol.com

Nina Ebert
A Word's Worth Resume & Writing Srv
808 Lowell Avenue
Toms River, NJ 08753
732-349-2225
wrdswrth@gbsias.com

Penne Gabel
Business Training Institute
170 Hillman Avenue
Glen Rock, NJ 07452
201-447-9782
hrpenne@aol.com

Susan Guarneri, NCC, NCCC, LPC,
CPRW, IJCTC, CCM
Guarneri Associates/Resumagic
1101 Lawrence Road
Lawrenceville, NJ 08648
609-771-1669
Resumagic@aol.com
www.resume-magic.com

Fran Kelley
The Resume Works
71 Highwood Avenue
Waldwick, NJ 07463
201-670-9643
TwoFreeSpirits@worldnet.att.net
www.careermuse.com

Rhoda Kopy, CPRW
A Hire Image Resume & Writing Service
26 Main Street, Suite E
Toms River, NJ 08753
732-505-9515
ahi@infi.net
www.jobwinningresumes.com

Judith McLaughlin
ResumeWizards.com, Inc.
27 Lavern Street
Sayreville, NJ 08872
732-432-4000
2wizards@resumewizards.com
www.resumewizards.com

Igor Shpudejko, CPRW, JCTC, MBA
Career Focus
842 Juniper Way
Mahwah, NJ 07430
201-825-2865
ishpudejko@aol.com

Pat Traina
The Resume Writer
PO Box 351
Vallejo, CA 94590
732-239-8533
ptraina@aol.com
www.theresumewriter.com

Kathy Vandenburg
Prosperous Futures
16 Hill Hollow Road
Milford, NJ 08848
908-995-2193
jvandenburg@blast.net

NEW MEXICO

Tricia Miller, CPRW
Albuquerque T.V.I.
525 Buena Vista S.E., Albuquerque
NM 87106-4096
505-224-3069
tmiller@tvi.cc.nm.us

NEW YORK

Ann Baehr, CPRW
Best Resumes
122 Sheridan Street
Brentwood, NY 11717
631-435-1879
resumesbest@earthlink.net

Etta Barmann, CPRW, JCTC, MSW, CSW
Compu-Craft Business Services, Inc.
124 E. 40th Street, Suite 403
New York, NY 10016
212-697-4005
erbarmann@aol.com

Liz Benuscak
Bi-Coastal Resumes, Inc.
32 Old Schoolhouse Road
New City, NY 10956
914-708-9134
bi-coastal@prodigy.net

Mark Berkowitz, MS, NCC, NCCC, CPRW,
IJCTC, CEIP
Career Development Resources
1312 Walter Road
Yorktown Height, NY 10598
914-962-1548
cardevres@aol.com

Arnold Boldt, CPRW
Arnold-Smith Associates
625 Panorama TraIL Bldg. Two, Suite 200
Rochester, NY 14625
716-383-0350
arnoldsmth@aol.com

Kirsten Dixson, JCTC, CPRW
New Leaf Career Solutions
PO Box 991
Bronxville, NY 10708
888-887-7166
kdixson@newleafcareer.com
www.newleafcareer.com

Donna Farrise
Dynamic Resumes of Long Island, Inc.
300 Motor Parkway, Suite 200
Hauppauge, NY 11788
631-951-4120
donna@dynamicresumes.com
www.dynamicresumes.com

Judy Friedler, NCRW, CPRW, JCTC, CCM
CareerPro New York
56 Barrow Street, #G-1
New York, NY 10014
212-647-8726
judy@rezcoach.com
www.rezcoach.com

Margaret Lawson
Resume Processing & Career Services
PO Box 2664
New York, NY 10027
212-862-0053
Resumepr@aol.com

Ken Lawson
Partners in Human Resources International
9 East 37th Street, 7th Floor
New York, NY 10016
212-685-0400
klawson@partners-international.com
www.partners-international.com

Linsey Levine, MS, JCTC
CareerCounsel
11 Hillside Place
Chappaqua, NY 10514
914-238-1065
LinZlev@aol.com

Kim Little, JCTC
Fast Track Resumes
1281 Courtney Drive
Victor, NY 14564
716-742-2467
info@fast-trackresumes.com
www.fast-trackresumes.com

Jane Lockshin
YourMissingLink.com
60 Sutton Place South, #14BN
New York, NY 10022-4168
800-445-3557
jlockshin@yourmissinglink.com
www.yourmissinglink.com

Christine Magnus, CPRW
Business Services Plus
1346 E. Gun Hill Road
Bronx, NY 10469
718-519-0477
BizServ@aol.com

Linda Matias, JCTC, CEIP
CareerStrides
34 E. Main Street, #276
Smithtown, NY 11787
631-382-2425
careerstrides@worldnet.att.net
www.careerstrides.com

Michele Mattia
Philips Electronics
1251 Avenue of the Americas
New York, NY 10020
212-536-0573
michele.mattia@philips.com

Dorothy Mueller, Ph.D.
The Strickland Group
1420 York Avenue, #4B
New York, NY 10021
212-861-1623
dmueller@stricklandgroup.com
www.stricklandgroup.com

Peter Newfield
Career Resumes
PO Box 509
Goldens Bridge, NY 10526
800-800-1220
peter@career-resumes.com
www.career-resumes.com

Beth Stefani, MBA, Ed.M, JCTC
Orison Professional Services
265 Union Street, Suite 101
Hamburg, NY 14075
716-649-0094
info@orisonservices.com
www.orisonservices.com

Darby Townsend
257 W. 86th Street
New York, NY 10024
212-787-7757
dtowns5901@aol.com

Salome Tripi, CPRW
Careers TOO
3123 Moyer Road
Mount Morris, NY 14510
716-658-2480
srttoo@frontiernet.net
www.frontier.net/~srttoo

Marty Weitzman, NCRW, CPRW, JCTC
Gilbert Career Resumes Ltd.
275 Madison Avenue
New York, NY 10017
212-661-6878
gilcareer@aol.com
www.resumepro.com

Deborah Wile Dib, NCRW, CPRW, JCTC, CCM
Advantage Resumes of New York
77 Buffalo Avenue
Medford, NY 11763
631-475-8513
gethired@advantageresumes.com
www.advantageresumes.com

Martin Yate
Peregrine McCoy
PO Box 70
Sea Cliff, NY 11579
516-674-3329
mccoy007@earthlink.net

OHIO

Hanan Akra, CPRW
DocuMall,
4102 N. Main Street
Findlay, OH 45840
419-423-0259
documall@aol.com

Susan Anderson
US Air Force - Family Support Center
88 MSS/DFP, 2000 Allbrook Dr. #3
Wright Patterson AFB, OH 45433
937-656-0939
susan.anderson@wpafb.af.mil

Pierre Daunic, Ph.D.
R.L. Stevens & Associates, Inc.
1674 Quail Meadows Drive
Lancaster, OH 43130
740-689-8056
pdaunic@rlstevens.com

Richard Haid, Ph.D., PCC
Adult Mentor
157 E. Fairway Drive
Hamilton, OH 45013
513-868-1488
dickhaid@adultmentor.com
www.adultmentor.com

Alice-Kay Hilderbrand, JCTC
Ohio Northern University
Career Services Center
Ada, OH 45810
419-772-2145
a-hilderbrand@onu.edu
www.onu.ed/admin-offices/

Susan Hoopes
Cuyahoga Valley Career Center
8001 Brecksville Road
Brecksville, OH 44141
440-526-5200
cvccshoopes@netscape.net

Barrie Hubbard
Centennial, Inc.
1014 Vine Street, Suite 1525
Cincinnati, OH 45202
513-381-4411
barrie@centennial-inc.com

Deborah James
Leading Edge Resume & Career Services
1010 Schreier Road
Rossford, OH 43460
419-666-4518
OhioResGal@aol.com
www.leadingedgeresumes.com

Andrea Kay
PO Box 6834
Cincinnati, OH 45206
606-781-2228
AskAndrea@fuse.net

Louise Kursmark, CPRW, JCTC, CCM
Best Impression Career Services, Inc.
9847 Catalpa Woods Court
Cincinnati, OH 45242
513-792-0030
LK@yourbestimpression.com

Sue Montgomery, CPRW, IJCTC
Resume Plus
4140 Linden Avenue, #112
Dayton, OH 45432
937-254-5627
resumeplus@siscom.net
www.resumeplus.com

Jerry Tisovic
R.L. Stevens & Associates
5005 Rockside Road
Independence, OH 44131
216-642-1933
gtisovic@rlstevens.com

Caitlin Williams, M.Ed., Ph.D.
Successful Working Women, Inc.
24408 Westwood Road
Westlake, OH 44145-4838
440-716-0929
cpwms@aol.com

Janice Worthington-Loranca, MA, CPRW, JCTC
Fortune 500 Communications
6636 Belleshire Street
Columbus, OH 43229
614-890-1645
janice@fortune500resumes.com
www.fortune500resumes.com

PENNSYLVANIA

Jewel Bracy DeMaio, CPRW
A Perfect Resume.com
419 Valley Road
Elkins Park, PA 19027
800-227-5131
mail@aperfectresume.com
www.aperfectresume.com

Paula Brandt, CPRW
The Resume Lady
183 Valleyview Drive
Belle Vernon, PA 15012
724-872-9030
paula@resumelady.com
www.resumelady.com (in process)

Barbaraanne Breithaupt, IJCTC, CPRW, CO
Barbaraanne's Lasting Impressions
3202 Holyoke Road
Philadelphia, PA 19114-3522
215-676-7742
Tiger4PARW@aol.com

Bob Bronstein, MBA
Pro/File Research
548 Bethlehem Pike
Fort Washington, PA 19034
215-643-3411
bronsteinr@aol.com

Patricia Harrington, CPRW, JCTC
Accent Resume Design
567 Lenape Circle
Langhorne, PA 19047
215-860-5345
accentp@aol.com

Jeffrey Lewin
Bernard Haldane Associates
1150 First Avenue, #385
King of Prussia, PA 19401
610-491-9050
LewinJ@bhaldane.com

Jane Roqueplot, CBC
JaneCo's Sensible Solutions
194 North Oakland Avenue
Sharon, PA 16146
724-342-0100
janeir@janecos.com
www.janecos.com

Robert Wolk
Bernard Haldane Associates
5100 S. Convent Lane, #502
Philadelphia, PA 19114
610-491-9050
perryxx@aol.com
www.jobhunting.com

PUERTO RICO

Myrna Muriel Gonzalez
Professional Office Support Srvcs.
Murcia #251
Vistamar, Carolina, PR 00983
787-750-4926
myrnaelena@hotmail.com

SOUTH CAROLINA

Kim Erwin
Clemson University
101 Barre Hall
Clemson, SC 29634
864-656-5727
kerwn@clemson.edu

Karen Swann, CPRW
TypeRight
384-4 College Avenue
Clemson, SC 29631
864-653-7901
karzim@carol.net

TENNESSEE

Carolyn Braden, CPRW
Braden Resume Solutions
108 La Plaza Drive
Hendersonville, TN 37075
615-822-3317
bradenresume@home.com

Marta Driesslein, CPRW
Cambridge Career Services, Inc.
300 Montvue Road, Suite A
Knoxville, TN 37919
865-539-9538
careerhope@aol.com
www.careerhope.com

Randall Howard
Randall Howard & Associates, Inc.
PO Box 382397
Memphis, TN 38183-2397
901-754-3333
RHAssociates@aol.com

Lynn Jackson
Russell, Montgomery & Associates/OI Worldwide
5050 Poplar Avenue, #328
Memphis, TN 38157
901-763-1818
Ljackson@oiworldwide.com
oiworldwide.com

Angela Majors
1137 Nelson Drive
Madison, TN 37115
615-868-8847
admajors@msn.com

TEXAS

Tracy Bumpus, CPRW, JCTC
RezAMAZE.com
1807 Slaughter Lane, #200, PMB 366
Austin, TX 78748
512-291-1404
tbumpus@rezamaze.com
www.rezamaze.com

Marsha Camp, CPRW, CCM
Accent on Success
711 N. Carancahua, Suite 700
Corpus Christi, TX 78475
361-884-7027
MarshaCamp@aol.com

Melinda Coker
6701 La Costa Drive
Tyler, TX 75703
903-561-5694
melinda_75703@yahoo.com

Mike Fernandes, CPRW
Resumes And More
13101 Preston Road, Suite 300, Dallas
TX 75240-5229
972-239-1991
MikeFernan@aol.com

Cheryl Harland, CPRW, JCTC
Resumes By Design
25227 Grogan's Mill Road, Suite 125
The Woodlands, TX 77380
888-213-1650
CAH@resumesbydesign.com

Lynn Hughes, MA
A Resume and Career Service, Inc.
PO Box 53932
Lubbock, TX 79453
806-785-9800
lynn@aresumeservice.com
www.aresumeservice.com

Shanna Kemp, M.Ed., IJCTC, CPRW
Kemp Career Services
2105 Via Del Norte
Carollton, TX 75006
972-416-9089
respro@aresumepro.com
www.aresumpro.com

Ann Klint, NCRW, CPRW
Ann's Professional Resume Service
1608 Cimmarron Trail
Tyler, TX 75703
903-509-8333
Resumes-Ann@tyler.net

Monique LaCour
Career Management Services
4800 Sugar Grove Blvd., #290
Stafford, TX 77477
713-270-6056
careermgt@usa.net

Peggy Mathias, CPRW, JCTC
Peggy's Paper Works
2525 Johnson, Suite A
San Angelo, TX 76904
915-224-2733
pege@wcc.net

Gerald Moore, CPRW
5536 Longview Circle
El Paso, TX 79924
915-821-1036
jmoore@dzn.com
www.thewritejob.com

William Murdock
The Employment Coach
7770 Meadow Road, Suite 109
Bedford, TX 76021
214-750-4781
bmurdock@swbell.net

Helen Newell
10101 South Gessner, #304
Houston, TX 77071
713-777-3715
helious21@aol.com

Joann Nix, CPRW, JCTC, CEIP
Beaumont Resume Service
7825 Fox Cove
Beaumont, TX 77713
409-899-1932
Info@agreatresume.com
www.agreatresume.com

Kelley Smith, CPRW
Advantage Resume Services
PO Box 391
Sugarland, TX 77487
281-494-3330
info@advantage-resume.com
www.advantage-resume.com

Ann Stewart, CPRW
Advantage Services
PO Box 535
Roanoke, TX 76262
817-424-1448
ASresume@aol.com

Kim Thompson, LPC, NBCC
New Avenues Career Management Programs
13811 Burgoyne
Houston, TX 77077
281-752-4015
kmathomp@aol.com

UTAH

Lynn Andenoro, CPRW, JCTC, CCM
My Career Resource
1214 Fenway
Salt Lake City, UT 84102
801-883-2011
Lynn@MyCareerResource.com
www.MyCareerResource.com

Diana LeGere
Executive Final Copy
PO Box 171311
Salt Lake City, UT 84117
801-277-6299
execfinalcopy@email.msn.com
www.executivefinalcopy.com

VIRGINIA

Herbert Crowder
Darden Graduate School of Business Administration
PO Box 6550
Charlottesville, VA 22906
804-924-4878
CrowderH@darden.gbus.virginia.edu
www.darden.virginia.edu

Jack Dunne, CMP, RCC
JJD Enterprises, Inc.
2600 13th Rd. S., #397
Arlington, VA 22204
703-685-6068
jjdent@erols.com

Bonnie Miller, LPC
The BrownMiller Group
312 Granite Avenue
Richmond, VA 23226
804-288-2157
TBMGroup@aol.com

Emily Saunders
SunTrust Bank
1001 Semmes Avenue, RVW 4131
Richmond, VA 23224
804-319-4454
emily.saunders@suntrust.com
www.suntrust.com

Laurie Smith, CPRW, IJCTC
Creative Keystrokes
3904 Flagstone Terrace
Alexandria, VA 22306
703-768-7210
ljsmith@creativekeystrokes.com
www.creativekeystrokes.com

Becky Stokes, CPRW
The Advantage, Inc.
401 Mill Lane
Lynchburg, VA 24503
800-922-5353
advanresume@earthlink.net
www.advantageresume.com

Betty Williams, CPRW, NCRW
BW Custom Resumes
18 Clarke Road
Richmond, VA 23226
804-359-1065
vabhw@aol.com

WASHINGTON

Valorie Hanousek
Northwest Secretarial Service
82 E. Mountain View Road
Camano Island, WA 98292
360-387-3631
nwsecretarial@tgi.net

Julie Mellen, MA
JM Consulting
3940 N.E. Surber Drive
Seattle, WA 98105
206-525-1923
jmcons@serv.net

Janice Shepherd
Write On
2628 East Crestline Drive
Bellingham, WA 98226
360-738-7958
resumesbywriteon@earthlink.net
www.resumesbywriteon.com

Lonnie Swanson, CPRW, IJCTC
A Career Advantage
21590 Clear Creek Road NW
Poulsbo, WA 98370
360-779-2877
resumewriter@amouse.net

WISCONSIN

Michele Haffner, CPRW, JCTC
Advanced Resume Services
1314 W. Paradise Court
Glendale, WI 53209
414-247-1677
michele@resumeservices.com
www.resumeservices.com

Kathy Keshemberg
A Career Advantage
1615 E. Roeland Avenue, #3
Appleton, WI 54915
920-731-5167
KathyKC@aol.com
www.Acareeradvantage.com

Joan Rogers
Brilliant Resumes
3616 N. Morris Boulevard, Milwaukee, WI 53211
414-963-0440
jrogers@execpc.com

Roberta Stafne, CPRW
Briarwood Consultants
827 S. Hillcrest Parkway
Altoona, WI 54720
715-834-2200
bwood@execpc.com

Julie Walraven
Design Resumes
1202 Elm Street
Wausau, WI 54401
715-845-5664
design@dwave.net
www.dwave.net/~design

WEST VIRGINIA

Lois Jobe
ASAP Resume Services
5915 Ohio Road
Huntington, WV 25702
304-529-1009
LoisCJ@aol.com

CANADA

Diana Bradford, IJCTC
CareerBound
1898 Flintlock Court
Mississauga, Ontario, L5L 3E1
905-820-1024
career_bound@hotmail.com
www.careerbound.org

Martin Buckland, CPRW, JCTC, CEIP
Elite Resumes
1428 Stationmaster Lane
Oakville, Ontario, L6M 3A7
905-825-0490
resumes@fox.nstn.ca

Maxwell Chernyak, CPRW
Best Services Group, Inc.
180 Dundas Street West #310
Toronto, Ontario, M5G 1Z8
416-340-9500
bestserv@yesic.com

Tanya Civiero
Encore Resumes
19870 Horseshoe Hill Road
Calendon, Ontario, L0N 1C0
519-941-9887
tciviero@hotmail.com

Candace Davies, BBA, CPRW, FCI
Cando Career Coaching & Resume Writing
10710 90th Street
Grande Prairie, Alberta, T8X 1J8
780-513-0010
candoco@telusplanet.net
www.candocareer.com

Sandra Lim CPRW, CCM
A Better Impression
24 Wellesley Street W, Suite 2302
Toronto, Ontario, M4Y 2X6
416-961-8840
a_better_impression@myna.com

Leslie Lumsden
Richard Ivey School of Business/Univ. of Western Ontario
1151 Richmond Street
London, Ontario, N6A 3K7
519-661-2111
Llumsden@ivey.uwo.ca

Ross MacPherson, MA, CPRW, JCTC, CEIP
Career Quest
1586 Major Oaks Road
Pickering, Ontario, L1X 2J6
905-426-8548
careerquest@primus.ca

Sylvia Mastromartino
Resume Excellence
643 16th Avenue
Richmond Hill, Ontario, L4C 7A8
905-709-8887
resumeexcellence@home.com

Nicole Miller
Mil-Roy Consultants
1729 Hunter's Run Drive
Orleans, Ontario, K1C 6W2
613-834-2160
resumesbymilroy@hotmail.com

INTERNATIONAL

Cristina Mejias
Career Managers S.A.
Talcahauano 833 7 A (1013)
Cap., Fed., Argentina
11-481-67500
consultores@careermanagers.com.ar
www.careermanagers.com.ar

Rick Browning
Rick Browning The Career Doctor
PO Box 523
Kings Cross NSW, 2010, Australia
coach@careerdoctor.com.au
www.careerdoctor.com.au

Gayle Howard, CPRW
Top Margin Resumes Online
7 Commerford Place
Chirnside Park, Melbourne, 3116, Australia
getinterviews@topmargin.com
www.topmargin.com

Paul Stevens
The Centre for Worklife Counselling
PO Box 407
Spit Junction, Sydney, 2088, Australia
worklife@ozemail.com.au
www.worklife.ozemail.com.au

Mohamed Sadik
Jolie Ville Hotels & Resorts
Sharm El-Sheikh
South Sinai, Egypt
206-260-0100
sadik1959@hotmail.com

Gilles Dagorn
Job Strategy
80 Avenue Charles de Gaulle
Neuilly, 92200, France
info@jobstrategy.fr
www.jobstrategy.fr

Paula Stenberg
CV Style
Level 5B, 9 Victoria St. East
Auckland, New Zealand
0064-9-377-3348
paula@cvstyle.co.nz
www.cvstyle.co.nz

Han Kwang, MBA, CCM
Personal Mastery Resources
196 Bishan Street 13 #03-559
Singapore, 570196
065-352-8756
haninc@magix.com.sg

John Read, JCTC
What Career Next!
Robinson Road, PO Box 1040
Singapore, 902040
065-354-3551
career@magix.com.sg
www.ecircles.com/magic

Christina Kuenzle
Coutts Career Consultants
Hauserstrasse 14
Zurich, 8006, Switzerland
411-268-8844
christine.kuenzle@coutts-consulting.ch

Career Resources

THE FOLLOWING CAREER RESOURCES ARE AVAILABLE, directly from Impact Publications. Complete the following form or list the titles, include postage (see formula at end), enclose payment, and send to:

IMPACT PUBLICATIONS
9104 Manassas Drive, Suite N
Manassas Park, VA 20111-5211
1-800-361-1055 (orders only)
Tel. 703-361-7300 or Fax 703-335-9486
Email address: *info@impactpublications.com*
Quick & easy online ordering: ***www.impactpublications.com***

Orders from individuals must be prepaid by check, money order, Visa, MasterCard, or American Express. We accept telephone and fax orders.

Qty.	TITLES	Price	TOTAL
Cover Letters and Resumes			
____	201 Dynamite Job Search Letters	$19.95	____
____	1500+ KeyWords For $100,000+ Jobs	14.95	____
____	**Best Cover Letters For $100,000+ Jobs**	24.95	____
____	Best Resumes For $100,000+ Jobs	24.95	____
____	Dynamite Cover Letters	14.95	____
____	Dynamite Resumes	14.95	____
____	Haldane's Best Cover Letters For Professionals	15.95	____
____	Haldane's Best Resumes For Professionals	15.95	____
____	High Impact Resumes & Letters	19.95	____
____	Military Resumes and Cover Letters	19.95	____
____	Resume Shortcuts	14.95	____
____	Resume Winners From the Pros	17.95	____
____	Resumes For Re-Entry	10.95	____
____	Savvy Resume Writer	10.95	____
____	Sure-Hire Resumes	14.95	____
Interviews, Networking, Salary Negotiations			
____	101 Dynamite Answers to Interview Questions	12.95	____
____	101 Dynamite Questions to Ask At Your Job Interview	13.95	____
____	Dynamite Salary Negotiations	15.95	____

Career Resources

_____	Haldane's Best Answers to Tough Interview Questions	15.95	_____
_____	Get a Raise in 7 Days	14.95	_____
_____	Interview For Success	15.95	_____
_____	Proof of Performance	17.95	_____
_____	Savvy Interviewer	10.95	_____
_____	The Savvy Networker	14.95	_____
_____	Winning Interviews For $100,000+ Jobs	17.95	_____

Job Search Strategies and Tactics

_____	100 Top Internet Job Sites	12.95	_____
_____	America's Top Internet Job Sites	19.95	_____
_____	Change Your Job, Change Your Life	17.95	_____
_____	Discover the Best Jobs For You	15.95	_____

Government, International, and Nonprofit

_____	Complete Guide to Public Employment	19.95	_____
_____	Directory of Federal Jobs and Employers	21.95	_____
_____	International Jobs Directory	19.95	_____
_____	Jobs and Careers With Nonprofit Organizations	17.95	_____
_____	Jobs For People Who Love to Travel	15.95	_____

SUBTOTAL _____

Virginia residents add 4½% sales tax _____

POSTAGE/HANDLING ($5 for first
product and 8% of SUBTOTAL over $30) $5.00

8% of SUBTOTAL over $30 ------------------------------------ _____

TOTAL ENCLOSED ------------------------------------- _____

NAME _____

ADDRESS _____

_____

_____

❑ I enclose check/money order for $ _____ made payable to
IMPACT PUBLICATIONS.

❑ Please charge $ _____ to my credit card:
❑ Visa   ❑ MasterCard   ❑ American Express   ❑ Discover

Card # _____ Expiration date: _____/_____

Quick and easy online ordering...

24 hours a day!

Books, videos, software, training materials, articles, and advice for job seekers, employers, HR professionals, schools and libraries

Visit us online for all your career and travel needs:

www.impactpublications.com
career superstore and Impact Publications

www.winningthejob.com
career articles and advice

www.contentforcareers.com
syndicated career content for job seekers, employers, and intranets

www.greentogray.com
www.bluetogray.com
military transition databases and content

www.ishoparoundtheworld.com
unique international travel-shopping center